ARCHITECTURAL
plants

ARCHITECTURAL
plants

christine shaw

Collins

DEDICATION

This book is for my daft cousin Steve, whose knowledge of horticulture could be written on a small postage stamp, and also for my learned chum Angus White, whose extensive plant knowledge has been a pleasure to share.

First published in 2005 by Collins
an imprint of HarperCollins*Publishers* Ltd
77–85 Fulham Palace Road,
London W6 8JB

The Collins website is:
www.collins.co.uk

Text copyright © Christine Shaw
Design and layout copyright
©HarperCollins*Publishers* Ltd

Editor: Helen Ridge
Designer: Alison Fenton

For HarperCollins
Senior Managing Editor: Angela Newton
Assistant Editor: Lisa John
Production Controller: Chris Gurney

A CIP catalogue record for this book is available from the British Library

ISBN 0-00-720470-1

Colour reproduction by Colourscan
Printed and bound in Great Britain
by The Bath Press Ltd

Hardiness colour codes

All the plants featured in this book have been given a hardiness colour code. This is to help you select plants that are capable of surviving the winters in your area.

■	GREEN	hardy down to -20°C (-4°F)
■	ORANGE	hardy down to -10°C (14°F)
■	RED	hardy down to -5°C (23°F)
■ ■	DOUBLE RED	hardy down to 0°C (32°F)

PAGE 1
Alocasia
macrorrhiza
PAGE 2
Phyllostachys nigra
PAGE 5
Yucca gloriosa
variegata
PAGE 6/7
Alocasia
macrorrhiza

Contents

Architectural plants are currently enjoying a massive wave of popularity, and quite rightly so. In fact, this type of gardening is the fastest-growing area of horticulture. More and more gardeners are realizing that these types of plants can have a dramatic effect on an ordinary garden, transforming it into something much more exciting.

I have always had an interest in gardening and, after six years of dealing with various company accounts and other financial shenanigans, followed by a rather lengthy stint as a croupier, decided that a career in horticulture was long overdue. The usual channels of night school and part-time college courses resulted in a job at the local garden centre, but I quickly came to the conclusion that fruit trees and roses weren't as interesting as I had first thought and that it was time to move on. So, off I went for an interview at a company called Architectural Plants. As soon as I approached the premises, I knew this was where I wanted to be. The whole place was stuffed to the gunwales with exotic-looking trees, banana plants (*Musa*), spiky *Yucca* and all manner of wonderful things. Nearly fifteen years later, I still enjoy every aspect of working with these incredible plants.

For a plant to be considered architectural, it needs to have either a strong shape, an exotic appearance, an evergreen presence or an unusual quality that can visually improve its surroundings.

Some plants such as palms, *Agave*, *Yucca* and tree ferns (*Dicksonia*) have obvious architectural traits. They have a strong, shapely outline and are completely different from the sort of plants most gardeners are used to. They are very noticeable in the garden, and have year-round appeal. As they are

evergreen, their theatrical allure is particularly valuable during the winter when other more traditional gardens in the neighbourhood look tired and dull, with most plants having shed their leaves.

Then there are architectural plants that have more subtle qualities while still remaining highly desirable. The red, peeling bark and the winter flowers of the evergreen Strawberry Tree (*Arbutus* x *andrachnoides*) make this tree one of the most coveted plants in the gardening world. The billowing shapeliness of the mature Green Olive (*Phillyrea latifolia*) makes this evergreen tree an essential choice for any small garden. The huge, glossy leaves of a *Fatsia* are perfect for adding an evergreen, tropical air to a dark corner. And an evergreen, jungly bamboo not only looks beautiful, but there is also the bonus of the gentle rustling of its leaves whenever there's a light breeze.

There are also plants here which, although not evergreen, are so loud, brash and vibrant, and add such an exciting impact to the garden, they could be called nothing less than architectural. The absurd, massive leaves of the Hardy Japanese Banana (*Musa basjoo*), the fabulous flowers of the Ginger Lilies (*Hedychium*), the colourful tropical-looking *Canna* and the large velvety foliage of the Foxglove Tree (*Paulownia tomentosa*) all have the capability of injecting some obvious glamour and pizazz to even the most pedestrian of gardens.

RIGHT
Chusquea breviglumis is a fabulous South American bamboo.

ABOVE
Pinus montezumae has soft luxuriant foliage of vivid emerald-green.

BELOW
The large leathery leaves of *Fatsia japonica* make a fine jungly addition to the shadiest corner of the garden.

Apart from their architectural qualities, many of these plants have the added extras of exquisite fragrance, fat berries or juicy fruits. Many are useful for groundcover or screening purposes. Some can help to mask unwanted noise from passing traffic, while a large number can withstand the harsh conditions often found on the coast.

The plants featured in this book have been chosen for many reasons. To start with, they are all personal favourites, and they are all beautiful and exciting. Most of them are easy to grow and maintain, although a few challenges have been included just to make life even more interesting. Most of them are widely available from specialist nurseries and, due to their accelerating popularity, are now starting to make their way into some garden centres too.

These plants have appeal for beginners and experts alike. Novice gardeners like them because they are easy to care for, while experts love them because they are so unusual. Busy gardeners adore them because of their low-maintenance requirements. Even non-gardeners are drawn towards these plants: people who would rather be found dead in a ditch than deadhead roses or double-dig an herbaceous border suddenly realize that gardening can be pleasurable after all.

These architectural plants have also been selected with all types of climate and soil conditions in mind. If a plant can be grown successfully only in a special kind of soil and in an exceptionally mild climate, and also needs insatiable amounts of care and attention in order to thrive, it has not been included, no matter how beautiful it may be. Most of us want unusual and interesting plants for our gardens, but we can all do without difficult subjects that have a limited chance of success. Virtually all the plants here should be a permanent feature in the garden, with more than a sporting chance of reaching old age.

Although many of these plants are reasonably priced, some of the larger specimens can carry a hefty price tag. This usually applies to slow-growing plants that have taken many years to reach a decent size. For example, a palm tree from a nursery that is 12ft (3.7m) tall could easily be twenty years old. Someone has had the expense of propagating it, repotting it several times during its life, feeding, watering and generally caring for it to keep it looking lush and verdant, until it is considered ready enough to become the main feature of someone's garden. The fact that it costs several hundred pounds should come as no surprise whatsoever. The expression 'you get what you pay for' is exactly right. It may help to work out how much it would cost to keep an area of the garden planted with seasonal bedding plants during the summer and again in the winter for a period of twenty years. Although these plants seem relatively cheap when bought individually, the total cost can come as quite a surprise.

Although architectural plants are becoming more and more popular, so far very little information has been written about them. This book is the first fully comprehensive guide to all aspects of gardening with these lovely plants. Although many of them were well known in Victorian times, most subsequent generations of gardeners have been completely oblivious to their fine qualities. It is only in the last fifteen years that they have been fully appreciated.

ABOVE
Catalpa bignonioides 'Nana' is a good choice as a large-leaved specimen tree.

LEFT
Yucca gloriosa variegata is essential for any garden design involving a spiky element.

This book lists the best possible choices of architectural plants. There are photographs of every one, with a full description of what they look like and what they do throughout the seasons. All sorts of practical information is given regarding hardiness, soil conditions, light levels and maintenance. There is advice on buying, siting and using these plants in the garden to provide different effects and planting schemes. Information has also been given on the less glamorous side of horticulture, namely which pests and diseases to look out for on each particular plant. A Rogues' Gallery at the back of the book helps in the identification of various ailments and other annoying, unwanted presences that can be the bane of a gardener's life.

Wherever possible I have avoided mentioning the kind of horticultural descriptions that require a glossary to explain what they mean – so very few references to culms, petioles and clustered node bases, and just basic easy-to-understand descriptions with all the emphasis on how to succeed in growing these plants, without being bogged down with unnecessary complications. However, all of the plants are listed alphabetically using their formal botanical names.

I would like to put up a spirited defence of the use of Latin in horticulture. Although no one detests rules and regulations of any kind more than I do, using the correct Latin names for all plants is essential. Apart from a few lapses in the naming of bamboos, most plants have only one Latin name. No matter which country you live in, this name is always the same, and there can be no confusion about which plant is being referred to. This might be stating the obvious, but this revelation didn't really dawn on me until I worked abroad. The common names of plants are different in every part of every country, and it's impossible to learn them all. Sometimes the common name of a plant in England refers to a totally different plant in Australia, and even in Scotland.

Despite the long words, horticultural Latin really isn't as intimidating as it first appears. It is not as strict as Classical Latin, so all the horrors of Latin classes at school can be forgotten. Of course, some people like to spout Latin just because they enjoy sounding pompous, but pomposity isn't a quality solely restricted to horticulture.

This book is intended to inspire confidence in growing these amazing plants and to enable any gardener to create some stunning effects with them. Whether you plant just one or two strategically to liven up a border or opt completely for this type of planting and transform the entire garden, this book offers all the advice and help required to do so. But, be warned, this type of gardening is addictive. The addition of just a few plants to start with can make ordinary garden plants seem so tame and lacklustre that more and more will probably be acquired until a whole new look has been achieved.

TOP
Cortaderia richardia looks beautiful in a breezy garden, adding movement to any planting plan as the wind swishes through the foliage.

ABOVE
Trachelospermum jasminoides provides strong fragrance in the garden throughout the summer.

Making the right decisions

Before charging off to your favourite architectural plants nursery, just spend a short while contemplating a few points. This chapter will help you come to the right decisions about the suitability of your choice of plants for their intended positions.

With such a dazzling array of architectural plants to choose from, making your initial selection can be a bit daunting, especially for those who are new to this type of gardening. Apart from spending time learning as much as you can from books, such as this one, visiting local botanic gardens and specialist nurseries to see how the plants are sited and how they grow will help with the choice.

Suitability of site

It is important to assess the suitability of your own garden for the plants that you are considering. Planting spiky desert plants in a boggy position in full shade is bound to end in failure. Similarly, planting bamboos in bone-dry soil on the top of a windy hill will guarantee their survival for only about ten minutes.

Unless you are especially stubborn, there is little point buying plants that have only a slim chance of surviving in your particular plot.

Some sites can be changed fairly easily. For instance, if your soil is poor, it can be enriched with large dollops of food. If the drainage is bad, digging in piles of grit can help enormously. If your garden is on an exposed coast, planting salt-resistant trees to act as a windbreak will hugely increase the possible choice of plants. But, basically, learning as much as you can about every aspect of your garden is a good starting point. Few gardens have just one characteristic. There are nearly always shady corners. There is usually a spot that remains boggy after heavy rain. And it is rare to find a garden without a sun-baked section somewhere.

The soil type should also be ascertained. Most plants in this book will grow in either acid, neutral or alkaline conditions. Some have preferences towards one end of the scale, but are not too fussed. Occasionally, one will be listed as being a lime-hating plant, which means that alkaline soil is not an option. Sometimes, if gardeners are really determined, large planting holes can be dug out and the existing soil replaced with something more suitable to allow their chosen plant to succeed. But this is really only a temporary solution. Eventually, the plant roots will grow down into the natural soil and start to suffer accordingly. This is not, therefore, something I would recommend.

Irrigation is another point to consider. If the chosen plants need frequent watering, then making this task as easy as possible for yourself means that you are more likely to attend to it. If full watering cans have to be lugged up the entire length of the garden every day during a hot summer, your enthusiasm for this chore will soon wane. By installing a nearby tap or automatic irrigation system, the plants will thrive with much less effort.

OPPOSITE
A well-stocked specialist nursery full of mouthwatering horticultural goodies.

Choosing & buying

After inspecting the garden thoroughly, reading through the plant descriptions and making a final decision about what you'd like to grow, the much more exciting task of buying the plants can proceed. There are a couple of things to think about, though, before embarking on the buying expedition. Firstly, where to buy the plants from, and secondly, what size of plants to buy.

Specialist nurseries vs garden centres

Specialist nurseries are great fun to visit. They stock only the plants they are interested in. There'll be no barbecues, pot-pourri or Christmas decorations in sight – just lots and lots of lovely plants. Nurseries selling architectural plants will be visited by like-minded customers, and experiences and gardening tips can be talked about and shared. The nursery owners and staff can offer expert advice and usually have enough time and enthusiasm to assist with the selection and purchase of any plant required.

The staff at nurseries will also be experienced in wrapping and packing awkward or unfamiliar plants, and can usually arrange the delivery of any large specimens that you're unable to take home yourself. Delivery is normally expertly done by strong young chaps, who are used to dealing with weighty

BELOW
Some plants
are much
more successful
in containers
than others.

palm trees and giant bamboos. These plants will be delivered to your door and manoeuvred to any part of the garden, as requested.

All in all, specialist nurseries are hard to beat and, because most of the plants are produced on site, the cost is reasonable and the full range of stock is usually available.

However, garden centres shouldn't be automatically dismissed. Many of them are becoming much more adventurous in the plants they stock, and increasing numbers of architectural plants can be found on their premises. Garden centres are also convenient places for buying compost, garden tools, irrigation equipment, lighting and anything else that might be required for the garden, all of which can be bought at the same time as the plants.

Financial constraints

Gone are the days when everyone lived at the same address for several decades and was able to grow plants from tiny specimens until maturity. Nowadays, many of us are impatient for an 'instant fix', and television gardening programmes have encouraged us all to buy large plants for immediate impact. This is fine if your budget is open-ended, in which case buy the largest of everything. Most of us, though, can't spend our hard-earned cash with such reckless abandon and need to be a bit more cautious.

ABOVE
There's a wide choice of exciting plants for growing indoors too.

If your budget is limited, work out from your list of requirements which are the fast-growing plants and which are the slowest. If a plant is a rapid grower, putting on several feet of new growth per season, such as a *Eucalyptus*, then buying a smaller, cheaper plant makes sense. For plants that are tediously slow, such as palm trees, put as much money as possible into buying a decent-sized specimen. Watching a small palm put on just a few inches of growth per year is a maddeningly frustrating experience, as you know that it will be years before it flourishes enough to become a focal feature in the garden.

One last thing to give some thought to is that some of the larger plants can be extremely heavy and quite tricky to plant. So, there is often the added expense of employing a professional team of capable gardeners to do the hard work for you. It's a choice between parting with yet more cash or risking personal injury by doing the job yourself.

RIGHT
Aeonium
'Schwarzkopf' is
a popular and
easy choice for
a terracotta pot.

Plants in pots

Growing plants in containers has always been popular, but the difficulties of cultivating plants in this way are often glossed over. Magazine articles and advertisements for conservatories and terracotta pots make it look so easy, and gardeners usually blame themselves when plants become unhealthy or die. But it cannot be overemphasized exactly how unhappy plants can become when forced to spend their lives in such an unnatural environment.

Plants are at least a hundred times happier when planted in the ground, where they belong, than when they are planted in pots.

The roots of plants growing in containers are far nearer the elements than they were designed for, which is tucked away snugly underground. They experience more frost, more heat from the sun and more rain, which doesn't always drain away quickly enough. So the chances of these plants suffering from freezing, drought and rotting are far higher than if they were growing in the garden. Plant roots also like to spread out, not to be cramped in a small space, which causes the plant additional stress. A stressed plant has reduced resistance to pests and diseases. Plants in containers have to be sprayed for bugs far more often than those in the ground. Insects can detect a weakened plant a mile off and zoom in for the kill with astonishing speed.

The most common cause of failure, however, is lack of water. Watering in the summer is something we all know has to be done, but sometimes watering twice a day in periods of extreme heat is too much of a chore. During the winter, when we assume that plants are looking after themselves more, watering is a task easily forgotten. Just because it has been raining for days on end doesn't mean our containers are being adequately supplied with moisture. The rain can bounce straight off leafy plants without any water going directly into the pot.

Sometimes, though, containers are unavoidable. If your garden consists of a roof terrace or balcony, then they are the only choice. Pots on either side of the front door or along a terrace are always popular, too. By choosing suitable containers and understanding why certain plants should be avoided, the whole process can be turned into a successful venture.

Selecting suitable containers

The traditional flower pot is a carefully chosen shape, not because of its looks, but because of its practicality. The fact that it is wide at the top, narrow at the base and has smooth straight sides means that however pot-bound a plant becomes, it can always be pulled out. This should be given serious consideration when choosing a pot for your prize specimens.

Although there are some beautifully shaped pots on the market, containers with extravagantly curved sides should be used only as ornaments for the garden. Otherwise, when it is time for the plant to be moved into something larger, the only options are either to smash the pot or to chop off a considerable amount of the plant's root system.

Whether a pot is plastic, terracotta, ceramic or stainless steel, good drainage is vital. Unless there are really good-sized drainage holes drilled into the bottom, leave it in the shop – it is useless!

Also, bear in mind that the larger the pot, the wider the choice of plants that can be grown in it successfully.

It is interesting to remember that the French king Louis XIV had figured all this out years ago with his famous Versailles pots. They were brilliant designs that enabled plants to be kept in them for decades. Each of their four sides could be removed, which gave his gardeners access to the roots. Every year, one side only was lifted off, any dead roots were cut out and the old compost was gently tweezed out with a specially made implement – something like a small curved fork. This was replaced with fresh compost, which gave the plant a new lease of life. This meant that every four years, all sides of the plant received this treatment, which ensured that the king's precious *Citrus* trees remained healthy and in peak condition.

A genuine Versailles planter costs a small fortune, but there are some good replicas on the market. Before you buy, check first that they have removable sides, otherwise they rather miss the point.

Choosing plants for pots

Seasonal plants such as *Canna*, *Zantedeschia*, *Agapanthus* and *Hedychium* that die back each year after flowering can all live in pots for years. Once they become too large for their pots, haul them out, divide the clumps into several plants, replant what is required and give the rest away to a gardening chum.

However, the idea of buying a splendid new pot, often at considerable expense, is usually for it to be a permanently planted focal feature, looking attractive all year round, not for just a few months in the summer.

Plants that never get any bigger are ideal. Box (*Buxus*) balls, bay (*Laurus nobilis*) lollipops, yew (*Taxus*) cones and Japanese pom-poms such as *Ilex crenata* are perfect, as long as they are clipped regularly to keep them in shape. During the growing season, clipping must be done little and often so that the foliage doesn't become straggly and unkempt. If the foliage is allowed to grow, more stress is put upon the root system as it struggles to support the extra leaves.

RIGHT
Japanese topiary such as *Ilex crenata* are blissfully content in large terracotta pots.

LEFT
Slow-growing
plants like
*Trochodendron
aralioides* are
happy to spend
the first four
years of their lives
in containers.

For something a little more unusual, try the silver-leaved *Corokia* x *virgata* from New Zealand or the dense form of *Euonymus japonicus* 'Compactus'.

Another category that contains some interesting choices are those that are very slow-growing and evergreen. There really is little point in choosing anything deciduous: nobody wants to look at a pile of sticks in the winter if the container is in a prominent part of the garden. The Dwarf Fan Palm, *Chamaerops humilis*, is happy in a pot for years. So is the dwarf *Pittosporum tobira* 'Nanum'. This lovely glossy-leaved plant has highly scented flowers in the summer and can be grown in a pot quite easily. Tree ferns such as *Dicksonia antarctica* are happy enough, too, as their root system takes years to outgrow a large pot. *Hebe rakaiensis* is another good choice. This plant grows to a 90cm (3ft) mound and then stops, although clipping is still advisable to keep it extra tidy. Consider a rare tree as well: *Trochodendron aralioides* is slow-growing, tolerant of neglect and essential for any gardener wanting to grow something really unusual.

There is also a wide range of small succulent plants available, all of which are quite content to sit in pots. Try *Aloe aristata*, *Echeveria glauca*, *Aeonium arboreum* and the purple variety *Aeonium* 'Schwarzkopf'.

Finally, there are the strongly architectural spiky plants. Most of these come from desert regions, which mean they have had to adapt to burning hot sun during the day, freezing temperatures at night and long periods of

BELOW
*Euonymus
japonicus*
'Compactus' is
an unusual leafy
choice for a pot.

drought, making them admirable choices for containers. Most hardy *Yucca* suit this purpose for the first few years of their lives, especially *Yucca gloriosa* and *Yucca aloifolia*. The wonderfully spherical *Dasylirion acrotrichum* can live in a pot for years. Probably the most spectacular of all is *Agave americana*. This plant and its various coloured forms all look stunning in terracotta pots.

Compost

With the exception of tree ferns, which require a peaty compost, most plants are blissfully content in a loam-based compost, such as John Innes no. 3. Stir in up to 50 per cent of extra grit to provide really sharp drainage. This eliminates the need to fill the bottom few inches of your pot with large crocks as we are often advised to do. Loam-based compost is heavier than a peat-based mix, which helps to stop pots blowing over in the wind. It also has more nutrients and is easier to re-wet if the whole pot dries out.

Feeding

Plants in pots need all the help they can get, and this includes regular feeding throughout the growing season. In spring, start off by giving each pot a good dollop of something strong, such as a mix of blood, fish and bone. Thereafter, add a small dose of foliar feed to each watering can and use every time you water, even if it's every day. Vital nutrients are easily leached out of pots, leaving plants prone to yellowing. The aim is to have handsome foliage that looks in the peak of health, not jaundiced and miserable.

Watering

The all-important task of irrigation must be taken seriously. The compost should never be allowed to dry out completely, which is quite an onerous task in the middle of a heat wave. Having pots within easy reach of a hose helps, so does having a garden tap. Plants in pots need watering virtually every day during the summer months, so careful planning is needed. Don't wait for the summer to realize that each plant is a long way from a water supply – carrying heavy watering cans soon becomes a chore.

Alternatively, think about installing an automatic drip-irrigation system. Each pot has the recommended number of 'drips' pushed into it, all of which are connected to a long length of tubing plumbed into the water supply. The timer is then set to come on for as long and as often as you wish. The cost of these irrigation systems has decreased considerably as their popularity has increased, and they are now available at all good garden centres. Most are now fairly easy to install without expensive plumbing costs.

LEFT
With regular
irrigation, *Cycas
revoluta* can look
fantastic in a pot.

Pests & diseases in pots

Plants in pots are much more prone to attacks from various beasts and general disorders than plants in the ground. Keep a constant watchful eye and catch them at the first sign. (See the chapter on pests, diseases and other disorders on pages 334–347.) One particularly nasty horror is the dreaded vine weevil. This sneaky, vicious brute lurks under the soil feeding on the roots of your precious specimens. One day, your plant collapses with no warning and the top comes off in your hand – no roots left at all! By scraping around under the soil, large fat white grubs can be found (they're large and fat because they have been gorging on the entire root system). Other signs to watch out for are nibbled notched leaves, which are made by the adult form of this nocturnal creature.

Once found, dispose of the entire contents of the pot, fill it with fresh compost and start again. There are some exceptionally nasty chemicals around that can be added to the soil to ward off vine weevil, but using a loam-based compost and giving an occasional dose of a natural predator (a nematode worm that eats only the bad guys) works very well. Vine weevils are lazy things and prefer to burrow through soft, peaty compost rather than heavier loam.

Overwintering

No plant will stand having its roots frozen solid for weeks at a time. If you have a nice little courtyard garden in a warm inner city or if you live in a mild area near the sea, then this won't be a problem. In colder areas, pots may have to be moved indoors or wrapped up. Choosing very hardy plants is obviously sensible, but the roots would still remain vulnerable. If cold winters are a regular occurrence in your part of the world, before planting, line the inside of each pot (excluding the bottom) with a thick layer of bubble wrap. This is completely invisible once the pot is planted up and much more pleasing to the eye than an old blanket wrapped around the outside of the pot.

Moving a heavy pot that has been planted up to less cold conditions indoors can be rather a nuisance. There are various trolleys and sack barrows on the market, but the best one I've come across has a beautifully angled shape and heavy-duty pneumatic tyres, which make light work of the whole procedure.

ABOVE
Canna indica
can easily be
overwintered
under glass if
it is planted in
a container.

ABOVE LEFT
Aspidistra elatior
is a nice leafy
choice for a pot.

LEFT
The blue form of
Agave americana
looks beautiful
next to the colour
of terracotta.

Conservatories

Conservatories have never been more popular. Having a garden room attached to the house, where one can wander into a different climate and enjoy all the leafy and floral delights that are too tender for outdoors, is a splendid idea. The image often includes reclining in comfy chairs and occasionally reaching out languidly to pick a home-grown juicy citrus fruit or maybe a ripe fig. A place where the last rays of the setting sun can be observed at the end of the day...

If only reality could match the dream. Nothing prepares conservatory owners for the difficulties of growing plants in this kind of environment. The glossy adverts are taken at face value, and the fact that there are myriad problems to overcome can be a bit of a shock. The previous pages dealt with growing plants in pots, but growing plants in pots and under glass takes the art of cultivation into a new league altogether. Plants hate the excessive heat, dry atmosphere, lack of ventilation and the extreme variations of seasonal temperatures often found in conservatories.

The better the environment in the conservatory, the larger the range of plants that can be grown successfully.

Choosing a conservatory

Buy the largest conservatory that you can accommodate and afford. The larger the space, the easier it is to maintain a balanced climate. Instead of automatically siting a conservatory on the sunniest side of the house, consider a shadier spot where the heat of the summer is less intense. If possible, choose a structure with a door at each end. This will allow a good flow of air during the summer to help keep the interior cooler. Gentle breezes are what we are aiming for, not howling gales, so a sheltered part of the garden is required, not an exposed corner.

Ventilation is a boring, but essential, subject to think about as well. It is almost impossible to have too much ventilation, especially in the summer. Most conservatories are not well designed in this department, offering just one or two feebly inadequate vents in the roof, if you're lucky. It is worth paying extra to have as many fixed panes of glass in the roof as possible converted into movable ones that open. If the design allows, have some side vents fitted as well, to catch the breeze from all directions.

Flooring

As all plants are much happier growing in the ground than they are in containers, leaving some space in the conservatory floor, where small trees and faster-growing plants can be planted directly into the soil, is something

worth thinking about when you are planning your conservatory. The roots would have the benefit of being able to spread out naturally, while the glass overhead would protect tender foliage from the frost.

Also consider choosing the sort of flooring that can be hosed down in the summer. This would help to lessen the heat while increasing the humidity, both of which would benefit the plants. Fluffy rugs might look okay flung on the conservatory floor, but they are not exactly practical.

Watering

Having a hose pipe right where it is needed will make watering much less of a chore, and your plants are therefore more likely to be irrigated when they need it, rather than having to wait until it is convenient.

Automatic irrigation systems have improved hugely during the last few years. Available from all good garden centres, they are easy to install, reliable and reasonably priced. A main pipe is placed all around the conservatory, and from this numerous drip nozzles can be pushed into each container. The timer is as easy as any domestic central heating or hot water system. They are the perfect solution for anyone who is frequently away from home or who would prefer spending their time doing other things.

ABOVE
Tropical, lush verdancy is what we're aiming for in a conservatory.

ABOVE LEFT
Strelitzia reginae
adds an exotic
air to any
conservatory.

ABOVE RIGHT
The size, aspect,
ventilation and
maintenance of
a conservatory
have a direct
bearing on what
can be grown
successfully.

Heating

From being boiling hot in the summer, the temperature in many conservatories plummets during the winter when the heat is quickly lost through the glass. Many plants can cope with almost freezing conditions, but a few degrees above freezing will make life more pleasant for plants and humans alike.

Whether the conservatory is heated by leaving the door to the adjoining house open, or by radiators, hot pipes, portable gas heaters or anything else, it is important to remember that plants do not like direct heat, so keep them some distance away from any heating source. Avoid heating systems that blow hot dry air directly onto the plants' foliage as this can make the leaves turn brown and crispy.

If possible, avoid underfloor heating as well. Although this is nice for cats and people to walk on, plants hate this much heat so near to their roots – they will start to shed their leaves almost immediately. The only plants able to tolerate underfloor heating are spiky and succulent ones that are used to coping with the heat of their native habitats, such as the Sonoran Desert in Arizona or the warm plains of South Africa. Lovely though these plants are, most gardeners prefer to grow a variety of plants under glass, and the sharp spines of *Yucca* and *Agave* can be inconvenient indoors.

Conservatory plants

By checking the cultivation requirements of the various plants featured in this book and by reading the section on how to grow plants in pots (see pages 20–27), you can soon assemble a list of suitable plants for growing under glass. If the heating, ventilation and irrigation topics have been addressed, you will have more than a sporting chance of attaining the dream of a conservatory filled with lush, healthy, exotic plants.

The single most useful and beneficial thing that you can do in the heat of the summer is to move all your plants outside for the hottest months. They will appreciate not only the fresh air, but also the rain, which helps to clean any dust from the leaves.

Pests & diseases under glass

The unnatural conditions of being under glass, the hostile environment of fluctuating temperatures and the problems of growing plants in containers mean that pests and diseases are virtually guaranteed at some time or other. Once bugs are happily ensconced, they can breed with alarming rapidity. Some insects, such as whitefly, can produce another generation mature enough for laying its own eggs within three days.

Check all plants at least once a week, looking not just for insects, but also for any signs of fungal infections, moulds, rotting or any other maladies. Dealing with any problems at the very first sign saves all sorts of trouble for the future. There's no point ignoring it and hoping it will go away – it won't. The more an infestation takes hold, the harder it is to deal with.

The chapter on pests and diseases (see pages 334–347) gives more comprehensive information, and there is also a Rogues' Gallery (see pages 340–347) to help you identify exactly which horrors to look out for.

TOP
Sparmannia africana is a fine plant for filling a corner of a large conservatory.

ABOVE
Tibouchina urvilleana adores lots of heat and humidity.

Professional maintenance contracts

The difficulties of looking after plants grown in conservatories are well known in the horticultural trade. As a result, teams of marvellous people are always available to help gardeners keep everything looking healthy. They will visit your home regularly to check that all is well in the conservatory. They will water, feed and clean plants whenever necessary and dispense valuable advice at the same time. They take all the hard work out of looking after plants, leaving you just to enjoy the results.

Architectural plants in the garden

Gardening with architectural plants is no different from any other type of gardening, but I can appreciate that planting a garden with unfamiliar plants might be a bit daunting. The usual rules still apply, although I prefer to think of them as tips and helpful advice.

Walking into an architectural plants nursery for the first time can be overwhelming. When faced with plants that look so big, bold and different, it's easy to assume that all those on sale are fully grown, mature specimens. Although such a nursery is not for the timid, closer inspection will reveal that this type of gardening is not just about large plants.

You will also find on display a massive selection of smaller, easily affordable plants lurking throughout and underneath all the greenery. There is usually plenty of stock readily available that doesn't require a second mortgage. So, if you're new to this type of gardening and are bowled over by the choice of plants on offer, where do you start?

Garden design

There is a lot of pretentious nonsense bandied about garden design. If someone thinks that a selection of plants looks good together, who's to say that they are wrong? As long as the gardener or client is happy with the result, that should be all that matters. But, many of us are happier with a few guidelines to assist, so here are just a few.

Choose plants that suit your type of garden and learn as much as you can about what keeps them happy.

It is important to choose plants that are right for your garden and to learn as much as possible about the growing conditions that would suit them best. (This is discussed in detail on page 16 and also in the individual plant entries.) Also, try to learn a bit about their eventual size – there is little point planting small plants near the back of the border where they will be obscured from view in a couple of years. This is, of course, all common sense that applies to any type of gardening, not just gardening with architectural plants.

Another common-sense strategy when planting – but one that I completely ignore – is to allow space around each plant so that it can spread without being crowded by its neighbours after a few seasons. Common sense it may be but, to impatient people like myself, this is something far too boring even to contemplate. I like to see a wonderful lush garden within two years, not ten. If plants start to crowd together, then I either get out the shears and do some serious pruning or, better still, thin out the number of plants and transplant the spare ones somewhere else.

Using the same plants throughout the garden to carry on a theme, rather than just having one of each type of plant, is something I am very keen on. It is much more pleasing and organized to look at. If one of your favourite plants happens to be, for instance, a *Yucca gloriosa*, start by planting one in a position

where it is easily seen, and then plant several more along the length of the border or garden at various intervals. This effect gives the impression that a deliberate planting plan has been thought about, rather than appearing as a random hotchpotch. It is a commonly held misapprehension that using the same plant more than once is boring and shows a lack of imagination. Plant one of each only if you are an avid collector or the curator of a botanic garden.

Still on the subject of multiple planting, small plants such as some ferns, grasses or groundcover plants are much more noticeable and give a more dramatic effect when planted in large sweeping groups of all the same type.

And, when using architectural plants as screening, groups and rows of bamboos or trees do the job very well but, again, the effect is less messy if all the same types of bamboo or tree are selected. Not only is the result more visually appealing, but the growth rates will be the same, keeping the screening more uniform as it matures.

Using the same types of climbing plants across a fence or over a pergola also looks tidier, but I usually fail miserably in persuading clients to go for this option. Gardeners expect climbers to work hard, providing screening, flowers, fragrance and a bit of colour for the whole growing season. Indeed, choosing from the range of climbing plants in this book, this is certainly possible to achieve but, from an aesthetic point of view, lots of the same is easier on the eye. And if they all intermingle with each other, it doesn't matter at all.

Larger plants such as trees, palms and bamboos look perfectly okay when planted as single specimens and as the main focal feature of the garden, but they can also be effective in small groups. Palm trees look particularly good planted together in groves, with all the plants of slightly different heights. Grouped in this way, you can almost kid yourself that they grew there naturally.

With architectural plants, the emphasis is on the foliage, not the flowers, so it can be great fun experimenting with all the different shapes, textures and shades of green to make different effects. For example, in a shady corner, the large glossy leaves of a *Fatsia japonica*, the fat crinkly foliage of *Eriobotrya japonica*, the blue-green spiky leaves of *Yucca* x *floribunda* and the emerald-green, soft foliage of *Hebe parviflora angustifolia* look lovely all grouped together.

In a sunnier position, the combination of the small, bright green foliage of a bamboo such as *Phyllostachys aurea*, the spiky sword-shaped leaves of *Phormium tenax*, the large, shiny leaves of *Acanthus mollis* all underplanted with the dense groundcover of *Rosmarinus repens* makes an interesting mix.

Generally, because of the lack of too many gaudy flowers, architectural plants can be mixed and matched in almost limitless combinations. At this point, it is time to throw in a few words about variegated plants. With architectural plants, the colour green obviously dominates, and with all the hundreds of shades of green, little else is really needed. Even the absence of a constant array of flowers is not much of a loss. But, just occasionally, introducing a contrasting plant can add that bit of extra interest. If a coloured-leaved

ABOVE
Pleioblastus variegatus makes a pretty contrast to other larger bamboos.

LEFT
Strongly shaped architectural plants do not need flowers or colour to make them noticeable.

Architectural Plants · 37

LEFT
Beautifully shaped
palms are striking
enough to grab
anyone's attention.

BELOW
This photo shows
a perfect choice
of plants for a
layered effect in
a small garden.

plant such as *Rhamnus alaternus variegata*, *Yucca gloriosa variegata* or *Phormium tenax variegata* is planted among masses of green, the effect can be quite stunning. However, if too many coloured-leaved plants are added, the whole contrasting effect can be diluted to the point of being lost. So, think green, and you can't go far wrong.

After introducing architectural plants to a garden, other ordinary garden plants can start to look dull, which usually leads to the buying and planting of more and more shapely specimens. If you plan to turn the whole garden over to architectural plants but you are on a fairly tight budget that allows only a gradual transformation, spend your cash on planting the garden in sections. Completely finishing one small area can make a much more rewarding difference than spreading out your new plants in just ones and twos around the garden.

If you prefer a more traditional garden that just needs a little oomph, architectural plants can fit in surprisingly well with existing planting. A shapely, evergreen architectural tree will not seem out of place as a focal feature in any style of garden. A couple of palms or a large *Yucca* can enliven the dullest of herbaceous borders without appearing at all alien. An olive tree can look wonderful in any sun-baked courtyard. And bamboos or large grasses planted around ponds look totally acceptable, even if the rest of the garden is turned over to lawn and vegetables.

If space is a bit limited, it is surprising how many large plants can fit into one small area if the varying heights are taken into account. The photo shown opposite below is a brilliant illustration of professional design and imagination (alas, not mine!). A canopy of tall *Eucalyptus glaucescens* provides the first layer. Underneath these, a few *Cordyline australis* nestle to provide the next layer and also provide shade and shelter for tree ferns (*Dicksonia antarctica*), which are tall enough to leave room for ground-level plants such as *Astelia*. It's inspirational stuff indeed, and there's no reason why amateur gardeners can't create something reasonably similar.

Beautiful as architectural plants are by day, they still have some hidden talents up their sleeves. It is easy to forget about the garden once the sun sets, but some of these plants are so sculptural and shapely that they can even look fantastic at night with some carefully positioned up-lighting to accentuate their silhouettes. The plants with the strongest shapes such as palms, *Yucca* and *Agave* work best with spotlights on them.

One last comment to add about planning your own garden is not to be too strict in your choice of plants. After reading up on plants you like the look of, it's usual to write down a few favourites and compile a list of those that you'd really like. The longer the list, the less chance there is of obtaining them all during one shopping trip. However good your preferred nursery is, to expect it to stock every size of every plant all year round is being unrealistic. It is better to make a very short list of essentials, then visit the nursery and spend time looking around to see what looks good at the time. Make your final selection from what you see on the day. Otherwise you could spend a long time tracking down every single plant on a long wish-list.

Themed planting

Most architectural plants enthusiasts start with just one or two specimens at a time and gradually build up a wider selection later on. It is not unusual for the entire garden to be filled with these beautiful plants eventually. Some gardeners take things one step further and theme their garden in one particular foreign style. This is often done straight after a particularly enjoyable holiday when you are wishing you were still there. Theming the garden allows the mind to be transported back to whichever part of the world you recently visited.

Settlers new to a particular country sometimes like to be reminded of their homeland, and they plant their gardens accordingly: New Zealanders and Australians living away from home seem to have a special passion for doing this. As the choice of architectural plants is wide, it is easy to develop gardens that are reminiscent of one particular country or region. The provenance of the plants doesn't have to be strictly correct as long as the look of it suits what you are trying to create. For example, a Mediterranean-style garden could be created using plants such as Italian Cypress (*Cupressus sempervirens*), Umbrella Pines (*Pinus pinea*), *Magnolia grandiflora*, olives and palms, together with *Trachelospermum jasminoides* and *Pittosporum tobira* to add the familiar scent found in Tuscany or the south of France.

Some might prefer a Japanese look, with the emphasis on Black Bamboo (*Phyllostachys nigra*), together with trees such as *Podocarpus macrophyllus* and *Phillyrea latifolia*, and maybe some Japanese topiary as well, such as *Ilex crenata* and formally clipped *Buxus sempervirens* or curved mounds of *Hebe rakaiensis*.

Jungly gardens can be very dramatic using palms, bamboos, Banana Plants (*Musa basjoo*) and anything else with large leaves such as the Foxglove Tree (*Paulownia tomentosa*) and Rice Paper Plant (*Tetrapanax papyrifera*). Loud splashes of colour can be introduced with any of the *Canna* or Ginger Lilies (*Hedychium*), and all types of large-leaved ferns could be used for the underplanting.

Australian-type gardens would have masses of all types of *Eucalyptus*, *Acacia dealbata*, *Acacia pravissima*, *Callistemon subulatus* and *Solanum laciniatum*, probably planted densely around a summer house with a corrugated iron roof and a shady verandah.

New Zealand gardens can easily be created in cooler areas that have a high rainfall. With a mix of *Cordyline australis*, *Dicksonia squarrosa*, *Phormium*, *Astelia* and the fabulously weird and wonderful *Pseudopanax crassifolius*, pulling back the curtains every morning and gazing out on plants such as these could make you forget which country you actually live in.

My favourite group of plants is the spiky and succulent one, and any choice of these can look fab together. To look out of the window and see a scene that could easily be from the Sonoran Desert in Arizona always gives me a real buzz. A mix of *Agave*, *Yucca* and *Dasylirion* can be used to good effect, although postmen, meter readers and visitors to the house don't seem to share my enthusiasm for these plants – they've probably been on the receiving end of the sharp thorns once too often.

LEFT
Leafy tree canopies
underplanted
with palms give
a jungly feel.

BELOW
Loud and vibrant
flowers remind
us of trips to
the Caribbean.

LEFT
Rows of formal
Cupressus have
an air of the
Mediterranean
about them.

BELOW
The rich scent
of *Magnolia
grandiflora* flowers
fills the air in
Italianate gardens.

There are enough plants in this book to create gardens with Chilean and South African themes too. Depending on how vivid your imagination is, you could replicate the planting of just about any country in the world. There are also plenty of plants that can be used to make much more traditional gardens, as well as those where the emphasis is on fragrance. Believe it or not, it is possible to create unusual, bright, flowery gardens – there are just about enough exotic blooms among these plants to satisfy the floral needs of gardeners, despite the emphasis being on their foliage. There are also lots of plants here that have excellent salt resistance, which makes them very practical for seaside gardens.

Last of all, even bog gardens can get a look in with a selection of moisture-loving specimens such as *Gunnera manicata*, *Acorus gramineus variegata*, *Zantedeschia aethiopica* 'Crowborough' and *Arundo donax*.

I can't think of any garden anywhere that wouldn't benefit from at least a small selection of architectural plants.

Garden designers

If you really can't bear the thought of choosing your own plants and would prefer someone else to create a beautiful garden for you, then it's worth considering bringing in a professional.

There are lots of garden designers out there, and although many of them are talented and dedicated people, some of them are not quite so marvellous. So, how do you choose one?

There is nothing to beat a verbal recommendation from a chum or neighbour who has recently had their garden revamped. And it's usually a fairly safe bet to employ someone who's been in the business for a long time. He or she will have the benefit of years of experience and, hopefully, will still retain a certain amount of enthusiasm for the task.

Don't just accept quotes from one designer; it pays to shop around. It is also reasonable to ask to see their portfolio of recent commissions. If their photos are beautifully presented in a well-cared for album, this bodes well. If their portfolio consists of a few faded pictures stuffed into a tatty old envelope, then their attention to detail probably won't amount to much.

Within reason, try not to be too influenced by the cost quoted. To dismiss a quote purely because it's expensive can definitely be the wrong thing to do. You might miss out on the best, tidiest, nicest and most professional teams of chaps or ladies in existence. Sometimes a very cheap quote might not include various hidden extras that will be tacked on at the end of the job. In other words, the gardening world is no different from anything else when it comes to employing someone's service.

Finally, just because someone is a designer, don't assume they are a gardener. Some designers never leave their office desk and will present you with a garden plan only. The planting and hard graft might still have to be done by you.

New gardens & borders

Sometimes the opportunity arises to create a completely new section of garden. If a reasonably large area is being considered for this type of planting, its preparation should be given some careful thought. Architectural plants need the same kind of preparation as most other types of plant, but it's useful to offer a couple of tips on the subject here.

Fashionable advice is often given about the use of some kind of membrane cover, such as Mypex. This is placed over all of the soil in a large sheet and is used to suppress weeds and slow down water evaporation. *Please, please, I beg of you*, don't use this ghastly stuff. It's truly awful and, although it does keep the weeds from growing, the disadvantages far outweigh any benefits. Although useful for large commercial areas, it has no place in a private garden. Once *in situ* it becomes impossible to condition the soil in any way. Digging can't be done – this won't hurt for a couple of years but, long-term, it isn't a good thing, as the soil will gradually become more compacted and stagnant. Feeding, except with foliar food, isn't possible. Worms can't work the soil, as they cannot pass back and forth through the material. Adding any new plants

is a bore because the material has to be uncovered and cut before a planting hole can be dug. And, lastly, it's hideous to look at. Even when top-dressed with a mulch of pea shingle or bark chippings, the weather and local wildlife will soon shift this around, exposing areas of it to public view. Well, I think I've probably made my views on it more than clear, so enough said.

When a new border has been dug over and levelled, it's a useful opportunity to be able to feed the whole area in one go prior to any planting. Numerous references throughout the book are made to using copious quantities of well-rottted manure. This is excellent for providing all sorts of nutrients for practically all types of architectural plant. But, make sure it is well rotted and has reached the stage where it is dryish and crumbly. If it is runny and smells bad enough to make your eyes water, then don't use it. When it is this fresh, it needs nitrogen to help it to rot down further. So, instead of adding much-needed nitrogen to the soil, it is actually taking it away. Also, very fresh manure can scorch delicate foliage and roots. If well-rotted manure is difficult to obtain, buy sacks of 6X from the local garden centre. It works just as well and is easy and pleasant to use. It also stinks out the entire neighbourhood for about a week but, what the hell... Blood, fish and bone also gets talked about a lot in these pages. It is bought as a powdered mix and sprinkled over the surface of the soil. It smells awful, but the horrible pong will soon fade. If you keep a pet dog, this powder will have to be forked in lightly otherwise the greedy mutt will feast on it.

Before planting, take some time to arrange all of the plants across the new area. While they are still in their pots, they are easy to move around until their exact positions have been decided on.

A few thoughts

Although the following are completely random thoughts, I do think that they are worth mentioning.

Tools & equipment

Whatever tools or gardening equipment you choose to purchase, please try to buy the best and most expensive offered. Good-quality garden tools should only have to be bought once, whereas cheap tools seldom last for more than a few years. This, of course, applies to almost all types of gardening. However, architectural plants are such a special range that they deserve the very best aftercare. An architectural plants garden often dispenses with the traditional lawn, as grass takes up valuable planting space. So, the money saved from not needing an expensive mower can go into the few really useful tools that are regularly required.

Strong sturdy ladders are a must, and there are some beautifully made, lightweight Japanese ones currently on the market, which are worth every penny of the asking price. Similarly, if your choice of plants includes lots that require frequent clipping, such as *Buxus* or any topiary, it is worth buying a pair of lightweight, super-sharp secateurs to make the task more pleasurable. And expensive secateurs are a joy to use. They can be taken to pieces and sharpened to keep them in pristine condition for decades, and they usually come with a smart leather holster to keep them in.

To help in moving some of the larger plants in and out of the conservatory or around the garden prior to planting, a superior type of sack truck is essential. Buy one that is beautifully balanced, easy to use and has nice thick pneumatic tyres for bouncing over uneven ground or gravel.

Pruning & chopping

If lots of herbaceous plants such as *Canna* and *Hedychium* are used, after they have turned brown for the winter, instead of cutting them right down to ground level, leave a couple of inches of stem showing above the ground. These will remind you of their whereabouts so that other plants aren't mistakenly planted in the same place. This might sound drearily obvious, but it's something I read in a gardening magazine years ago and I found it a useful tip.

Pruning or clipping plants little and often keeps them in shape and encourages bushy, tight new growth. This is also important with some plants such as *Hebe parviflora angustifolia* that won't tolerate hard pruning back into old wood. In fact, such action could kill them. With plants such as *Buxus sempervirens* that have been grown as spheres, if the growth is allowed to get out of hand, cutting it back into its original curvy shape can be quite tricky.

Maintenance

Finally, my last word on the subject of gardening. *There is no such thing as a no-maintenance garden.* The reason for stating this is because I'm often asked to supply one. Television has a lot to answer for...

BELOW
Formally clipped plants such as this *Hebe rakaiensis* are always a feature of Japanese-style gardens.

Palms

Palm trees are the ultimate
architectural plant: they are
shapely, evergreen, and add
an exotic touch to any garden.
Although they are associated
with steamy jungles or baking
hot deserts, many are hardy
enough for average gardens
in much cooler climates.

OPPOSITE
Phoenix canariensis
is a large, stately
palm that is
suitable for mild
gardens only.

The palms that are featured on the following pages have all been selected for their hardiness and availability, as well as for their good looks and ease of cultivation.

Choosing the correct palms for your particular garden is important. If very cold temperatures down to -20°C (-4°F) are regularly experienced, then *Trachycarpus fortunei* would be the palm to choose if it is to stay unprotected for the entire winter. Looking out into the garden during a cold snowy winter and seeing a perfectly happy palm tree is a sight that always lifts the spirits.

Palms are always best planted directly into the ground, rather than grown in containers. In the ground they can grow unchecked to their full stature. The foliage of palm trees planted in the garden always looks greener and healthier

As long as it is given an adequate supply of water and protection from the wind, a healthy palm should live for many decades.

BELOW
*Chamaerops
humilis* is a slow-
growing dwarf
palm, perfect for
small gardens.

than the foliage of those kept in tubs. But if planting in pots is your only option – to stand on the paving around a swimming pool or for a roof terrace, for example – then choose the largest pot possible. Palms kept in small pots not only suffer from having their roots cramped, but the ends of each leaf tip are also much more likely to go brown due to lack of food and uneven amounts of watering. Plants in pots are totally dependent on us for food and water, whereas plants in the ground can usually find their own sources of nourishment and moisture once they are established.

Although palms are reasonably easy to propagate from seed, this method is not for the impatient gardener. Years can be spent waiting for specimens to mature enough to make a real difference to the view from the house windows. Buying a good-sized palm that is at least eight years old ensures instant appeal, and larger palms are also much hardier than small seedlings.

Chamaerops humilis and *Trachycarpus fortunei* can grow in either sun or shade, but all of the other palms featured in this chapter need some sunshine to look their best. All palms need adequate moisture but they hate to have their roots permanently soggy.

Whether you are planting in the ground or in pots, check that the soil contains enough grit, flint, rock or gravel to make sure that excess water can drain away. Virtually all palms, with the exception of *Chamaerops humilis* and *Phoenix canariensis*, need to be sited in a sheltered position away from coastal gales and exposed hilltops. Strong winds can leave the leaves looking battered and messy. Large palm foliage, whether fan-shaped or feathered, looks so much better if it is straight and undamaged.

Palms appreciate a good feed in late spring, when they are actively growing. Sprinkling a few handfuls of a blood, fish and bone mixture on the surface of the soil around each trunk is usually sufficient. Palms rarely need any means of staking and support; each trunk is usually sturdy enough to take care of itself.

When the lower leaves become brown and scruffy, usually because of age, some maintenance is required. The leaf tips are the first part to look untidy, but this can be remedied by lightly trimming them off with a sharp pair of scissors or secateurs (see photograph, top right). This process can be repeated several times as the leaf ages, until so much of the leaf has been removed that more drastic surgery becomes necessary. Once this stage has been reached, the removal of the entire leaf right down to its base becomes desirable. Using a very sharp pair of secateurs, or a saw if the leaf base is especially thick, cut as close to the trunk of the tree as possible, leaving a nice tidy cut. This cut piece will be visible for years, so care should be taken to make it as pleasing to the eye as possible. As the palm matures, and more leaves are removed, these cut leaf bases become numerous along the entire length of the trunk. If the cuts are all made carefully and to the same size, a pattern starts to form, which gives each palm a cared-for appearance (see photograph, below right).

If you have plenty of space in the garden and a reasonably generous budget, instead of just planting individual specimens, go for a more natural look. Palms look so much nicer planted in groves of all the same type but of many different sizes. With a bit of imagination, palms grouped together in various stages of maturity can give the impression of having been there for years, with the smaller trees the result of seedlings produced by larger ones.

Although large palms aren't the cheapest plants around, if they are looked after properly, it will be money well spent, as healthy palms can live for many decades. Palms should always remain a focal point of the garden, adding more of an exotic presence with each extra year's growth.

Palms are low-maintenance plants that suffer very little from pests and diseases. If grown under glass in a greenhouse or conservatory, red spider mites can be a problem. Outside, if the climate is too cold and wet for the chosen type of palm, then leaf spot can become unsightly and spread throughout the entire plant if left unchecked.

If a very cold winter is forecast and the hardiness of palms selected for planting outside is in doubt, emergency tactics can be applied. Gather all the palm leaves together vertically and tie them up fairly tightly with string. Then wrap hessian, horticultural fleece or any suitable porous material many times around the whole lot and fasten it securely (see page 155). This should protect the most vulnerable parts of the plant – the innermost younger leaf shoots – until the worst of the cold spell is over. Do not use bubble-wrap or polythene, as this could trap excess moisture and lead to rotting.

ABOVE
Manicuring palm leaves using a pair of secateurs removes any brown leaf tips that can look unsightly.

BELOW
Butia capitata has had many old leaves removed over several decades, leaving a tidy arrangement of leaf bases.

Brahea armata
Blue Hesper Palm

SYN. *Brahea glauca*
Erythea armata

A beautiful silvery blue desert palm, native to southern California and Mexico, and named in honour of Tycho Brahe, a Danish astronomer. It is one of the prettiest palms that can be grown in colder climates, and is often in short supply due to popular demand.

As well as being one of the most desirable palms, it is also one of the slowest-growing: it can take 15 years to reach 1.8m (6ft) and is therefore usually one of the most expensive to acquire. Buying a decent-sized specimen is essential unless you have great patience and youth on your side.

In its native environment, *Brahea armata* can cope with temperatures as low as -10°C (14°F), but the desert conditions mean that it is used to dry, crisp air with just short spells of really cold weather. If it is grown outside in places that experience high rainfall, foggy conditions and prolonged periods of cold during the winter months, then it becomes much trickier getting it to survive.

Unless warm, dryish winters can be guaranteed, the best way of cultivating *Brahea armata* is to grow it in a large container. It can then be put outside during the summer and overwintered under glass. Make sure the compost has masses of grit stirred into it to make the drainage exceptionally good. Soil-based compost is preferable to peat. Water the pot well during late spring and summer, and keep fairly dry in late autumn and winter. It is important to feed any palm, especially if it is grown permanently in a container. A couple of handfuls of blood, fish and bone applied in late spring will keep it looking healthy. If *Brahea armata* is grown outside all year round, choose a warm, sunny spot in a sheltered position.

Although some huge 12m (40ft) tall specimens can be seen in the wild, *Brahea armata* palms in general cultivation are unlikely to exceed 3m (10ft).

ABOVE
The unusual colouring of *Brahea armata* makes this palm a desirable acquisition.

BELOW
A close-up of the blue, fan-shaped leaves.

Butia capitata
Jelly Palm

SYN. *Cocos australis*
Cocos capitata
Cocos corinata

Butia capitata is an impressively sturdy palm, with large, blue-grey leaves that take the form of arching, feathery fronds. Plants that are raised from seed have a wide colour variation, ranging from greenish-grey through to a pale silvery blue.

Away from its native habitats of Brazil and Argentina, it is maddeningly slow-growing if planted outside. Regardless of its size when purchased and how long it is nurtured and loved for, the wretched thing seems to stay exactly the same size. Each year new fronds are formed with the promise of adding a little extra height but, as they unfurl and arch gracefully downwards, no visible increase in stature is ever observed.

With this in mind, buying a good-sized specimen is essential. In temperate climates, plants over 4m (13ft) are rarely seen. Although not very hardy, *Butia capitata* is such a splendid palm that it is well worth considering even for a cold garden. Planted out in a sunny, sheltered spot, it can be cosseted during the winter by pulling all the leaves up vertically and tying them together, then surrounding the whole plant with layers of horticultural fleece (see page 155). This will keep it cosy until warmer weather returns.

Alternatively, plant it in a container – the larger the better – and wheel it inside under glass when the temperature drops. Mature plants can be rather weighty, so the purchase of a purpose-built, plant-moving sack barrow would make this job less of a chore. Stand containers in the lightest, sunniest part of the conservatory or greenhouse, where the palms will be quite happy for several months. As soon as the very worst of the winter weather is over, move them back outside. If left for too long inside, they can become susceptible to attacks from red spider mites and scale insects.

ABOVE
Butia capitata has elegant, arching blue-grey fronds, and is a good choice for mild gardens.

Chamaerops humilis
Dwarf Fan Palm

Instead of the usual palm tree shape of a mass of leaves on top of a single trunk, *Chamaerops humilis* is a low-growing, bushy palm with numerous stems coming from the same root system to create its own natural grove. The foliage is made up of copious, stiff fans that form a dense clump. Each leaf petiole (stem) is covered with sharp barbs along the entire length. The leaf colour ranges from green, silvery green to almost blue. The bluest plants are sometimes given a separate identity, namely *Chamaerops cerifera*.

Chamaerops humilis is the only Mediterranean palm that really thrives in colder climates. Its natural habitats include Spain, Morocco and Sicily. A tough, hardy palm, it can be grown in a variety of conditions. Because of its density, it is able to shrug off strong winds and salty gales without developing a battered and shredded appearance, as happens with many palms grown in exposed positions. This makes it a perfect choice for any coastal garden.

It is extremely slow-growing – a twenty-year-old specimen is unlikely to be more than 1.2m (4ft) tall and 1.2m (4ft) across – which makes it suitable for containers. *Chamaerops humilis* is unfussy about light levels. A sunny planting position would produce the fastest growth, and older plants would eventually produce little yellow flowers, followed by fat bunches of large, glossy, orange berries. Light shade is also perfectly acceptable, where the leaves take on a deeper, prettier green hue. *Chamaerops humilis* can even cope with conditions indoors, where light levels are quite poor. However, without a few months outside during the summer, new growth would be minimal.

Mature plants start to form little trunks that are usually hidden among the foliage. These are often rather attractive and can be made visible by trimming away some of the external, lower leaves. If one of the central trunks happens to be very straight, then all the outside stems can be sliced off with a saw or sharp knife, to leave just one central, more traditional-looking, single-stemmed palm tree. Any side stems with a piece of root attached can be used for propagation.

ABOVE
The leaf stems of *Chamaerops humilis* are covered with sharp barbs along their entire length.

This method of propagation produces decent-sized plants far more quickly than the usual seed-grown method.

Chamaerops humilis grown outside in very cold and wet conditions can sometimes develop chocolate-brown spots on the leaves. These can spread throughout the entire plant if the disease is not dealt with quickly by removing affected leaves and drenching the whole plant with a systemic fungicide.

Cycas revoluta
Sago Palm

Cycas revoluta is difficult to categorize. Its appearance is somewhere between a palm and a tree fern, although it is actually neither. As it tends to resemble the former slightly more, it fits rather well into this chapter.

This primitive plant has been around for several hundred million years. Its natural habitat is nowadays restricted to China and parts of the East Indies. *Cycas revoluta* is one of the world's slowest-growing plants, taking about fifty years to reach 1.5m (5ft) tall. Because of this, it is a good contender for growing in a terracotta pot in the conservatory.

Its base is similar to that of a coconut, and from this will emerge palm-like fronds covered in a waxy coating, giving it an almost artificial look. The number of new leaves sent out each year could be anything from nil to thirty, depending on its mood, but the year's growth is produced within a few weeks, rather than gradually throughout a whole season.

Growing *Cycas revoluta* is a bit of a challenge. It is almost best neglected, as it is tempting to fuss over such a special plant and give it far more attention than it requires. It is very easy to overwater, and the leaves will show their displeasure quite quickly by turning yellow. If this happens, there is little to be done except to cut them off and learn from the experience. Hopefully, the following year new, fresh green ones will sprout once more from the base.

Cycas revoluta can be grown outside only in very mild areas that rarely get any frost. If your garden is so favoured, plant in a sunny, well-drained spot. In colder climates, keep it in a shady part of the conservatory where direct sunlight through the glass cannot scorch it. Water sparingly until new fronds start to emerge, then water regularly until growth stops. Apart from a light dose of nitrogen in late spring, the only care needed is an occasional wipe over with a cloth to keep the leaves free from dust, and periodic inspections for scale insects.

An important point worth noting is that plants must never be moved when new fronds are unfurling because this upsets their growing pattern as they try to follow the sun's direction. Instead of being symmetrical and curved, the leaves can end up crooked and twisted.

Jubaea chilensis
Chilean Wine Palm

A huge, vast tree that has the thickest trunk of any palm. The wondrous sight of a mature plant can bring a tear to the eye – in the world of palms, its majesty is unrivalled.

The trunk, which can grow up to 1.5m (5ft) in diameter, is pale grey in colour with a rumpled appearance, making it look a bit like the leg of an enormous elephant. Large, waxy fronds of foliage arch out from the top of the trunk.

This tree is painfully slow-growing, and buying anything less than 1.8m (6ft) tall to start with requires patience and perseverance. In its native Chile, it can reach 18m (60ft), but in cooler climates it is unlikely to exceed 9m (30ft), even after a hundred years.

Jubaea chilensis used to be a familiar sight all over Chile but now, alas, it is a rare and protected species. Its exploitation for the production of palm wine – the trunk of a mature plant contains about 450 litres (100 gallons) of the sugary sap that is the main ingredient of this alcoholic beverage – has led to its sad decline. Unfortunately, the harvesting of this sap results in the death of the tree.

Propagation is from the palm's miniature edible coconuts. Seedlings and young plants are very tender, but they become surprisingly hardy as they mature.

Giving this palm perfect growing conditions will help to speed up its growth a little. Rich, moist, fertile soil always gives the best results. It also grows faster in a warm, sun-baked spot, although being in a lightly shaded position will do no harm. The surrounding soil should be kept moist for the first couple of years after planting. The roots can then usually find their own water supply once established. Younger plants could spend the first few years of their life in a container but they should never be allowed to dry out.

Phoenix canariensis
Canary Island Date Palm

This beautiful, shapely palm is extremely popular with enthusiasts of architectural plants – it seems to sum up everything that is exotic in the gardening world. Massive, arching fronds explode out of what looks like a huge, thick pineapple. The foliage appears lush and soft as it swishes around in the wind, conjuring up images of windswept desert islands and Robinson Crusoe. It is one of the most frequently planted palms in the world, and is seen by numerous holidaymakers on their travels, who then wish to have their own specimen as a souvenir of a sunny vacation.

What a pity, then, that its hardiness is not that good. In temperate climates, this palm is reliably hardy only in warm inner cities and mild coastal regions. But, because it is so beautiful, many gardeners are prepared to take a risk and plant it anyway. If this is the case, purchase a plant as large as possible – the bigger the palm, the hardier it is – and find the sunniest spot in the garden.

For a palm, *Phoenix canariensis* is fairly quick-growing, so keeping it in a pot is a difficult task. If the winter is fairly dry, it can endure quite low temperatures. If it is a wet winter, this can lead to trouble, as the vulnerable part of the central growth point can rot and never recover. Wrapping the plant up for the winter can help: tie all the foliage together vertically and cover it with something warm but porous, such as hessian (see page 155). With all the leaves huddled together, the tougher outer ones shelter the more delicate inner ones.

When brown-bitting becomes necessary (the removal of the lower leaves that have become tatty with age), you will need a large saw. Every time a leaf is removed, saw it off at exactly the same distance away from the trunk and at exactly the same angle as all the others. This leads to quite a pleasing decorative effect around the trunk as it ages. Take care when getting too close to the ends of the fronds: they look soft and harmless but can give a surprisingly painful jab.

Older plants in colder climates can form trunks 4.5m (15ft) tall in around twenty years. Mature plants also form massive clusters of beautiful lush orange fruits. These are inedible, so leave them on the tree.

Trachycarpus fortunei
Chusan Palm

SYN. *Chamaerops excelsa*

An essential palm for all exotic gardens. This is by far the best palm for temperate gardens because it is the hardiest palm in the world. It is also one of the easiest to cultivate, coping with a wide range of conditions. It is usually on a single trunk, but multi-stemmed plants are sometimes seen. The entire trunk is covered with coarse, shaggy hair, making it instantly recognizable. The leaves are large and fan-shaped. Named in honour of Robert Fortune, the plant explorer, *Trachycarpus fortunei* is native to central China.

Although happiest in a sunny spot, this palm can be grown in light levels almost down to full shade, where it remains quite healthy, even if it grows more slowly than it would in a brighter position. Any well-drained soil will do, whether it is clay, loam, peat or chalk, but rich, fertile conditions will always give the best results. It is a greedy plant, and poor soils would benefit from regular applications of well-rotted manure in the spring and early summer.

Avoid planting where the ground can become waterlogged, as this would be detrimental to the roots. Also avoid planting in a position where it is constantly windy, such as on the seafront or the top of a hill. Although this won't cause any harm, it will give a battered appearance to the leaves, as they easily bend and shred if exposed to strong breezes, and the whole plant can end up looking miserable.

Considering that it's a palm, *Trachycarpus fortunei* can tolerate ridiculously low temperatures. As long as it is at least 1.2m (4ft) tall, it can cope with winters down to -20°C (-4°F), which is astonishing for such a tropical-looking tree.

Older plants can produce attractive flowers early in the season. They start off as lumps of yellow close to the trunk and emerge as large arching shapes, which have been wittily referred to as smoked haddocks. The flowers are small but numerous, and gradually ripen to blue-black berries. The whole flowering cycle is interesting to watch, but while this process is happening, the tree is having its energy drained. Ideally, a hardhearted approach should be adopted and the flower

RIGHT
Large, luscious
fan-shaped
leaves emerge
from the top of
a hairy trunk.

RIGHT
A healthy plant
could produce
ten new leaves
each year.

buds chopped off at the first sign, so that all available energy can be devoted to leaf production instead.

Very little maintenance is needed, apart from removing any older leaves as they turn brown. But for those who like a challenge, there is an interesting technique that can be used on the trunk. Popular though *Trachycarpus fortunei* is, few people would claim that it is beautiful. Its large, hairy trunk. just isn't that pretty. However, by removing all the hair and exposing the lower waxy layers, you can transform it into a much more tropical-looking addition to the garden. Removing the hair is in no way detrimental to the palm and doesn't appear to lessen its hardiness. A plant stripped in this way nearly eight years ago and growing in a frost pocket remains perfectly happy.

The instructions given opposite for this technique are for right-handed gardeners.

1. Starting at the base of the trunk, tear away at the hairy fibre at ground level until you uncover the first leaf base.

2. Hold the leaf base in your left hand and slice the right-hand side of it downwards using a very sharp, good-quality, serrated bread knife. Slice around the entire trunk clockwise while peeling away the fibrous surface.

3. You can now see the very first orangey-cream layer.

4. This photograph shows the trunk after three leaf bases have been cut away.

5. Repeat the process, working your way up the trunk.

6. This photograph is a close-up of the trunk with more of the leaf bases removed.

7. Keep working your way up the trunk. This photograph shows the finished result after an hour's work.

8. Just one trunk will yield a barrowful of fibre. There must be lots of uses for this material but, so far, I've failed to discover any!

There are a couple of interesting forms of *Trachycarpus fortunei* that are well worth mentioning. The first is *Trachycarpus wagnerianus*, which was once thought to be an entirely separate species.

The leaves of this palm are smaller than those of *Trachycarpus fortunei*, but straighter and stiffer, giving the tree a much tidier appearance. It can cope with windy positions slightly better, too, without tearing quite as much. It is slower-growing and can be fairly difficult to track down, which makes it more expensive to buy. If seeds are taken from one of these plants and germinated successfully, usually around 25 per cent will come true to form. The other 75 per cent look

exactly the same as *Trachycarpus fortunei*, giving weight to the argument that it is not a separate species.

Another form worthy of special mention is *Trachycarpus* 'Breppo'. It's not often seen, but worth hunting around for. The leaves are large, beautiful and fairly stiff, but it's the trunk that gives it a superior look. It is stockier than that of *Trachycarpus fortunei*, and the trunk hair is made up of much longer and fluffier tresses. Removing this would be a pity.

Washingtonia filifera
Cotton Palm

A splendid palm tree with huge fan-shaped leaves of vivid green. The fingers of each part of the leaf are tipped with white threads of 'cotton', which hang down from every frond, giving a graceful feel to the whole plant.

Named in honour of George Washington, *Washingtonia filifera* is native to California and all south-western parts of the USA. It is used heavily for municipal planting and is easily recognizable by the thatch of old leaves that hangs down vertically to cover the whole trunk. However, these old brown leaves are considered a fire hazard in some areas, and their removal by brown-bitting is becoming more commonplace. Seeing the clean stout trunks with a head of lush green foliage is a huge improvement on their appearance.

As it is a desert palm, *Washingtonia filifera* can cope very well with hot, dry atmospheres, making it an excellent choice for an atrium or a large conservatory. Its speed of growth and eventual size of at least 9m (30ft) even away from the desert mean that planting in the ground is by far the best option. When planning their conservatories, some gardeners leave planting spaces in the ground for such plants. If it really has to be grown in a pot, make sure it is a massive one. This palm takes around fifteen years to attain a height of 3.7m (12ft) but then it can speed up and become unmanageable very quickly. Large palms are far too heavy to keep repotting easily. However, this palm is so beautiful, it is tempting to buy one, grow it for ten years and then worry about what to do with it when the time comes.

Growing young plants from seed is very easy and quick. Observing the root system on even newly germinated seedlings will tell you that this palm is used to finding its own water supply: the tap root is about five times longer than the leaf section. But this drought-resistant quality applies only to plants growing in the ground – container-grown specimens must be watered regularly during the growing season.

Full sun is an essential requirement, too. The only maintenance needed is frequent inspections for red spider mites.

Ferns

Ferns are delightful additions to any garden. They do not flower, but their wide variety of leaf shape and their different shades of green bring something special to planting schemes.

ABOVE
The foliage of
Pteris cretica
consists of delicate
evergreen ribbons.

There are hundreds of different ferns generally offered for sale, but this chapter concentrates on the few that could be described as the most architectural, either because of their size and shape or because they are evergreen. All ferns have a certain presence and charm, but those giving year-round colour obviously have more benefit in the garden.

There are several categories of evergreen fern discussed in these pages. There are Tree Ferns such as *Dicksonia antarctica* and *Dicksonia squarrosa*, which have such a stately and imposing shape that they could easily be planted as single special specimens in any garden. Then there are the smaller ferns such as *Pteris cretica* and *Blechnum spicant*, which look especially effective in large numbers. There are also large, low-growing ferns such as *Blechnum chilense* and *Polystichum munitum*, which look fine planted singly in smaller gardens but would look very impressive in groups if you happen to have the luxury of larger grounds.

Ferns enjoy moist, shady conditions in corners of the garden where there is little wind and high humidity. They love being on sloping ground, where the water can drain away immediately without collecting around the roots. Although they need plenty of moisture, boggy places are not suitable.

Ferns are easy to maintain. They need little extra food, and pests and diseases are rare if the cultivation notes are followed. This is just as well because the foliage of ferns is often too delicate to cope with being sprayed with chemicals. If anything is found nibbling on ferns, it is better to remove the problem manually, as insecticides often cause more damage than the bugs.

A whole new language has been constructed around ferns, and some of the terms deserve explanation. The leaves are referred to as fronds. The new season's growth is tightly coiled up before gradually straightening out as it matures, and its curly stage is rather imaginatively referred to as a crozier (think of the large metal crooks, or staffs, brandished by bishops when they are in full

RIGHT
*Dicksonia
antarctica* adds
a loud presence
to any fernery.

regalia). Ferns don't have flowers or seeds or seed pods. They are propagated from spores, which is powdery dust contained in little sacs called sori. There are also fern societies to join if you're really keen, and these are referred to as pteridological societies. Unfortunately, I get the word pteridological mixed up with pterodactyl, which conjures up all sorts of mental images of the people attending their annual meetings.

Some fern collectors take their hobby as seriously as stamp collectors, delighting in obtaining as many different types of fern as possible. This is fine for a botanic collection, but no use at all for the amateur gardener or landscaper. Ferns look so much better if planted out in larger numbers. The effect is far more dramatic if ten of the same fern are planted together, rather than one each of ten different species.

Most ferns prefer to be planted in areas of the garden where many other plants refuse to grow, which makes them useful as well as desirable.

This group of plants adores soil containing lots of peat. The light texture suits their root systems admirably. With the natural sources of peat being stripped away, it seems irresponsible recommending such material. But, having tried many peat substitutes, there is nothing as good as the real stuff - not yet, anyway. Hopefully, this is something the compost industry is working towards. It would be wonderful to find something that is as cheap and pleasant to use, produces excellent results and doesn't have to be shipped from halfway around the globe using fuel-hungry means of transport.

The propagation of ferns is a tricky subject. Some ferns such as *Asplenium scolopendrium* conveniently form clumps as they mature. These can usually be divided up to obtain extra plants. Others such as *Woodwardia radicans* form baby ferns on the upper surface of mature fronds. These fronds can be pegged down over compost until the babies have formed their own root system. They can then be separated and grown on singly. The main method of fern production, though, is by using spores. These spores are stored on the backs of mature fronds usually in formal lines. The procedure of gathering spores, which are the size of tiny dust particles, sterilizing every piece of equipment you use, fiddling around with seed trays, using polythene covers to retain humidity, watching green slimy substances form, followed by microscopic plants, which have to be separated from all the sludge that has formed, is all too much for most gardeners, who are sensible enough to leave it to the experts. Apart from the Tree Ferns, most other types of fern are not expensive enough to warrant such a chore.

Asplenium scolopendrium
Hart's Tongue Fern

The fronds of *Asplenium scolopendrium* are fresh apple-green with a waxy surface and wavy edges. The undersides are often well covered with thick rows of chocolate-coloured sori (spore cases). It is not a large fern, reaching a maximum height and width of only around 60cm (2ft). In spacious gardens it can be planted in groups for more impact, although it is quite noticeable as a single specimen.

This evergreen fern is extremely tough and can cope with very low temperatures and a wide range of conditions that many other ferns would not tolerate. Large amounts of lime or chalk in the soil cause no problems at all. It also copes with more sun and less water than would normally be expected from a fern. I have a small plant that has grown from a spore blown by the wind into a tiny space between a concrete path and the bottom of a terracotta pot. I'm not sure what it lives on, and its size is certainly somewhat diminished, but it has lived there quite happily for three years.

Although this fern is tolerant of less than perfect conditions, much better results will be achieved with a light, alkaline soil, frequent watering and a shady, well-drained planting position. Ferns must be planted into the ground very gently, as the roots hate to grow through soil that has been heavily compacted. Fern roots are idle things that enjoy an easy journey.

Feeding is usually unnecessary unless the soil is really poor. A generous helping of leaf mould would help, but this isn't always easy to obtain. Alternatively, add a small amount of really well-rotted crumbly manure to the surrounding area, or add some liquid seaweed food to a watering can and use this mix every six to eight weeks during spring and summer.

Propagation from spores is best left to the experts, but large clumps of this fern can often be divided quite successfully. The best time for this would be early spring, just before the new season's growth commences. Pests and diseases are rarely a problem, especially with the straight form. There are lots of cultivars available, with fronds of varying widths and with different degrees of wavy edges. Some are quite acceptable, but they are generally less robust and less vigorous than the basic *Asplenium scolopendrium*.

ABOVE
Asplenium scolopendrium is a rather un-ferny-looking fern with entire fronds instead of the usual filigree style of foliage associated with ferns.

Blechnum chilense
Seersucker Fern

A great beast of a fern, essential to all jungly and leafy planting schemes. Given the right conditions, it could easily reach a height and spread of more than 1.2m (4ft).

Ferns can be fussy plants, and *Blechnum chilense* is no exception. Shade is essential to keep the fronds a good colour. Although low temperatures can be coped with, milder climates are preferred. The most vital factor for achieving ferns of colossal proportions is a super-abundance of water. The largest specimens of this Chilean monster are nearly always growing on the edges of ponds or streams, where the roots have constant access to water. Waterlogging won't be tolerated at all, though, so good drainage is important. Planting on a slope or bank in a high rainfall area out of the wind would be a perfect choice.

Soil should be light and crumbly, but using peat on its own won't be enough to sustain *Blechnum chilense*. An ideal mix would be equal quantities of leaf mould, peat (or peat substitute) and loam. Leaf mould is a bit of a luxury and not always easy to acquire, but the search is worth the effort. All ferns are happiest planted directly into the ground, but if this is not possible, use a very large container and never let it dry out. Watering ferns is never an easy undertaking, as they need constant moisture without ever becoming too boggy.

When planting, firm the roots in very gently. Fern roots prefer their journey through the soil to be made as easy as possible. Humidity is appreciated, but try to avoid getting the fronds too wet in very cold weather, as this can cause them to blacken. Feeding is not usually required, but the addition of some very old, well-rotted crumbly manure to the surrounding area in spring would be beneficial, especially to poor soils. The only other maintenance to consider is the removal of any older fronds that have turned brown with age. Cut them off with secateurs to keep the plant looking green and healthy.

Propagation is again best left to the experts, but even skilled propagators have trouble with this one, as the spores must be really fresh to succeed. Pests and diseases aren't usually a problem, although large green caterpillars occasionally feed on the fronds.

ABOVE
The surface of the fronds is rough to the touch, and puckered like seersucker, hence its common name.

Blechnum spicant
Hard Fern or **Deer Fern**

The bright emerald-green fronds of this fully hardy, evegreen fern add a bit of cheer to a dark corner of the garden, especially in winter. They also have an attractive glossy sheen to them. Individual clumps can spread very slowly to cover eventually only about 60sq cm (2sq ft), and the maximum height is unlikely to be much more than 45cm (18in). Because of its relatively small stature, planting just one single specimen gives no effect at all to a garden. *Blechnum spicant* must be planted in much larger groups to give visually pleasing results. In decent-sized gardens, a whole bank or border planted up with just these ferns would look splendid. In smaller gardens, there is still usually enough room to accommodate generous groups of them. Anything less than five would, in my opinion, look rather miserly.

These ferns should never be removed from their natural habitat, tempting as this may be. Apart from the responsible conservationist attitude, they tend not to appreciate being hauled out of the ground and transplanted elsewhere. The chance of damaging their roots and harming the plant is quite high. Instead,

always purchase them from a reputable and reliable nursery where they have been propagated professionally and grown on site. Propagating these ferns is quite tricky and is best left to the experts. If you enjoy a challenge, try growing them from freshly ripened spores removed from the parent plant in early autumn.

This fern is happiest in the shade, grown in moist peaty soil with a bit of leaf mould added. Although shade and moisture are preferred, this tough little fern can cope with drier conditions, and will even put up with some sunshine. Neutral to acid soil is necessary – chalk or lime in the soil will give very poor results.

If you can, give this plant a slightly sloping site, so that excess moisture can run away immediately. The planting area should never be allowed to dry out, but boggy conditions would be unsuitable. This is an exceptionally easy fern to grow, providing it has been planted correctly. No annual feeding is needed, and pests and diseases rarely cause problems. The only annual maintenance is removing any older brown fronds. Cut them off as far into the plant as possible with secateurs.

ABOVE
The leaf formation resembles the shape of a fish skeleton. This fern is a familiar sight in English woodlands.

Dicksonia antarctica
Tasmanian Tree Fern

Tree ferns are fabulous plants to own. Few plants are more exotic than this leafy giant. A thick, fibrous chocolate-brown trunk is topped with huge deeply cut fronds 2.2m (7ft) long. *Dicksonia antarctica* starts to form a trunk after five years, which then grows at only 30cm (1ft) every ten years, so buying a baby plant will need a lot of time and patience to see it develop into something spectacular. A plant this slow would be fine in a container for several years as long as the compost is kept moist at all times. Container-grown specimens look wonderful in a shady conservatory.

There are lots of mature plants offered for sale at nurseries and garden centres, and many thousands of *Dicksonia antarctica* are imported from forest clearance sites in Tasmania and Australia. Please buy from a reputable nursery to ensure that these plants are not illegal imports. If there is any doubt at all as to their origin, leave them where they are and buy from somewhere else.

This fern is extremely fussy in its requirements – it is almost like buying a pet. Shade is essential for the very best results.

A sheltered position is also important, not only shelter from the wind but also from anyone brushing past it. Humidity is necessary too – ideally, the trunk should be sprayed twice daily during the hot summer months.

The best soil is peat, or peat substitute, mixed with leaf mould and silver sand for drainage. This is usually not difficult to organize if the fern is being planted into a container, but it is a little unrealistic for most gardens. It will, in fact, grow in any light soil that holds some moisture without ever being boggy. Enrich it annually with either leaf mould or kitchen waste from the compost heap.

Watering should be done regularly to keep the soil just about moist. The occasional application of a balanced dilute feed poured into the top of the trunk can have a remarkable effect on how many new fronds are produced – twice the normal number can be expected. Feed weekly from mid-spring until mid-summer.

The fronds should remain evergreen for several years, but if ideal conditions cannot be met, they are quite likely to go brown. If this

happens, cut them off at their base and try to treat next year's fronds with a little more care. Propagation is difficult and best left to a specialist fern propagator. Pests and diseases are rarely a problem.

These plants are reliably hardy only in mild inner city gardens or those near the coast. In colder gardens, some winter protection will be needed. Tucking a handful of straw or fleece into the top of the trunk will be enough to protect next year's new fronds (see photograph, right). Push the straw down gently into the hollow bit where new fronds emerge. It should stay there without being fastened down.

The existing year's fronds can be allowed to frost and turn brown, and then be cut off at their base. A much better plan, however, would be to protect the fronds by wrapping them in horticultural fleece for the winter. Having several

years' worth of fronds on a tree fern makes it even more lush and splendid to look at.

To wrap *Dicksonia antartica* for winter, all you need is a ball of hessian string, a roll of horticultural fleece and, unless you are around 2m (6⅝ft) tall, a stepladder. Instructions for winter wrapping, together with some useful tips, are given on the opposite page.

1. Scoop the fronds up vertically and tie them together firmly with hessian string.

2. Tie one end of the roll of horticultural fleece to a leaf stem to act as a starting point.

3. Wrap the fleece around all the foliage several times.

4. Once you have wrapped the fern completely, fold some of the fleece over the top of the fern to protect the leaf tips, and secure it in place with string. Tie string around the fern in several more places to secure the rest of the fleece.

5. This photograph shows the finished ensemble.

Some points to remember

● Tie the string firmly but not too tightly to allow for its easy removal during the winter if a warm spell of weather approaches. The fronds would also appreciate a bit of fresh air now and again.

● Instead of using horticultural fleece, after tying up the fronds with string, stack straw bales around the whole plant instead. This looks more aesthetically pleasing than fleece, although obtaining straw bales isn't always practical if you live in a large town or city.

● If you use straw bales, remove them the minute the weather warms up. If they are left on for more than a couple of months at a time, the heat generated by the straw can cook the fronds, turning them into a mushy mess, which rather defeats the whole point of wrapping them up in the first place.

● If your tree fern is being grown in a container and not in the ground, the roots will need a bit of protection from the frost too. Either move both the plant and its pot into a shady porch or conservatory for the winter, or wrap it all up as described in the steps and, in addition, wrap a large thick blanket around the pot. Rolls of bubble wrap could be used instead, if preferred. This will keep everything – roots, fronds and next year's new growth – cosy for the winter.

Dicksonia squarrosa
New Zealand Tree Fern

A sumptuous-looking tree fern from New Zealand that is more delicate in appearance and less well known than the more familiar *Dicksonia antarctica* described on pages 71–73. The trunk is quite slim and of the very darkest chocolate-brown. The same colour is also found on the underside of each frond, running the length of the leaf veins and, unfortunately, hidden from view for most of the time. The fronds are large and spread out gracefully from the top of the trunk. These can easily be 1.5m (5ft) long.

Although home-grown tree ferns can be obtained as small specimens produced from spores, virtually all those sold commercially are imported from New Zealand. They usually arrive in huge quantities packed into containers and shipped across to retailers who are eager to get their hands on large, mature plants. Unfortunately, these fabulous plants are not as hardy and easy to grow as is often implied, and around 90 per cent of them end up dead, which is a sad end to something that has been growing happily for fifty or so years in its native country. Before buying a *Dicksonia squarrosa*, please spend some time thinking about its growing requirements to ensure that it has more than a sporting chance of survival.

A perfect soil mix would consist of peat (or peat substitute) with some leaf mould and silver sand mixed in, but most types of light, well-drained soil would be okay. Avoid very chalky soil, not because it particularly hates alkaline conditions, but because of this soil's inability to retain enough moisture. A quiet, shady, humid position, sheltered from wind is essential. Leave enough space around it for the fronds to spread out fully without touching anything. Keep the soil just moist. Humidity is vital, not just for the leaves, but also for the trunk, which should be sprayed regularly in hot weather. This fern could be kept in a large pot for many years, but much better results would be gained from planting directly into the ground. Pour diluted liquid feed into the top of the trunk every month throughout the growing season.

Leave propagation to the experts. Pests and diseases do not usually cause problems. Unless your garden is very mild, winter protection will be necessary. Use exactly the same methods as described for *Dicksonia antarctica*.

ABOVE
A beautiful tree fern with chocolate-brown veins across the back of the fronds.

Polystichum munitum
Western Sword Fern

Another huge fern that is evergreen and fully hardy. It grows in the traditional fern shape, resembling a massive shuttlecock bursting out of the ground. Long, leafy fronds can reach 90–120cm (3–4ft) if the growing conditions are perfect. The spread of each plant can also reach the same dimensions.

These massive ferns look wonderful if planted as giant groundcover beneath moisture-loving trees such as *Eucalyptus aggregata* or *Eriobotrya japonica*. The effect looks very natural, as it would in any jungly environment where the ground is usually totally concealed. The canopy of the trees would provide enough shade to keep any fern a good healthy colour.

A sloping site is preferred so that any rain can immediately drain away without collecting in puddles around the plant's base. Waterlogging would quickly lead to rotting, but ample supplies of water are essential to keep this fern happy enough to reach its maximum size. A site on a shady riverbank or by a pond would also make a good planting position. This plant must be kept out of the wind, which is true of most ferns, but particularly of larger ones.

Also, avoid planting where people might brush past the foliage, as this is not something that will improve its appearance.

Make sure the soil is light enough to enable the roots to penetrate easily. Peaty soil on its own is not enough to retain adequate supplies of moisture, and very light, poor soil should be enriched every spring. Either use large quantities of leaf mould or spread well-rotted, crumbly manure throughout the surrounding area.

If moisture is allowed to gather in the crown during the colder months, the fronds can become discoloured with fungal disease, which eventually leads to rotting. Spraying with fungicide should be avoided. Instead, chop the whole lot down to the base and let it start again. The following season, it will grow like mad and produce masses of new croziers. By the end of the season, its former glory will have been regained. This treatment can also be adopted if it has been allowed to dry out and the fronds have become tired and brown.

Propagation is best left to the experts. Apart from the fungal problems already mentioned, pests are not usually a problem.

ABOVE
This evergreen fern is so hardy that it has even been seen growing in parts of Alaska, which sounds almost unbelievable.

Polystichum polyblepharum
Polly-polly

A fern with such a ridiculous Latin name, I was tempted not to include it. But it is such a pretty plant and so popular that it couldn't possibly be omitted. It is quite a small fern, growing to no more than 60cm (2ft) in height and width. The fronds are dark green in colour and have a lovely sheen to the upper surface. Their glossy finish makes them very noticeable.

Forget about planting just one or two of these ferns – they must be planted in large swathes for maximum effect. Large groups of the same type of fern always look more natural. The effect is far from boring. In fact, it looks restful and serene.

This Japanese native fern enjoys the usual requirements expected of this group of plants. Light, crumbly soil with some leaf mould added to provide moisture retention and nutrients is ideal. A shady position is best, and shelter from strong drying winds is essential. It has no special requirements as to soil acidity, but avoid very chalky or sandy soils, as these tend to be too thin and well drained to satisfy such moisture-loving plants. *Polystichum polyblepharum* should never be allowed to

dry out. It needs a constant supply of water that can be allowed to drain away almost immediately. Water collecting around the roots or crown of the plant can lead to rotting.

Annual feeding is not normally necessary, but very poor soils can be enriched with more leaf mould or some well-rotted manure that has reached the crumbly moisture-free stage. If just a few ferns are being added to a place in the garden that is already planted up, they will have to be happy with whatever soil is there. If whole new areas or borders are being planned, then it is better to enrich all the soil thoroughly before any planting begins. If the soil is heavy, then dig in lots of peat or peat substitute to help with the drainage and to lighten the soil texture. If the soil is poor or very light and sandy, digging in lots of extra loam will help retain moisture and provide nutrients. Finish off by digging in either small amounts of manure or heaps of leaf mould, which really is as valuable as gold dust from a fern's point of view.

Propagation is by using the dreaded spore method. Pests and diseases are rarely a problem.

ABOVE
The fronds of Polly-polly have a lovely glossy sheen to them.

Polystichum setiferum
Soft Shield Fern

This European fern's appeal in both looks and size creeps up slowly on unsuspecting gardeners. For the first couple of years, it is a perfectly satisfactory addition to any garden. It is a fine evergreen fern that is well suited to those damp and shady corners that can sometimes be a bit of a challenge.

By year number three, it starts to get much more attention during the daily promenade around the garden. With the arrival of year number four, it suddenly becomes one of the most beautiful plants in the garden. By this age, its spread is almost 90cm (3ft) across. Its massive fronds unfurl out of tightly rolled-up fluffy, white balls, which are attractive in their own right. Each frond is very finely cut into a delicate filigree pattern. It is usually during late spring in its fourth season that you suddenly wonder why you didn't plant loads more.

There are masses of cultivars of this fern; some of the 'Divisilobum' and 'Plumoso-divisilobum' ones are particularly attractive with lots of soft, feathery fronds, which are excellent plants even when young. But for sheer bulk and splendour, the straight form remains a favourite. Although propagation of this fern is generally done using spores, some of the cultivars conveniently produce baby ferns along the surface of adult fronds.

When planting out *Polystichum setiferum*, make sure there is plenty of room around it to reach its mature size without being crowded. Ferns hate being transplanted and if too many have been placed closely together, plants may have to be thinned out and disposed of. They are unlikely to survive being replanted once their roots have been disturbed.

The usual fern requirements also apply to this species. Lots of moisture without waterlogging is essential. A quiet humid spot in the garden is also preferred, although this fern is quite forgiving of less than ideal conditions, coping reasonably well with the occasional dry spell. Light, peaty soil enriched with leaf mould would be a good planting medium; shelter from strong winds to prevent the tips of the fronds from drying out is also important. Pests and diseases are uncommon, although excess water gathering in the crown could lead to rotting.

ABOVE
The lovely arching shape of each frond gives the whole plant a very architectural quality almost unmatched in the fern world.

Pteris cretica
Ribbon Fern or **Table Fern**

At first sight, this pretty little fern looks more like a miniature bamboo. The fronds are quite flimsy 'ribbons' that are a fresh bright green in colour. Its height at maturity won't exceed much more than 60cm (2ft). It is a lovely fern to possess and makes a complete contrast to most others.

It can cope with more sun than many other ferns, but still prefers a shady aspect. Too much sunshine, particularly midday sun, would scorch the fronds and the fresh green colour would take on a yellowish tinge. Light shade would be perfect. It can also cope with more wind than many ferns, but a sheltered position would still be best. This fern seems to manage with less water than most too. Keeping the soil constantly moist would give better results, but if it dries out occasionally, no great harm seems to happen to it. Most soil types suit *Pteris cretica*, but avoid very heavy clay, which makes it hard work for the roots to penetrate, and poor chalky ones, which dry out too quickly. This fern is so forgiving, that once settled in the garden, little fernlettes will appear out of cracks in nearby paving or between the pointing of damp brick walls. If spores blow into such

places, they can mature quite happily, living on virtually nothing except the odd shower of rain.

Pteris cretica is another fern that deserves to be planted in large numbers. Groups of this beautiful foliage growing together look very effective. They provide excellent groundcover for planting underneath moisture-loving trees and make a good job of brightening up dark and dull corners of the garden.

Slugs and snails adore the foliage and can completely ruin the appearance of all the fronds. If your garden is prone to these slimy beasts, use a slug repellent regularly throughout spring and summer. If the fronds become too tatty, cut the whole plant back to its base. New croziers will soon grow up to regain the fern's former glory. The new spring growth is an added attraction – its colour is even more striking, and new fronds are produced in plentiful amounts.

Propagation can be done from spores, but there is an easier method. As the plants mature, they start to form large clumps. Where there is enough material on substantial older plants, bits can be sliced off and separated in the same way as for other clump-forming plants.

Woodwardia radicans
Chain Fern

A magnificent evergreen fern, with massive arching fronds up to 6ft (1.8m) long, which would love a mild, jungly garden to lounge in. Alternatively, it can make a dramatic addition to a steamy bathroom if suspended from the ceiling in a large hanging basket. As *Woodwardia radicans* needs very little heat, it would also make a fine plant for a cool conservatory.

This fern tolerates higher light levels than many ferns, but still needs to be protected from direct sun. It should never be allowed to dry out and, if grown indoors, appreciates frequent misting to keep the air around it humid. Plant in a sheltered spot. The huge foliage would fare badly in a windy position. An ideal soil mix would be one part peat (or peat substitute) one part loam, one part leaf mould and a handful of silver sand mixed in to help with the drainage. This is fairly easy to provide for indoor use, but for outdoors, any rich, light, moisture-retentive soil would give perfectly good results.

Older specimens planted outside can produce little fernlettes at the end of each mature frond. As they increase in size, they weigh the parent frond down so it touches the ground. In time,

the baby fern will be tempted by the compost directly underneath it to send out some roots. Eventually, the new plant will become self-sufficient until it matures enough to repeat the process with another generation. In the wild, they could cover quite a wide area using this method, with lots of ferns all linked together. Presumably, this is what gives us the common name of Chain Fern. Another explanation is that the sori (spore cases) form a pattern like a chain on the backs of the fronds, but that theory is a bit dull for my liking. Fortunately, as many of us would object to having the entire garden covered with giant fronds, the baby plants can be removed at any time and grown on separately.

Very little annual maintenance is needed, apart from removing the occasional older brown frond. Cut these right back into the plant so the cut end isn't visible, using secateurs. Pests and diseases are rarely a problem, especially if grown outdoors. The most important thing to worry about is the watering. Too much will lead to rotting; too little will cause the fronds to shrivel. Rainwater is preferred, particularly if you live in a hard water area.

Grasses

Grasses are currently enjoying immense popularity, but few could really be described as architectural because of their poor winter performance, with many of them turning a horrid brown colour as soon as autumn approaches. However, the grasses selected for this chapter are definitely architectural.

The following grasses are nearly all evergreen, thus creating a year-round presence wherever they are planted. They are all striking in some way, for example, *Ophiopogon planiscapus* 'Nigrescens' with its jet-black foliage or *Cyperus papyrus* with its tall stalks topped with huge fluffy tufts of flowers. And let's not forget an old favourite, *Cortaderia selloana*, the lovely Pampas Grass that for years has been snootily ignored but, at last, is enjoying new fame as gardeners once again start to appreciate its stately appearance.

The two non-evergreen grasses featured are here because, despite their lack of winter appeal, the statuesque quality of *Arundo donax* and the shapely outline of *Miscanthus sinensis* 'Gracillimus' are just too wonderful to overlook. Their stunning good looks during three quarters of the year are compensation enough to earn their inclusion.

The grasses in this chapter have a wide range of shapes and sizes, from the diminutive *Acorus gramineus* 'Variegata' to the decorous *Cortaderia richardii*. Their cultural requirements vary hugely too, from the water-loving *Cyperus alternifolius* to the unfussy *Luzula sylvatica* 'Marginata'.

One thing these grasses do all have in common is their ease of propagation. All of them grow as clump-forming plants and all can be divided up at almost any stage of maturity. The smaller grasses can have their clumps teased apart

by hand. Some will need the help of a sharp knife and some with heftier root systems will need the assistance of a strong spade to chop through each section. The propagation of grasses is more down to brute force than expertise, and even novice gardeners are capable of achieving successful results.

Apart from the *Cyperus* grasses, all of the plants described here are fully hardy, capable of coping with temperatures down to -20°C (-4°F). So, almost any gardener can take advantage of their beauty, especially as their hardiness is combined with a robust nature and ability to cope with hostile conditions. Their individual requirements are discussed in each plant entry, but it will be noted that many can cope with exposed and windy conditions, making them good choices for gardens near the coast and for those on open hilltops. This group of plants is far more forgiving than their close relatives, the bamboos.

Grasses are the perfect group of plants for beginners, although experts appreciate their fine qualities too.

Grasses can fit in with many different kinds of planting schemes. The larger grasses look splendid enough planted as single specimens to spice up unexciting borders or to act as a soft backdrop to other plants. The smaller ones will look good anywhere in the garden, but avoid dotting just single specimens around.

The smaller grasses look far better, more noticeable, more effective and more dramatic if they are planted in drifts or large groups. In a small space, five of the same species of plant look a hundred times more natural and pleasing to the eye than one each of five different species, which can give a bitty and undisciplined look to a garden.

The maintenance of most grasses is easy too, providing their individual needs have been catered for, and most are happy with a light annual dressing of blood, fish and bone in early spring. Older clumps can become a bit tatty and tired-looking after a few years. If this happens, they can be rejuvenated quite easily. Many can be hacked back to ground level with a sharp pair of shears in the autumn or early spring. This may sound a drastic thing to do, but you will be rewarded by a vigorous burst of new fresh foliage as soon as the new growing season commences. By the end of the season, a completely new clump will have formed. The remaining bases of the old foliage will, by this time, have dried out and gathered as a brown thatch throughout the bottom of the new leaves. This can be teased out by hand to keep everything looking fresh and tidy.

ABOVE
Miscanthus sinensis 'Gracillimus' looks and sounds wonderful as the breeze swishes through it.

BELOW
Luzula sylvatica 'Marginata' has a very forgiving nature, making it a good choice for beginners.

Acorus gramineus 'Variegatus'

For those gardeners who like their plants neat, tidy and compact, this tiny Japanese grass would fit the bill admirably. It reaches no more than about 25cm (10in) in height. It grows in fan-shaped sections, consisting of many individual blades of grass closely packed together. Gradually, these clumps bulk up and spread quite slowly to cover a distance of around 60cm (2ft) across. Each of these sections can be removed at any time of the year and used for propagation.

The grassy leaf blades are vertically striped with green and pale cream. The variegation is pleasantly subtle and, unlike many coloured-leaved plants, is not at all offensive to look at. Mature plants sometimes produce flowers, particularly during very warm weather. These are long and narrow and can be quite difficult to see, as they are the same colour as the cream bits on the foliage.

This plant is ideal for any moist or boggy spot in the garden. It loves moisture so much that it is even quite happy in a shallow pond, and makes a useful aquatic addition to water features and streams. It is fully evergreen and

as attractive in winter as it is in summer. As it is very slow-growing, it could be grown in a pot for the first few years of its life, but remembering to water it virtually every day could become too much of a chore. This grass is too small to be grown as a single specimen and needs to be in larger groups for maximum impact.

Full sun will give the best colouring, but light shade is quite acceptable. It will grow in any soil, but rich loam would give the best results. It must always be kept moist – it is almost impossible to overwater. Remove any older leaves as they turn brown. Apart from the odd aphid, this plant is usually trouble-free.

A word of warning: if this plant is being purchased with the intention of planting it near a pond or stream containing fish, check with the nursery as to what compost it has been grown in. Many nurseries mix a nasty chemical called Suscon Green into the soil. This is to kill vine weevils, which can be a real problem for plants grown in pots, but it will also harm other wildlife, so take care to wash the existing soil from the roots and repot the plant into something safer.

Arundo donax
Spanish Reed

A huge grass that looks a bit like sugar cane. It can grow to 4m (13ft) tall and has thick canes a good 3cm (1in) in diameter. The long, narrow blue-green leaves can be up to 60cm (2ft) long. It is probably the most dramatic inhabitant of the grass world that can be grown in temperate climates. Its energy goes into producing height, rather than width, and it is quite slow to bulk up enough to form a decent-sized clump. Unless you're very patient, plant at least three of these grasses together to speed up the effect.

The flowers are pale creamy brown, feathery plumes. They are a lovely bonus to growing this grass, but they seem to appear only on plants in warmer European countries such as Spain or Italy, where they are widespread.

Arundo donax is very hardy and is especially useful in coastal areas. Despite its stature, it can stand up to sea winds extremely well and, in a strong breeze, the leaves whip around the canes making a wonderful noise. It is a good choice for planting as a windbreak in exposed seaside gardens.

A variegated form is often available with pale cream stripes along the leaves. This is less hardy than the straight green form and reaches only 2.2m (7ft) in height. It is even slower to form decent-sized clumps than its green counterpart, and should therefore be planted in more generous groupings.

Plant in rich, moist soil for the fastest growth, although any soil would suffice. It is happy in either sun or shade, but the variegated form prefers more sun to keep the colouring brighter. Moisture is the main requirement, and watering should be done regularly for the first couple of seasons after planting. After this time, *Arundo donax* is quite capable of fending for itself, and feeding and watering can be dispensed with. Generally, this grass will grow almost anywhere. It is often seen in water-filled ditches and along riverbanks throughout Europe. But, it can also cope with the other extreme, tolerating sun-baked clay soil without much of a problem.

If the soil is very poor and growth is unsatisfactory, apply a good helping of blood, fish and bone in the spring. Well-rotted

ABOVE
The large canes of *Arundo donax* make a fantastic sound in windy weather.

manure will also help speed up the growth rate. Very little maintenance is required, apart from the removal of any brown leaves as they appear.

During the winter, the leaves turn brown and two choices can be made. Either cut the whole lot down to ground level, from where it will start to regrow in spring, quickly reaching its full height again in one season. Or, strip the foliage from the stems, to leave just the bare canes. This latter method has two advantages. Firstly, the space that the plants occupy won't be completely empty in the winter, and lots of bare stems are definitely much more attractive than a gap in the planting scheme. Secondly, during the following growing season, new canes will not only emerge from ground level, but side shoots from the old canes will also sprout, making an even bushier clump.

Pests and diseases are not usually a problem. Propagation can be done by dividing up existing clumps with a spade, by stem cuttings grown in water or from fresh seed.

ABOVE
In warmer climates, the flowery plumes of *Arundo donax* soar above the foliage.

RIGHT
The variegated version is smaller and less hardy.

Cortaderia richardii
Toe-Toe

This gorgeous grass is similar in many ways to the well-known Pampas Grass. But, instead of originating from South America, it hails from New Zealand, hence its Maori common name of toe-toe, which is actually pronounced 'toy-toy'.

Masses of long, grassy blades form great heaps of foliage that eventually reach dimensions of around 1.5m (5ft) in height and the same size across. Each blade is slightly serrated along the edges, enough to cause some discomfort if grabbed and pulled through your hands as you walk by. During the winter, this plant stays much greener than many grasses, making it highly attractive for the entire year.

The plumes of grassy flowers are also similar to the more familiar Pampas Grass, but those on this grass are sent up during mid-summer instead of early autumn. They are shorter and a much nicer colour – a kind of bronzy-beige. They are lovely and fluffy, and can be cut off for using in dried flower arrangements, where they look good for many months until they start to gather dust.

Cortaderia richardii is a very easy plant to cultivate. It is largely unfussy, although it hates being in the shade. It makes a good coastal plant, as salty winds do not seem to cause any harm. However, it stays much tidier if grown tucked out of the way from the strongest sea breezes. Good light levels are required – the more sunshine, the better. Most soils are fine, although the very best results will be from rich, moist loam. If the soil is very poor, enrich it annually in spring with a large dollop of well-rotted manure.

Moist conditions are preferred but, once established, much drier conditions can be tolerated, and watering is usually necessary only if the summer is excessively rain-free. Water regularly for its first season after planting until the roots have settled in.

Remove any old brown leaves and cut off the flower spikes when they become scruffy. Chop these off with secateurs as low as you can reach down into the centre of the plant.

Pests and diseases do not often cause any problems. Propagation can be by division or from fresh seed.

Cortaderia selloana
Pampas Grass

SYN. *Cortaderia argentea*

The 'prawn cocktail' of horticulture is how some gardeners describe *Cortaderia selloana*, but this seems to be very dismissive of a wonderful grass.

It can form massive clumps of glaucous green that make an imposing addition to any garden. Mature clumps can reach 2.5m (8ft) tall and 3m (10ft) across. Enormous quantities of long, arching evergreen leaves quickly pile up on themselves to form a graceful architectural shape. Each slender leaf blade is sharply edged along the entire length. The sharp bits are too small to be seen, but can be painfully experienced if you pull the leaves through your hands. In late summer, tall panicles start to emerge from the centre of mature plants. These can reach 3m (10ft) tall and open out into large fluffy plumes of a rich cream colour. They last for most of the autumn. They can be left on the plant to be enjoyed, or be cut and dried for indoor flower arrangements.

This is a very easy plant to grow and it is forgiving of most planting sites. However, it would prefer to be in a bright sunny planting position, sheltered away from strong winds. The soil should, ideally, be a rich loam, but most types will give adequate results. Really poor soil can be fed annually with any high nitrogen food in the spring. Water regularly until established. After the first couple of seasons, it can usually take care of itself.

Older clumps that become untidy can be given a savage haircut every few years in early spring. Cut the entire clump down to ground level with powerful electric hedge-cutters.

If this becomes too difficult, an alternative method is to set fire to the whole lot and burn it down. This quickly deals with all the brown thatch that gradually accumulates from old leaves. New foliage soon grows up again.

There are various coloured forms available but none manages to match the splendour of the true Pampas Grass. Propagation can be done by division and also from seed, but seed-grown plants can be very variable in habit and colour. A particularly good cultivar is 'Sunningdale Silver', which has beautifully pale plumes. *Cortaderia selloana* 'Pumila', a dwarf form, is a wonderfully stubby half-sized version for small gardens .

Pests and diseases rarely bother this grass.

Cyperus alternifolius
Dwarf Papyrus

A pretty little perennial grass that resembles a miniature Papyrus, but is much tougher. It is reliably hardy, though, only in mild inner city gardens and coastal areas. It forms clumps of long, bright green stalks that can reach 90–120cm (3–4ft) tall. These are topped with spreading 'umbrellas' of grass, so that the whole plant looks like tiny palm trees. The flowers are typical grassy tufts and not terribly exciting.

Outdoors, grow it either in a pond or a very boggy site, where it has permanent access to water. It will die down every year and send up new shoots in spring. This plant can also be grown very successfully in a conservatory, where it will remain evergreen. Stand it in a large saucer of water and never let it dry out. It is also suitable for gardeners who kill through 'kindness', as it is impossible to overwater.

Cyperus alternifolius can be propagated by seed or division, but there is another way that is much more fun to try, especially for children. Chop off one of the heads (from the plant, not the children!) with a long piece of stalk attached. Turn it upside down and push it into a bottle full of water. Roots will form from what was the top, and new shoots will start to form. Keep the water fresh and clean so that the whole process can be observed. When a manageable-sized plant has developed, remove it from the bottle and pot it up in fresh compost.

This grass will grow in virtually any soil, and can be sited in full sun or light shade. Keep away from strong winds, otherwise the fragile stems will be blown flat. It is easy to maintain; watering is the only thing to worry about. Older leaves can turn brown and fall down. Cut these right back to their base with secateurs to keep a tidy appearance. Aphids can be a nuisance on new growth in spring and early summer.

A word of warning: if this plant is being purchased with the intention of planting it near a pond or stream containing fish, check with the nursery as to what compost it has been grown in. Many nurseries mix a nasty chemical called Suscon Green into the soil. This is to kill vine weevils, which can be a real problem for plants grown in pots, but it will also harm other wildlife, so take care to wash the existing soil from the roots and repot the plant into something safer.

ABOVE
Although this grass is native to Madagascar, it can be grown successfully in much cooler climates.

Cyperus papyrus
Papyrus

An enormous plant, big enough at maturity to fill a spacious corner in even the most generously proportioned conservatory. Thick, fleshy stems are sent up from the rootstock to a height of 2.5m (8ft), quickly making a thick clump that gradually spreads out across the surface of the pot and beyond its perimeter.

This plant is ideal for gardeners who tend to be heavy-handed with their watering – it is virtually impossible to overwater, and needs a constant supply. During its growing season from early spring to the end of summer, a large saucer or shallow trough placed underneath each pot and kept full of water will prove beneficial. Keep this water clean – if it starts going green or cloudy, change it immediately, as murky, stagnant water could lead to root problems. It will also start to smell unpleasant.

Full bright light is essential, especially from above. If the light levels are too low indoors, the stems will not remain upright. Instead, they will collapse and become very untidy. If grown in the correct position, the stems will fall over only when they are old or damaged. These should then be chopped off at the base with a sharp knife. Regular repotting each spring will be required, until its size makes this impractical. The clumps can then be divided up instead to make smaller plants.

Older plants send out new growth from around the perimeter of the pot, which grows horizontally as if it is trying to escape. These can be removed to keep the clump tidy as an alternative to constant repotting. These plants enjoy being potted into a loam-based soil such as John Innes no. 2, which should give good results. Feed annually in spring with a liquid nitrogen-based food. Aphids can be a bit of a problem during spring and summer.

Although almost freezing temperatures can be tolerated, *Cyperus papyrus* is much happier if the temperature can be maintained at no lower than 6°C (43°F). Any less than this means that watering should be almost withdrawn, so that the compost dries out slightly until the weather warms up again.

Luzula sylvatica 'Marginata'
Woodrush

A low-growing grass, native to northern Europe, that is perfect for small gardens. Individual plants will spread out to only around 60cm (2ft) and will take at least three years to do so. If a larger space can be provided, these plants look wonderful in large groups and used as groundcover. They are also very effective in groups underneath and around trees, where they appreciate the dappled shade provided by the tree canopy. If planted close together, they form thick-enough masses to suppress all but the most ruthless of weeds.

Each leaf, which is about 45cm (18in) long and 1cm (½in) wide, is bright, shiny green with a narrow band of white along both edges. An occasional wispy filament appears along the length. Foliage is produced in substantial amounts to form dense mounds around 30cm (1ft) high. Flowers appear in summer, but as they're insignificant brown offerings, they can be chopped off.

Although *Luzula sylvatica* 'Marginata' is evergreen, clumps can start to look a bit scruffy after a few years and benefit from being chopped down to ground level with a pair of shears. This will encourage new shoots to regenerate from the base.

This is a very easy plant to cultivate, as it will grow practically anywhere and can tolerate a wide range of conditions. However, if subjected to too much stress caused by infrequent watering or by baking in too much sun, it is more likely to suffer from rust disease. Well-fed plants that are regularly watered and grown in fertile soil are much more capable of shrugging off this unsightly discoloration. Instead of spending time spraying affected foliage, cut it all back to the base and let it start again. Improved care should prevent the disease from returning the next season.

Light woodland shade will provide the richest-coloured foliage. Any soil will do, but a well-drained loamy one would be best. For optimum results, keep the soil fairly moist, but avoid making the ground too boggy. An annual dose of well-rotted manure in spring gives excellent results. Propagation is easy to do by dividing up existing clumps with a sharp knife.

Apart from rust disease, little else seems to cause this grass any problems.

ABOVE
This grass is much more effective if planted in groups, rather than as single specimens.

Miscanthus sinensis 'Gracillimus'

A delicate-looking oriental grass made up of lots of narrow leaves that arch over gracefully to form a dense clump. The overall height is around 90–120cm (3–4ft). The leaf edges are slightly serrated, making them rough to the touch and sharp enough to cut the skin if you pull them through your hands. They are sage-green in colour with a barely noticeable white stripe running along the centre. These grasses bulk up fairly quickly – a five-year-old plant could fill a circle 90cm (3ft) in diameter.

At the end of a hot summer, pretty tufts of reddish grassy flowers appear, reaching up to just above the foliage. These last many weeks. Soon after flowering, the foliage starts to change colour, taking on various red or bronzy hues until it turns yellow and brown. At this stage, it is best cut down to ground level for winter. New growth starts early the following season, and the fresh green shoots soon reach their full height. There is only a short period of time, just a few weeks, when this grass is doing nothing of interest.

Miscanthus sinensis 'Gracillimus' is a very easy plant to cultivate and will grow just about anywhere. It can cope with clay, peat or chalk.

For the very best results, however, grow it in fertile, loamy soil that stays moist at all times, without ever becoming boggy. It prefers a sunny position. Watering is more important for the first couple of seasons after planting. Mature plants that have become established can usually fend for themselves.

This grass can cope with windy positions quite well, but avoid really exposed sites, where strong winds can leave it looking decidedly battered. It doesn't mind salty air, so is a good choice for seaside gardens. This is a versatile plant that looks good in all sorts of gardens: it can add structure to herbaceous borders, looks marvellous when planted with other grasses, and is large enough to be planted as a specimen plant in a focal part of the garden.

An annual feed can be given in spring, if desired. Use a light helping of blood, fish and bone sprinkled around its base. There is little other maintenance to worry about, and pests and diseases are not usually a problem.

Propagation is by division, which can be done in spring when the new shoots are just bursting into growth.

ABOVE
Miscanthus sinensis 'Gracillimus' is grand enough to be planted as a single specimen in a focal position in the garden.

Ophiopogon planiscapus 'Nigrescens'
Black Grass

The Latin name of this grass took me years to be able to pronounce fluently – it really makes you wonder who's responsible sometimes....

Despite its daft name, this splendid plant would please even the most design-conscious gardener. The leaves really are jet-black. They form tufts of coal-coloured clumps that spread slowly to cover areas of no more than around 90cm (3ft), with a maximum height of only 15cm (6in). Groups of this lovely grass look particularly effective in beds mulched with light-coloured grit or stones, to show off their deep colour fully. They also look best planted in large numbers – just dotting one or two around a garden would make them look a bit lost. In a local municipal planting scheme that I saw recently, a circular bed 2.5m (8ft) in diameter had been dug out of a lawn. In the centre was a small tree, and the rest of the space had been completely filled with nothing but this grass. The effect was wonderful.

Apart from the unusual-coloured foliage, this evergreen has attractive sprigs of lilac flowers in late summer, followed by small, shiny berries that last for months.

These Japanese plants perform best on light, well-drained soil. If the soil tends to be heavy, stir in some extra grit or silver sand to improve drainage. Full sun is preferred, but their colour holds well in light shade. Once established, they are remarkably drought-tolerant. Their size makes them a good choice for growing in a terracotta pot, but they are much slower to spread when grown this way than when they are planted directly into the ground.

This plant is very easy to cultivate and almost maintenance-free. Annual feeding is not really necessary, but a small amount of general fertilizer can be applied in spring, if you wish. Pests and diseases are not usually a problem, although aphids can sometimes be a nuisance in the summer, and regular inspections should be made for them.

Propagation is easy by division but, as these plants are so slow to spread, very little spare material is available for this purpose.

ABOVE
This unusual-coloured grass is small and slow-growing, making it suitable for a pot.

BELOW
The berries are jet-black, shiny beads.

Bamboos

Bamboos add a lush, jungly feel to any garden. Their evergreen leaves and beautiful canes combine to create a permanently exotic presence. They are also immensely versatile plants and can be used in a wide number of ways.

Bamboos can be used as single, ornamental specimens to liven up a dull corner of the garden or create interest in boring beds and borders. They are an essential ingredient of Japanese-style gardens, and make excellent screening plants for blotting out unsightly views or nosy neighbours. Planted between garden and roadside, they can help to mask the sound of noisy traffic.

They can be grown as informal hedges, coping well with light clipping. They are also a good choice for play areas in the garden because they can take a fair amount of rough treatment from rampaging children. Since they harmonize well with water, they look especially effective planted near streams or ponds. If you're lucky enough to own a lake, large sweeps of bamboo planted along the edge make a fine sight. And, although bamboos are not good at coping with very windy, exposed positions, if they're planted where light breezes can swish through them, the rustling sound is very soothing.

The idea of introducing bamboos to gardening schemes fills some people with horror, as they imagine wild, invasive plants taking over every corner, ripping up ponds and patios in their wake. Although some of the fast-growing tropical species have the potential for doing this, most bamboos behave in a much more restrained and dignified manner. In fact, many of the bamboos in this chapter stay in a nice tight clump even after a couple of decades.

Most bamboos are not invasive plants, but well behaved and dignified.

All of the bamboos featured here are fully hardy down to -20°C (-4°F), so there is a good choice of bamboo for even the coldest garden, ranging from the lofty heights of *Semiarundinaria fastuosa* to the delicate form of *Pleioblastus variegata*. These plants have been chosen for their suitability for average temperate gardens, their ornamental qualities and ease of cultivation. There is also a good chance that specialist nurseries will stock them.

Choose a decent-sized plant for transplanting into the garden. Seedlings are slow to get started, and it can take around five years for a clump to become noticeable. Bamboos prefer a sunny spot, although most will tolerate some shade. For really shady spots, choose *Pseudosasa japonica* or *Sasa palmata nebulosa*, which are the least fussy to cultivate.

All bamboos look much better planted away from strong winds. Permanently breezy conditions won't kill them, but the wind can scorch the leaf edges, leaving them brown and crispy. Plants look much greener and healthier in a sheltered spot. An exception to this is the robust *Pseudosasa japonica*, which can take an astonishing amount of battering from seasonal storms.

Bamboos are very thirsty plants and need permanent access to irrigation. However, they will not stand very waterlogged conditions, so good drainage is important. Pools of water stagnating around the roots will lead to rotting.

LEFT
Sasa palmata
'Nebulosa' has the
largest leaves of
any hardy bamboo.

The best examples of green and healthy bamboos with enormous canes are always to be found in gardens that have a high water table or alongside rivers or streams. In these positions, water is constantly available for them to help themselves whenever it's required.

With this in mind, growing bamboos in pots is a very bad idea. If they dry out, they die – it's as simple as that. Once they reach that brown, parched look, you've had it. Just think how a lawn looks after a hot dry summer. Bamboo reacts in the same way. Recovery from a brown, crisp specimen takes such a long time that the best thing to do is dispose of it and start again, as any new growth that might occur will have to regenerate from the old root system. If growing in a container is unavoidable, choose a massive pot and install an automatic irrigation system.

Bamboos are also greedy plants and appreciate lavish quantities of well-rotted manure or a blood, fish and bone mix applied during spring and early summer. Never apply seaweed or seaweed extract – the salt in this can kill bamboos. The only other maintenance required is to remove any old, brown leaves and to keep a lookout for aphids. These horrid creatures enjoy feeding on the new shoots during early summer. If not dealt with, they excrete a sticky substance, politely referred to as honeydew. This honeydew can speedily turn black from sooty mould, giving an unsightly appearance to the plant.

Bamboos grown as a hedge or screen can be clipped lightly with shears along the top of the clump after the main growing season, which lasts from spring through to early summer. If a mature bamboo has grown taller than required, use secateurs to cut through any woody canes.

New canes
of *Phyllostachys
aureosulcata*
'Aureocaulis'.

New canes emerge from the ground during each new season. The width of
these new canes remains the same throughout the bamboo's life; small ones
do not become fatter with age. Therefore, if you spot small, skinny canes, it
would be a good idea to chop them off at ground level as soon as they appear,
so that the plant can put all its energies into the larger ones. Each year,
bamboos produce canes that are generally slightly fatter and taller than the
previous year. The really huge canes found on bamboos are the result of two
things: copious amounts of water and age. A really large clump of tall canes
with a good circumference could be at least thirty years old.

As will be noted, the Latin names of bamboos are absurdly complicated to
learn. Horticultural boffins have had a field day with this type of plant. Even
worse, just as you've mastered a particularly silly name, some rotter goes
and changes it again! It's very annoying. Unfortunately, bamboos flower so
infrequently that the chance to study them is rare. This means that mistakes
in categorizing them have occurred in the past. Renaming them is not done
out of vindictiveness or pomposity, but as a result of the latest studies.

On the subject of flowering, this is an unusual event that, from a gardener's
point of view, is a bit of a disaster. Generally, once a bamboo has flowered,
it dies. Each type of bamboo tends to flower at the same time, wherever
it is. For example, if *Fargesia murieliae* is flowering in one country, the chance
of it flowering at the same time elsewhere in the world is very high. This

phenomenon was once attributed to the supposedly supernatural powers of bamboo. Although various other theories abound, a much more boring explanation is likely. After flowering, bamboos set seed. As this happens perhaps only once every hundred years, bamboo enthusiasts seize the opportunity to obtain fresh supplies and a new batch of planting using seed of the same age starts all over the world. So, all new plants are likely to mature and flower again at the same time. I rest my case.

If a small number of different types of bamboo are planted throughout a garden, flowering shouldn't really be a concern. If you want a screen or hedge of about a hundred plants, then it is important to check at specialist nurseries if anyone has reported seeing your chosen bamboo in flower. To lose one or two plants is not so bad, but to lose an entire hedge would be an expensive mistake. In recent years, *Fargesia murieliae* and *Pseudosasa japonica* have both flowered, so, unless you are planning to live an exceptionally long life, it is safe to plant both of them again.

Keen gardeners always want to have a go at propagating their favourite plants. But when it comes to bamboos, the whole process is so tedious and unrewarding that my advice is to leave it to the experts. If you remain undeterred, growing from fresh seed is probably the easiest method. Best sown in spring, the seed is slow to germinate and, after one year, all you'll have to show for it will be an extremely small tuft of leaves. At the end of the second year, you'll have a tuft of leaves only slightly less small. After three years, you'll start to have something resembling a small bamboo, but it won't exactly be taking up much space.

Another method of propagation is by division. The easiest time to do this is right at the seedling stage, before plants develop strong roots and canes. But the idea of spending a couple of years nurturing a small plant from seed and then slicing it in two seems madness to me unless you're a commercial grower. Another method, which is great fun to watch but torture to do yourself, is to try to divide large plants. The sheer effort required, the strength to slice through roots and canes using axes, hammers, chisels and God knows what else easily outweighs the benefits of getting a couple of extra plants. I have watched people turn purple and have to lie down to recover from their exertions after trying to divide a bamboo – it's a guaranteed trip to Hernia City as far as I can see. Please, just save some money and buy a decent-sized plant from a bamboo specialist who has done all the hard work for you.

A question often asked is whether canes can be harvested for use in the garden. The answer is that established bamboos may have one or two older ripe canes that would be better removed, but most canes are best left on the plant. Generally, the only time canes are removed is when they are young and too small to be of much use.

Arundinaria anceps
Himalayan Bamboo

SYN. *Sinarundinaria anceps*
Sinarundinaria jaunsarensis
Yushania anceps

Grown primarily for its luscious cascades of evergreen foliage, this is a very easy bamboo for beginners. It consists of masses of tiny leaves, densely packed together, which give a soft look to the whole plant. Grown as a single clump, it makes a fine addition to the garden, especially near a pond where it looks resplendent trailing over the edge. And, because of its denseness, it is an excellent candidate for growing as a bamboo hedge.

Arundinaria anceps is a slow plant to get going and seedlings aren't always successful. Therefore it makes sense to buy a reasonable-sized plant with a well-established root system. Bamboos can be planted at any time of the year unless the ground is frozen or waterlogged, although planting is perhaps best avoided during hot, dry summers, when watering would become a real chore.

For hedging, choose well-established plants with a good root system that are growing in at least 10- or 15-litre pots. Ideally, plants should be at least 90cm (3ft) tall. Spacing depends on your impatience and your budget, but no fewer than one plant per 1.2m (4ft) would be advised. Try to buy plants of a similar size so that when planted out they have a uniform appearance from the start.

Arundinaria anceps is best planted in the spring to give the plants a whole season to start resembling a hedge. Feed and water regularly throughout the growing season, and trim lightly with shears along the top and front whenever necessary, depending on the height and depth eventually required. As with any hedge, not just bamboo, trimming little and often is much better than cutting back hard just occasionally. The more that is cut from the top and sides, the more growth that will be encouraged widthways, which fills in the gaps between individual plants.

After two or three seasons, when the final shape has been attained, regular light trimming twice a year should suffice to keep things looking tidy. *Arundinaria anceps* is not a tall bamboo and could take at least six years to reach 3.7m (12ft). Away from its native habitat in the north-west Himalayas, this is likely to be its maximum height in an average temperate garden.

ABOVE
Lush heaps of shaggy foliage make *Arundinaria anceps* a popular choice of bamboo.

Chusquea breviglumis

SYN. *Chusquea gigantea*

A truly awesome plant and an essential acquisition for those who take their bamboos seriously. Currently, *Chusquea breviglumis* seems to be in the process of having another name change, but whatever name it ends up with, its appearance is unmistakable.

This bamboo is grown mainly for its canes, which are very tall, very thick and very straight. Providing the growing conditions are right, they are produced in prolific quantities. They are fresh green in colour, but the papery sheaths that wrap tightly around them give the whole plant an attractively striped effect. The foliage is dense and bushy, and can cope with coastal conditions slightly better than most bamboos, although a sheltered spot keeps the leaves in optimum condition.

This bamboo is also known as *Chusquea gigantea*, which is an excellent name. Not only is it easy to remember, but it is also very apt. Although its vital statistics can make alarming reading, they usually refer to what can be achieved in its native country of Chile. In an average temperate garden, its eventual size will be somewhat diminished, although it can

still be impressive. Expect a maximum height of around 5m (16ft) and a spread of about 3m (10ft) after ten years.

The stunning example in the photo is of a thirty-year-old plant growing in a garden in southern England, which produces more than fifty new canes per year. This is not only because of its age, but also because it is growing in a sheltered, fertile area with an exceptionally high water table. It never dries out, so it just keeps growing.

Chusquea breviglumis can be planted in sun or light shade, and prefers a position where the ground is constantly moist. All bamboos need copious amounts of water until they are established, but this bamboo needs regular water even in adulthood for it to reach its full potential. Generous feeding throughout the growing season will also help to give good results. Use either well-rotted manure, organic kitchen waste or a mix of blood, fish and bone.

ABOVE
The magnificent canes of *Chusquea breviglumis* are unrivalled in the bamboo world.

Fargesia murieliae

SYN. *Arundinaria murieliae*
Sinarundinaria murieliae

This lovely native of China is one of the most popular choices for bamboo lovers around the world and probably the most widely planted by amateur gardeners. It is also one of the easiest and prettiest bamboos that can be grown in colder climates. Fast-growing, it produces masses of very slim canes that form dense thickets within just a few years.

Although *Fargesia murieliae* can spread itself across the garden if left unchecked, it can easily be controlled to prevent it becoming invasive. The small and delicate-looking leaves clothe the whole plant almost down to ground level. This makes it ideal as a screen, creating a solid barrier up to 3.7m (12ft) tall.

Although evergreen, for a short period of about four weeks, usually at the end of the summer, alarmingly large quantities of leaves turn yellow and drop. Fortunately, this plant is so bushy that, even by losing such a large amount of foliage, it never becomes straggly, and its fresh green colour is soon restored.

A few years ago, *Fargesia murieliae* lost its popularity because its flowering season started (see page 98). However, this is now over and,

as it's unlikely to occur for many decades, gardeners can safely plant this bamboo again without fear of wasting their money.

There are some good cultivars on the market. One of the best is 'Jumbo'. I have no idea as to whether 'Jumbo' refers to the very slightly larger leaves it produces or if it is supposed to conjure up images of elephants and things of a general jungly nature.

As with all bamboos, the best results will be gained from planting in rich, fertile soil, where there is shelter from strong winds, and giving plenty of water until it is established. *Fargesia murieliae* will grow in sun or light shade. Unwanted canes can be cut off at ground level, while unwanted spread can be controlled by using a sharp spade to slice off chunks that extend beyond their allocated territory. Unusually for bamboos, this is not an unpleasantly difficult task, and the offsets can be used for propagation.

ABOVE
Fargesia murieliae produces copious amounts of luxuriant foliage.

BELOW
The dainty canes make this bamboo an elegant addition to the garden.

Phyllostachys aurea
Golden Bamboo

Phyllostachys aurea is a good all-rounder of a bamboo, performing well even at an early age. It is also an easy and reliable plant for beginners. The foliage is attractive and bushy, and the canes are unusual. Instead of being smooth, they are misshapen and knobbly, but in a pleasing way. The knobbly bits are where the leaf bases have clustered together, giving *Phyllostachys aurea* its distinctive appearance. (Please note that growers who take their bamboos seriously call these formations 'clustered node bases'.)

Its upright habit and long, straight canes make it an excellent choice for screening. A tidy boundary up to 5m (16ft) high can be created quite quickly by planting in a row, with plants no more than 1.5m (5ft) apart. If your budget allows, plant at half this distance for a more instant effect.

Phyllostachys aurea can also be used as a specimen showpiece for even the smallest space, as it is naturally clump-forming and does not spread. It could just about be considered suitable for a pot, but only if the container were huge and had access to automatic irrigation.

Plant in full sun if possible, although light shade is okay. Choose a sheltered spot away from wind in a fertile soil; rich clay gives excellent results. Despite its common name, the canes and foliage should remain green, except in very hot climates, where older plants can take on a golden hue.

Phyllostachys aurea behaves in a courteous manner and does not become invasive, even after many years. The clump in the photo has been allowed to spread a little but, after ten years, it is still well under control, expanding to a width of 3m (10ft). Chopping off new canes as they emerge keeps even elderly plants detained within a 90cm (3ft) perimeter. Newly produced canes are soft as they surface and can be snapped off or cut with secateurs.

As the canes are the main feature of this bamboo, any lower leaves can be trimmed away to make them more visible. The leaves can be removed up to any height to show off the canes, as required.

ABOVE
Phyllostachys aurea is a good screening plant with an upright habit and long knobbly canes.

BELOW
The knobbly canes are a distinctive feature.

Phyllostachys aureosulcata 'Aureocaulis'

One of my favourite bamboos and one of the prettiest for colder gardens. It is fast-growing and easy to keep confined to a single clump.

This is one of the first bamboos to send up new growth in early spring. The striking new canes are fat, even on quite young plants, with a reddish-pink tinge to them. They shoot out of the ground at extraordinary speed, putting on noticeable growth daily. As they age, canes from the current season continue to have a reddish blush, which looks even better when all the new canes have emerged. Prolific numbers are produced – a clump of mine has sent up around eighty canes in five years.

As the canes age, either at the end of their first season or into their second one, the colour changes into a strong, buttery yellow, which contrasts beautifully with the darkish green foliage. Any new canes that are weak and spindly should be cut off at ground level as soon as they appear. Occasionally, runners are sent out quite some distance from the parent plant. If new canes are spotted growing from these, chop them off to encourage a tight, single clump.

Masses of thick leaves pile up above the canes, making it dense enough to clip into shape, almost like topiary, if required. The whole plant could be given a clipped, curved top. Once in shape, an annual shearing of new growth protruding above the canopy is enough to keep it looking trim. Left unclipped, plants will reach no more than 5m (16ft) tall.

Plant in a sunny spot, and water only until established. In periods of prolonged drought, though, even mature plants will need extra irrigation. Although the foliage can cope with some shade, good light and sunshine will result in superior colouring of the canes. The dense foliage means that it can tolerate slightly breezier conditions than many bamboos, but sheltered positions away from strong winds always give better results. It is too fast-growing for life in a container.

Any foliage around the bottom metre can be clipped away to expose as many of the canes as possible.

Phyllostachys aureosulcata 'Spectabilis'

This is another bamboo with a complicated name, which is grown mainly for its lovely canes that are good to look at and also produced in profuse amounts. Masses of slim canes are sent up from the main clump; these are predominantly butter-yellow with the occasional green stripe. Although mostly straight, there are sometimes some odd-shaped ones that develop a zigzag effect.

The maximum height, even in cooler climates, could still exceed 5m (16ft) if grown in the right conditions. Once the plant is established, lots of new growth should be expected annually, but the whole plant should remain in a manageable clump unless you happen to live in an exceptionally warm climate, in which case it can become something of a nuisance.

Lots of fresh green foliage is also produced, which, if a dense clump is required for screening purposes, can be left as it forms. Alternatively, the leaves can be stripped from the lower parts of the plant to allow more of the coloured canes to become visible and make more of a statement.

Grown as a single specimen, *Phyllostachys aureosulcata* 'Spectabilis' can be the main feature in a small garden. In a larger garden, try planting a grove of them in a central spot, so that they can be admired from all angles. They also make brilliant choices for planting around the edge of the garden to cover up any ugly fence panels or to provide some privacy from neighbours.

As for so many other bamboos, choose a sheltered spot away from strong winds to keep it looking its best. Full sun is also preferred to get the maximum colouring on the canes, but light shade will suffice if full sun isn't an option. The soil should be kept as moist and as well nourished as possible throughout the growing season.

This is an easy bamboo to keep in a tight clump. Any new runners sent up outside the required area should be either sliced off with secateurs at ground level as soon as they appear or snapped off by hand while still soft.

Phyllostachys dulcis

The largest, fattest, most impressive canes on any bamboo that can be grown in a temperate climate belong to this lofty giant, and it's my favourite bamboo by miles. Several years ago, the sight of a mature clump growing in a local garden virtually brought me skidding to a halt to stop and stare at it in disbelief. This photo shows quite clearly how large the canes are compared with my hand.

Phyllostachys dulcis needs to be planted where there is ample room for it to spread out. Although far from being invasive, it can grow into quite a hefty clump. It is reasonably quick to get established, but planting this bamboo with a view to getting it to look like the one in the photo is rather a long-term project.

Once it is settled and growing happily in a suitable site, the super-sized matt green canes start to emerge after just a few years, but at the rate of only one or two per season. The bamboo illustrated has been growing on land with a high water table for thirty years. Its overall height is around 8m (26ft).

To get the best results from this bamboo, plant it in a very sheltered position where it won't be blown about by the wind. Choose a place in the garden where it can grow permanently – moving this beast is practically impossible. Plant it in the garden of a house where you intend to live for a long time so that you will see it in its full glory at maturity.

Constant access to copious amounts of water is essential, although take care to prevent waterlogging because this could rot the roots. Never let it dry out because it is the combination of water and maturity that produces these amazing canes. Any undersized canes that are sent up should be cut off immediately – only large canes are permitted when growing this bamboo. Either sun or light shade is suitable.

The foliage is the real underdog here. There's nothing wrong with it at all but, compared with the canes, it's almost irrelevant.

Phyllostachys nigra
Black Bamboo

This bamboo is grown primarily for its dark and glossy canes. Mature clumps have numerous straight, thick canes of ebony-black. It is one of the most popular bamboos grown in gardens all over the world. After a shower of rain, the canes become even darker and glossier, making a truly spectacular sight.

In the garden, it is usually grown as a single specimen where it can easily be seen and admired. It is quite slow to get going, so it's not really suitable for screening, unless you're happy to wait about five years for it to achieve enough bushy growth. The foliage is darkish green and, although sparse to start with, thickens up as the clump matures. If you must grow a bamboo in a container, this would be one of the better choices because of its slow speed of growth. The pot would still need to be a generous size, though, and preferably plugged in to automatic irrigation.

Buy plants labelled *Phyllostachys nigra* and ignore any with added names, such as 'Henonis' or 'Boryana'. Lovely though these two varieties are, their canes are speckled and brown, rather than the coveted deep black colour.

Phyllostachys nigra is an essential ingredient of a Japanese-style garden. Not only does it look the part, but it also benefits from being manicured in a way that comes naturally to Japanese gardeners but seems rather alien to the rest of us. Instead of leaving plants to grow in whatever way they develop naturally, selective clipping and pruning can improve them without too much effort.

Firstly, remove all lower foliage up to at least 90cm (3ft) from the ground, so that as much of the black colouring as possible is on view. Secondly, remove any weak and spindly growth as soon as it appears above the ground. Thirdly, retain just the very fattest canes from a mature clump, cutting the rest down to ground level. Leave ample space between each cane, to give a more managed, minimalist effect, which so suits this plant. Finally, keep the whole plant as a fairly short clump. The point of this is that the new canes emerge as olive-green or brownish in colour and turn black as they ripen. Cutting off canes before they reach their full height of 5m (16ft) speeds up the ripening process, without harming the plant.

ABOVE
The glossy black canes of *Phyllostachys nigra* are a beautiful addition to any garden.

Phyllostachys propinqua

For any gardener who thinks that bamboos without coloured canes are dull, *Phyllostachys propinqua* might just make you change your mind. Observing this bamboo brings to mind images of giant pandas and bamboo forests in China. The canes are mid-green and beautifully matt. They are also tall, straight, fat and meaty, and a long way from being boring. Exceptionally hardy, this bamboo can withstand some seriously low temperatures.

It is fairly quick to establish itself, if growing conditions are good, and canes of a decent width can be produced on plants just a few years old. The height of an adult plant could reach 6–8m (20–26ft), even in cool climates. The foliage wouldn't win any prizes but it is perfectly acceptable and reasonably bushy. The leaves are small, mid-green and rather shapely, being longer and narrower than most *Phyllostachys* bamboos.

Phyllostachys propinqua would make a splendid choice as a specimen bamboo for a small, sheltered garden tucked out of the way of strong breezes. Windy conditions give the foliage a desiccated look, leaving brown edges to all leaves that bear the brunt of the weather. Its height makes it more susceptible to damage from passing gales, and the whole clump can end up looking distinctly windswept.

It is happy growing in full sun or light shade. As always when growing bamboo, keep an eye on the irrigation and never let the roots dry out. Good helpings of food during the growing season help with the laborious task of cane production. Anything to assist with the supply of nitrogen will do, whether it is well-rotted manure, a mix of blood, fish and bone, or kitchen waste from the compost heap. The lovely old-fashioned mix of hoof and horn works wonderfully well, but shop assistants these days tend to shudder at its mention and adopt a horrified expression.

This plant is well behaved and unlikely to spread itself around the garden where it is not wanted. Clumps tend to huddle together, and new canes are usually sent up from the middle of the plant or very close to its outer perimeter.

If, for some reason, its ultimate lofty height becomes overpowering, chopping a few feet off the top of the plant will do no harm at all.

Phyllostachys vivax 'Aureocaulis'

Don't waste this stunning bamboo by using it as a screen or in a group at the back of the garden. Plant it as a main focal feature, where it can be admired from all angles and generally swooned over. It would hold the pride-of-place tag in the gardens of even the most rabid bamboo fanatics.

The canes of this bamboo are truly tropical-looking, reaching up to 5.5m (18ft) and almost 8cm (3in) in diameter. The colouring is mostly a rich, buttery yellow, although some canes are streaked with green stripes and occasionally a plain green one is sent up. The result is a wonderful mix of colour all in the same planting area.

The foliage is pleasant enough, but strip away as much as possible from the bottom of the plant, so that the full glory of the canes can be seen clearly.

It is always tempting to buy a large-sized plant for the garden, as the huge canes are irresistible even to the most impoverished gardener. Transporting a mature specimen home from the nursery can be tricky – new canes that are not fully ripened can be soft and easy to break. Instead of trying to cram it into a small car, either hire a large van or get the nursery to arrange delivery.

Choose the planting position carefully, allowing plenty of space around it so that the whole clump is fully accessible for all-round viewing. Unless you are lucky enough to have a garden that consists of rich, loamy soil packed full of nutrients, some soil preparation should be carried out before planting. Incorporate plenty of well-rotted manure or composted kitchen waste and dig it in thoroughly. If your garden also happens to have a high water table, then even better. Otherwise, ensure that the chosen planting spot will receive regular irrigation, either from a nearby tap or by making sure it is within easy reach of a hosepipe. You could also consider a 'leaky pipe' type of automatic irrigation threaded around the garden.

Because of its unwieldy nature, don't even think about trying to grow this bamboo in a pot.

Pleioblastus variegatus

SYN. *Pleioblastus fortunei*

This bamboo is a complete contrast to all the others featured here, and it's perhaps a welcome alternative for gardeners who feel that some of the larger bamboos can be too imposing. Mentioning *Pleioblastus* can bring a flicker of alarm to experienced bamboo growers, though, as some of the plants in this family can be seriously invasive. However, *Pleioblastus variegatus* is positively angelic and poses no threat whatsoever in a small garden.

Growth is a bushy mass of striped leaves, heavily variegated with pale creamy white. The variegation is pleasantly tasteful – there's nothing loud or vulgar about it. Clumps grow from a compact rootstock to a height of around only 90cm (3ft) with a spread of about 1.2m (4ft).

For a variegated plant, it performs surprisingly well in light shade, which gives it a much sharper colouring than if grown in full sun, where it can sometimes look a bit washed out.

This is a very easy plant to cultivate and much less fussy than many bamboos. Rich, moist soil would always be its number one preference, but most soil types can be tolerated. Light shade is best, in a sheltered spot away from very strong winds. After a few years, clumps can sometimes look rather tired and faded, but its youthful vigour can easily be restored by chopping the whole plant down to ground level with a pair of shears. Do this in early spring, just as the new season's growth is about to start. By the end of the growing period, it will look lush and leafy once more.

Chopping the plant down to start again is also a fast and easy remedy for rust disease, which this plant is prone to, and much better than spraying it repeatedly with some horrid chemical. If left unchecked, rust disease can spread throughout the whole plant. It should be noted, though, that well-fed and well-watered plants growing in the ground are much more likely to shrug off this disfiguring malady than those forced to live in a pot.

Pleioblastus variegatus is ideal for growing along the edges of garden beds and borders. It blends in well with other bamboos but can look perfectly fine on its own. Propagation is easy by division, even with mature plants. Don't bother with seed: the resulting seedlings will nearly always be plain green.

ABOVE
The foliage of *Pleioblastus variegatus* is attractively striped with pale creamy white.

Pseudosasa japonica
Arrow Bamboo or **Metake**

A handsome bamboo with large pointed leaves that can be 30cm (1ft) long on mature plants, giving a lush, jungly appearance. *Pseudosasa japonica* is robust and can stand rough treatment, making it the perfect bamboo for planting in avenues or groves for children's play areas, where kids can hurtle through them without harming the plants or themselves. Any trampled canes are soon replaced with new ones. It is very fast-growing, reaching a height of around 4m (13ft) within five years. It also spreads along the ground sideways but in a way that can be controlled quite easily by cutting out new shoots as soon as they appear.

Pseudosasa japonica is also suitable for planting as a fast-growing screen because the foliage stays bushy even at ground level. It is ideal for planting on the banks of streams or large ponds, where it can gradually spread to give an informal and natural look. Although not tolerant of windy conditions to start with, if the whole plant is regularly trimmed along the top and down all the sides to the ground, it can develop quite a dense form, which will then

stand up to strong winds very successfully. Once it reaches this stage, it will cope with constant coastal breezes and even the occasional fierce gale. However, don't plant it so near to the sea that it gets splashed with salt spray – no bamboo likes salt on its leaves.

Although the canes on this bamboo aren't attractive enough to be classed as ornamental, they are not without charm. Produced in large numbers, each green cane is partially covered with pale papery sheaths, giving a striped effect along the length of every one. The canes are thin and flexible, and easily swished about by passing gusts of wind. As the foliage is large enough to catch any passing breeze, too, this means that lots of lovely rustling noises are frequently heard coming from each clump.

Pseudosasa japonica is one of the most forgiving bamboos to cultivate. It copes well with virtually any soil and, once it has become established, can more or less be ignored and left to fend for itself. However, hefty helpings of food in the spring and plenty of irrigation will always give optimum results.

Sasa palmata 'Nebulosa'

A stunning bamboo with enormous leaves that look far too tropical to survive a cold winter. They are huge, even from an early age, and can be 30cm (1ft) long and 8cm (3in) across, making this the largest leaf of any hardy bamboo.

Sasa palmata 'Nebulosa' grows to its full height within three or four years, which is no more than 2.5m (8ft) in colder climates, and the whole plant is a mass of big, glossy leaves. But, be warned, it has a dark side. It spreads rapidly, and can be difficult to remove once it has a grip on its corner of the garden. It is not at all suitable for small gardens – it needs space to roam – but if you really can't live without it, try growing it in a large raised bed or huge pot to restrict its root growth. Once it has filled this confined space, haul it out, divide it into chunks, throw most of them away and replant just a small section to restart the process.

Every few years, to encourage new, fresh growth, hack the whole plant back to ground level and let it start again. Such large, lush foliage needs generous doses of nitrogen to stay a nice shade of dark green. Start feeding in early spring, just as new growth begins, and continue every four weeks until mid-summer. A mix of blood, fish and bone is as good as anything. Newly planted clumps need a lot of moisture at first but, after a couple of seasons, they can take care of themselves. Plants in raised beds will always need a helping hand to ensure they never dry out.

If this bamboo becomes too large, remove it at once. It is no easy process, though, and will take much digging. If it has been allowed to grow unchecked for years, removing it requires military-style tenacity. First of all, try cutting it back to the ground. When it regrows, cut it back again and again. This will weaken the clump and might just kill it. For more stubborn plants, dig a large trench all around its perimeter and fill it with something salty, such as fresh seaweed. This might at least stop it spreading further, but a couple of attempts might be necessary. To remove the existing root mass, either enlist the help of a few strong chums or hire a mechanical digger.

Sasa palmata 'Nebulosa' is such a tough plant that, even after flowering, it doesn't die but just carries on growing as normal.

ABOVE
Sasa palmata 'Nebulosa' has a tropical look to it, with the largest leaves of any hardy bamboo.

Semiarundinaria fastuosa

Semiarundinaria fastuosa is noted for being probably the tallest bamboo that can be grown in a temperate climate. Stems on a mature plant can reach the lofty dimensions of more than 6m (20ft). This Japanese species is also one of the hardiest bamboos in general cultivation. The canes are not only tall, but also very straight, giving individual clumps a somewhat regal air. They have large culm sheaths (the papery bits that curl around the canes) which, if peeled away, reveal an exceptionally attractive interior of iridescent pearly pink.

The slight disadvantage to growing this bamboo is that it is maddeningly slow to become established. It will take a minimum of five years to form a decent-sized clump, and a further five years to become a major feature of the garden. However, it is well worth the wait to witness such a majestic sight. Impatient gardeners should turn their attentions elsewhere.

Careful consideration should be given to where this bamboo is positioned. Make sure there is plenty of room for it to grow and

reach maturity without the need for it to be disturbed or transplanted later on. Choose a sheltered part of the garden, where it won't get buffeted by the wind. Food and water are required in massive quantities to get the best results from this plant, particularly in the early years after planting.

Something else to consider is the fact that, as with all bamboos, *Semiarundinaria fastuosa* is at its best just after the growing season has finished but before the winter storms set in. With this in mind, choose a planting position that will be viewed regularly during the autumn.

Canes are produced in large quantities once this bamboo becomes established. If a less dense clump is required, thin out the canes at any time of the year, cutting them right back to ground level with a sharp pair of secateurs.

Because *Semiarundinaria fastuosa* is so slow to spread and rarely sets seed, very little material is available for propagation purposes. The plant is therefore often in short supply at retail nurseries.

Climbers

Climbing plants have many uses, and it's rare to find a garden that doesn't have at least a couple growing somewhere.

Climbers, especially the faster-growing ones such as *Clematis armandii* and *Hedera canariensis* that cover everything at top speed, are invaluable for hiding hideous fence panels, sheds, drainpipes and other unsightly objects. With the exception of *Vitis coignetiae*, included because of its massive jungly leaves and stunning autumn colours, all the climbing plants in this chapter are evergreen, so the objects they are covering remain hidden all year round.

This group of plants can provide a third dimension to a garden, particularly a tiny one where some height is necessary to make the planting more interesting. As they are usually pinned flat against walls or other surfaces, they don't take up much space. There is, therefore, usually plenty of room left in front of them for other plants.

Climbers make an interesting backdrop to just about anything in the garden, whether herbaceous plants, palms, shrubs or trees.

BELOW
Holboellia coriacea
can be grown
in even the
coldest gardens.

The plants chosen here have all been included because of their architectural exoticness. Apart from their evergreen presence, many have exquisitely perfumed flowers. The delicious scent from *Trachelospermum jasminoides* or *Trachelospermum asiaticum* can waft all around the garden for the entire summer, while the delectable gardenia-like perfume of *Holboellia latifolia* can be detected from a considerable distance, filling the air all through the spring. These plants are also good choices to plant near the front door, so that they can be enjoyed fully every time you come home.

Most climbers need to have something to twine around, whether it's trellis or something more substantial, such as a pergola or archway. Some of the heavier climbers, such as *Fatshedera lizei*, may need to be tied to their chosen support as well. Some, such as *Pileostegia viburnoides*, are conveniently self-clinging, hanging onto walls with their little tendrils, and they generally look after themselves.

If your garden is by the sea, the salt-resistance of *Muehlenbeckia complexa* is almost unmatched. This tough plant can cope with the fiercest salty gales without any scorching to the leaves.

The conservatory hasn't been forgotten in this chapter either. *Ficus pumila* and *Tetrastigma voinierianum* are perfect for growing under glass and provide some much-needed height in an environment that is very often filled with just low-level potted plants.

All the climbers in this chapter are fairly easy to look after, as long as the individual cultivation instructions for each plant are followed. Their watering

needs careful checking, more so than for many other plants in the garden, especially if they are planted against house walls. Here the soil is often drier than in many other parts of the garden, as the overhang from the house shields these areas from much of the rain.

Care should also be taken to protect the bases of climbing plants. It would be a great pity, after waiting several years for them to provide a fine display of foliage and flowers, to see the whole lot collapse due to damage caused by strimmers or rabbits.

Don't try to grow climbing plants in pots, unless it really is unavoidable. For the first few years of their life, all is well, but as the plants mature and increase in height, keeping them supported on canes becomes quite tricky. Many climbers have brittle stems, making it difficult to transplant them into larger containers, which they will need every few years. Self-clinging climbers are even more awkward to repot into something else.

The propagation of this group of plants can be rewarding, even for amateurs. There is nothing too difficult to tackle in this chapter, and the requirements for each plant are given with the individual plant entries.

Finally, something that is often overlooked is the fact that, although these plants can be trained to grow up, they can also be used to trail along the ground, to provide underplanting to trees, shrubs and palms. The large-leaved *Fatshedera lizei* makes a lovely jungly groundcover plant, while the small leaves and tropical-looking flowers of *Mitraria coccinea* add an exotic feel beneath any planting scheme.

ABOVE LEFT
Mitraria coccinea bears fluorescent orange tubular flowers in summer.

ABOVE RIGHT
Vitis coignetiae has huge jungly leaves and brilliant autumn colour.

BELOW
Trachelospermum jasminoides can fill the garden with delicious perfume for many months.

Clematis armandii

A vigorous evergreen climber with large, shapely leaves, which are nicely arranged in groups of threes on each leaf stem They have a leathery texture to them and a glossy sheen across the upper surface. This plant is not self-clinging, but can quickly wind itself around drainpipes and trellis or up through trees, easily reaching a height of 4.5–6m (15-20ft). The flowers are borne throughout early spring and sometimes appear in late winter if the weather is mild. They are pure white, lightly fragrant and up to 5cm (2in) across.

Clematis armandii will grow almost anywhere. Virtually any soil will suffice, but this is one of those rare plants that actually seems to prefer chalky or alkaline conditions. Sun or shade are both acceptable, but more flowers will be produced if grown in a sunny spot.

There seem to be a lot of complicated pruning instructions for many *Clematis*, but not so for this one. Simply chop it back when it outgrows the space allotted for its height and spread. Flowers are produced on growth made the previous year, so do any pruning after the flowers have finished in late spring.

As older plants tend to get a bit woody around the base, it is a good idea to wind a few shoots downwards occasionally, to provide a constant replenishment of foliage to keep them from looking too bare. Never let this plant dry out. Watering should be done regularly, especially for the first couple of seasons after planting, until it becomes established. After this time, the roots should be capable of finding their own water, unless the summer is very hot and dry.

Give a light sprinkling of something like blood, fish and bone every year in late spring. Pests and diseases shouldn't be much of a problem. However, if the plant you are buying has been grown under glass, check for whitefly, which is rather partial to *Clematis*.

Propagation is usually from cuttings taken in late summer. They offer a bit of a challenge to many gardeners. Seed can also be used but plants raised in this way often produce plants with inferior flowers.

Clematis armandii 'Apple Blossom' has pale pink flowers. Pretty it may be, but it is prone to developing a virus that causes the leaves to curl and look unsightly.

ABOVE
This Chinese plant is easy to cultivate and a vigorous grower, quickly covering hideous fence panels.

Fatshedera lizei
Fat-headed Lizzie

An interesting cross between two plants, its parents being *Hedera helix* 'Hibernica', which provides its robust qualities, and *Fatsia japonica* 'Moseri', from which it inherits its good looks.

The large, jungly leaves have a leathery feel to them, and their glossy upper surfaces look as though they have been hand-polished. This evergreen climber can be attached to walls or trellis to provide a bright green backdrop to palms such as *Trachycarpus fortunei*, bamboos or *Cordyline*. Or it can be left to scramble across the ground, where it quickly tramples over every weed and covers every scrap of ground in its path. It looks good as groundcover interwoven between Banana Plants (*Musa*), *Pittosporum* and Loquats (*Eriobotrya japonica*).

This plant adores shady conditions. The lower the light levels, the richer emerald-green the leaves. Odd-looking cream-coloured flower spikes are produced in autumn, but as they are not things of great beauty, they can be removed so that all the energy goes into leaf production.

Plant in a sheltered spot away from strong winds, which could tear the large leaves. Rich, fertile soil, which is neutral to acid, is preferred.

Avoid chalky soil, as this is generally too poor and well drained to support these greedy plants. The soil should be rich enough to hold onto some moisture without being too boggy. Copious amounts of water will be required for the first couple of years until the roots settle in.

Feed regularly throughout the growing season using a food with a high nitrogen content. The surrounding soil can be enriched annually in late autumn or early spring with generous amounts of well-rotted manure. Remove any old leaves that have turned yellow or brown. These plants are easily raised from cuttings.

Although this plant is fully hardy, a late frost can burn the new growth. If this happens, chop off any damage – new shoots will soon be sent out to replace them. Black aphids love to gather around the new tips. They are such regular visitors that it is best to assume they will appear at some time. With this in mind, check the new shoots almost daily in late spring and early summer. At the very first sign, cut off the ends of the growing tips where they have congregated. Replacement shoots will soon be produced. Use chemicals only as a last resort.

Ficus pumila
Creeping Fig

A pretty, evergreen climber with lots of tiny, heart-shaped leaves. To start with, its presence in the garden is low-key, and it takes years for it to become large enough to contribute much to a planting scheme. However, when it has matured and spread out, it proves its worth, completely covering any surface that it clings to in a delicate way.

This plant needs no support at all; even young plants can cling onto walls or fences. It needs a shady spot in the garden, sheltered from cold winds that would scorch the fragile leaves. The best soil is one that is light and fertile and capable of holding onto some moisture without becoming waterlogged. Feed with a small helping of blood, fish and bone every spring.

Apart from an occasional aphid, little seems to bother *Ficus pumila*. Sometimes older plants take on a different form: the fruiting branches of mature plants can start to thicken up and produce much larger, fleshier leaves. These look perfectly acceptable, but can be removed if you prefer the smaller foliage. *Ficus pumila* is native to parts of China and Japan, and can be propagated from cuttings.

This plant is reliably hardy only in mild gardens. It does, however, make a good choice for a frost-free conservatory or greenhouse. Choose a shady wall for it to climb up, away from the glare of any direct sun. A shady position keeps the foliage a deeper green colour. If at all possible, consider planting *Ficus pumila* directly into the ground – much better results will be obtained if it is grown this way. The most likely planting spot, though, will be a container, but make sure it is a large one, so that repotting is needed only infrequently. Trying to repot any climber is a bit of a chore once it has reached a decent height and spread.

Under glass, annual feeding will still need to be done using blood, fish and bone, if you can bear the pong. Humidity is appreciated too, and occasional misting with lime-free water will keep the plant happy. Any lime or chalk in the water won't actually harm the leaves, but a powdery white deposit will gradually build up across the foliage. This is unsightly and, because the leaves are so tiny and delicate, washing it off would be difficult.

Hedera canariensis
Canary Island Ivy

An impressive jungly climber with large evergreen leaves up to 20cm (8in) across. Although it has a reputation for being tender, I've always found it to be reliably hardy enough to be worthy of its green hardiness colour code.

The foliage takes on different hues throughout the year. The new growth in spring is bright emerald-green, which gradually darkens to a much deeper green. Then, in the autumn, bronzy tints sometimes appear, especially if the ground is very dry. The reddish-bronze is usually a sign of some kind of stress, such as lack of rain during very cold weather, but the colouring is quite pleasing and no long-term harm seems evident as long as watering is resumed promptly.

This plant makes a wonderful backdrop to all sorts of planting schemes, whether exotic, jungly, leafy or traditional. It hides walls and fence panels speedily and can reach a height of 1.8m (6ft) within three years. It is self-clinging eventually, although young plants need a helping hand with canes or string to point them in the right direction until they become established.

Choose a planting position sheltered from any strong winds – the leaves are too big to be able to cope with constant battering from gales. A shady spot is best to ensure the leaves stay a rich dark colour, but some sun is acceptable. Rich, fertile, moist conditions are required to support this lush, leafy plant.

Annual feeding in spring with heaps of well-rotted manure or a generous helping of blood, fish and bone would be beneficial. A constant supply of moisture is also needed to get the very best results, although, like most ivies, it can tolerate quite a bit of neglect. The soil should be heavy enough to retain some moisture without ever becoming waterlogged.

Remove any older brown leaves as soon as they appear to maintain a tidy appearance. If the plant becomes too big for its allotted space, chop it back at any time using secateurs or shears.

Green aphids can be a nuisance on the new shoots in late spring and into summer, so make regular inspections for them. Instead of using chemicals, just chop off affected shoots – new ones will soon regrow. Propagation is very easy from cuttings taken at almost any time of year.

ABOVE
A good all-rounder for use in any type of planting scheme.

Holboellia coriacea

A vigorous, evergreen climber with dark green leathery leaves. Growth is dense, providing cover quickly, so that walls or fences are totally blotted out. It is not self-clinging, but is happy to wind around anything in its path. It can easily reach up into trees or climb to the top of drainpipes within just a few years. Its total height could be up to 6m (20ft). Instead of letting it grow up vertically, you could spread it along wires horizontally. Impatient gardeners wishing to conceal large areas should plant one *Holboellia coriacea* every 1.8–2.2m (6–7ft).

The flowers are different hues of greenish-white tinged with purple, depending on their gender. They start to appear in early spring and last for many weeks into the summer. After a particularly hot summer, mature plants sometimes start to produce odd swellings. These start off as green knobbly 'walnuts' and expand into long purple 'potatoes', which look quite bizarre. They are edible but, as they taste rather bland, they are best left on the plant.

This climber is unfussy and can cope with most conditions, but to get the very best results, plant in rich fertile soil. Although any degree of acidity or alkalinity can be tolerated, thin chalky soils need to be constantly fed and watered.

Newly planted specimens take a while to settle in, and all their energy goes into the roots for the first season. The following year, top growth is much more evident. Frequent watering is essential for the first year, but after that it largely takes care of itself. Feed every spring with generous amounts of any rich food such as well-rotted manure, composted kitchen waste or blood, fish and bone.

Holboellia coriacea seems just as happy in sun or shade. Shelter from very strong winds is essential, and exposed positions should be avoided. Pruning is necessary only if it outgrows its allocated space. This can be done at any time of year with secateurs, or use shears to control large areas.

Propagation can be from fresh seed or semi-ripe cuttings. Make regular inspections for green aphids, especially on new shoots.

Holboellia latifolia

SYN. *Stauntonia latifolia*

The fragrance from this beautiful evergreen climber is so strong that an entire garden can be filled with exquisite scent from just one mature plant.

There is nothing I would rather plant to cover unsightly larch-lap fencing than this climber. The dense mass of fresh green foliage lies quite flat against a fence or wall, leaving lots of space in front for other shrubs or trees. Growth is remarkably vigorous once the roots have settled in: an average-sized fence panel can be covered in three years. Stems can twine around wire or trellis quite easily if coaxed in the right direction. Individual shoots can reach 6m (20ft), so covering drainpipes is no challenge at all.

On mature plants after a very warm summer, peculiar-looking fruits appear in early autumn. They start off the same colour as the leaves, so are not immediately obvious. These knobbly 'potatoes' gradually enlarge until they are 10–13cm (4–5in) long, then ripen into a bright pinkish-purple colour. Although edible, they taste rather unexciting, so are best left on the plant .

Pruning can be done at any time of year by just chopping bits off when they are in the way or become untidy. This plant is usually sold with a bamboo cane in its pot for support. Leave this on when planting, rather than trying to unravel the stems; after a couple of seasons it will be completely concealed and you won't know it's there. *Holboellia latifolia* puts all its energy into the root system when first planted. It is in its second year that the reason for classing it as fast-growing becomes much more apparent.

This climber can cope with sun or shade, and is content with most types of soil. Shelter is required on permanently windy sites, although the occasional exposure to gales seems to cause little harm. For the very best results, plant in fertile soil that can hold onto some moisture without ever becoming waterlogged. Generous amounts of well-rotted manure or blood, fish and bone applied every spring would be greatly appreciated. Make regular inspections for green aphids on the new shoots. Propagation is easiest from semi-ripe cuttings.

Hydrangea seemannii
Evergreen Climbing Hydrangea

A handsome, large-leaved, evergreen climber from Mexico, which is surprisingly hardy, considering its provenance. It is a fairly recent introduction and deserves to be better known. It is self-supporting, clinging onto walls with aerial roots that form all along the stems.

Hydrangea seemannii is an unbelievably slow starter. Newly planted specimens do virtually nothing that is visible for the first full season – all the initial energy goes into establishing the roots. For the next three or four years, growth will still be slow, and its reach could be as little as 1.5m (5ft) in all directions. Thankfully, it then speeds up a bit so that, after ten years, it could easily be touching the gutters. The conditions also have a marked effect on this plant's performance, which will be faster on rich, moist soil than on drier, chalky ones.

Watering should be done regularly for the first two or three years after planting, after which time plants can usually start to fend for themselves and will need extra moisture only if the summer is especially hot and dry. This is an ideal plant for a shady spot. The foliage stays a deeper green in the shade, and it is also more likely to send out its aerial roots at an earlier age. Sunny walls can be coped with, but the plant will need some coaxing in the right direction before it gets a grip.

The splendid frothy masses of tiny, creamy white flowers are clustered together and usually appear in mid-summer. As they take a lot of energy away from the leaves, the flowers can be chopped off if you are hardhearted enough to be able to do so.

Although most conditions are suitable, the best and fastest results will be gained from planting in rich moist soil that is enriched each spring with hefty dollops of well-rotted manure. Little maintenance is required apart from removing old flower stalks and any older brown foliage. Young plants will need to be tied into position until they start to self-cling.

The most likely problem to be experienced is leaf spot, which can leave disfiguring brown circular spots across the foliage. Remove any affected leaves as soon as they are seen, to stop its spread throughout the plant. Propagation is reasonably easy from cuttings.

ABOVE
The big, glossy leaves of *Hydrangea seemannii* can completely smother a wall or even the entire front of a house, However, this will take many years, as growth is slow, especially for the first few years.

Mitraria coccinea

An unusual climbing plant from Chile with lots of tiny glossy leaves and fabulous exotic-looking flowers. The foliage is a dark racing green, which contrasts beautifully with the almost fluorescent scarlet-orange of its tubular flowers.

It can be tied onto wires or trellis and trained to cover fences and walls, and is ideal for softening archways and pergolas. It is also blissfully happy if left just to romp across the soil, providing groundcover underneath trees, palms or shrubs. It can spread across 2.5m (8ft) after five years, providing a dense covering capable of blotting out all the weeds.

To get the very best from this relatively fussy evergreen plant, the growing conditions need to be absolutely right. Moisture is the number one requirement. The water should preferably be lime-free – if you live in a hard-water area, use stored rainwater from a water butt. Ample amounts are needed to keep the plant healthy and contented, and it should never be allowed to dry out, even once established. It can cope with occasional boggy conditions, providing the soil doesn't remain waterlogged for more than a few days at a time.

A shady position is best to keep the colouring of the foliage a rich deep green. The type of soil is important too. Shallow, chalky soil would be hopeless. It needs soil that is rich, fertile and moisture-retentive. Avoid high alkaline chalky soil. Clay or loam would be best, and peat-based soil would also be fine if it were enriched annually. Feed each spring, preferably with well-rotted manure or composted kitchen waste. Blood, fish and bone can also be used but only in light doses – too much could result in the scorching and blackening of the leaves.

The flowering period can be any time throughout late spring and early autumn, and the flamboyant orange flowers are produced in copious amounts, providing the plant is well looked after.

This plant is very low-maintenance, and is generally free from pests and diseases. Propagation is from semi-ripe cuttings.

ABOVE
Mitraria coccinea can be used as an evergreen climber or jungly groundcover.

Muehlenbeckia complexa

Describing a plant as useful generally means that it's dead boring and not worth talking about. However, in this case, 'useful' means exactly that, plus a whole lot more. This exceptionally versatile plant will adapt to many different sites. The tiny evergreen leaves form a very tight mass, blotting out everything behind or underneath them; ugly fences, half-derelict walls and dry stony soil can soon become a distant memory. A single plant could attain a spread of 1.8–2.5m (6–8ft) and a height of 5m (16ft) after six or seven years.

It is just as happy growing along the ground as it is twining upwards on wires or through trees. It is even possible to use this plant as topiary by wrapping it around metal frames – its thin, wiry stems make it easy to clip into shape.

Muehlenbeckia complexa is hardy in most areas, except for bad frost pockets, and is one of the toughest plants around for coastal areas. Strong, salty gales are just shrugged off and, in its native New Zealand, it can be found growing on the beach. It can be grown in colder areas but it does not remain evergreen in really severe winters.

The white, waxy bell flowers are so incredibly tiny that they are difficult to spot. They usually appear during late summer or early autumn.

This plant really does grow anywhere, as long as it is in the ground. It is hopeless in a pot, unless the container is the size of a large bungalow. It can cope with bright sun or deep shade, is happy on clay or chalk, will grow in moist conditions or scramble over a dry beach. It is excellent groundcover too, quickly finding its way through and around other plants.

Water regularly during its first season. After that, watering can be largely ignored. It is very easy to look after, and even annual feeding can be dispensed with. Pruning isn't necessary unless it starts to grow where it isn't wanted, when it can be hacked back at any time of year with shears.

Keep a close watch for green aphids on new shoots during a hot summer. Little else causes problems. Propagation is easy from cuttings.

Pileostegia viburnoides

SYN. *Schizophragma viburnoides*

This rather classy evergreen climber, with a name that will test your Latin pronunciation, is one of the best possible climbing plants for a shady wall – the rich dark green foliage stays a much better colour in a shady aspect. It is such a fine-looking plant that it's a puzzle as to why it's not more widely grown. The large, elongated leaves are beautifully shaped, thick and leathery, and the upper surface of each one has a glossy finish. The foliage is plentiful, giving a dense covering for a wall or fence.

This plant is self-clinging, hanging onto damp walls with fuzzy aerial roots that grow along each stem. It is perfect for gardeners who can't be bothered with wires or trellis. It needs some persuasion to cling to drier surfaces but, after being pointed in the right direction, it usually takes hold eventually. It grows very slowly for the first few years, while all of its energy goes into the root system. Once it has settled in, growth speeds up a bit, and mature plants could cover the front of a house with ease.

The large frothy masses of creamy white flowers clustered together appear in late summer. They are fairly attractive but they

sap the plant's energy and can be chopped off as soon as they appear, if you wish.

Although less than ideal conditions can be tolerated, the very best results and the fastest growth will be from plants positioned in deep shade, where the sun doesn't reach at all. Moisture is important, and regular watering will be necessary for at least the first couple of seasons until it becomes established. After this time, watering will normally be needed only if the weather is especially hot and dry. Rich, fertile, moisture-retentive soil is preferred; shallow chalky soils should definitely be avoided. Clay or loam with good drainage would be best of all, and neutral to acid conditions are better than alkaline ones.

An annual feed of blood, fish and bone or a helping of well-rotted manure in spring will keep the colour and appearance tip-top. Pruning is unnecessary as a rule, and will need to be done only in the unlikely event of the plant becoming too big.

This plant has a robust nature, and little in the way of pests and diseases seem to bother it. Propagation is easy from cuttings.

ABOVE
A magnificent climbing plant that gets better and better each year.

Tetrastigma voinierianum
Lizard Vine

A beautiful leafy plant, despite its hellish Latin name. It is native to tropical habitats so, unless your garden is reliably frost-free, it must be grown indoors. As it can cope with very low light levels, it needn't be placed in a conservatory or greenhouse. It would be quite happy in the house if some humidity can be provided.

The leaves are enormous, especially on older plants. Thick and fleshy with nice wavy edges, they are supported on stout stems, and the whole plant can be rather weighty. It is self-clinging, as long as it can find something to wind around. By sending out long tendrils, it can gradually make its way across wires or trellis.

The flowers of this vine are so tiny and insignificant that it is best to class it as a foliage plant. This doesn't really matter, as the exotic, dense growth is interesting enough on its own. In shady conservatories, it can provide some height as a backdrop to other potted plants. It can also be left to cover a window, to provide even more shade to enable delicate plants such as ferns to grow more successfully.

Although a planting spot in the ground would be best, this plant is much more likely to have to make do with a large pot indoors. Make sure the container is enormous enough to support a mature plant – transplanting a large specimen would be very difficult without breaking any of the stems. Although a vigorous-growing plant, it can easily be controlled by chopping unwanted bits off it at any time of the year with secateurs.

For pot-grown plants, use a rich loam-based soil such as John Innes no. 3. No extra drainage is required, as the roots appreciate constant moisture in the soil. Water regularly enough to keep the compost almost permanently moist without becoming waterlogged. Feed every six weeks during the growing season with any high-nitrogen liquid food mixed in the watering can. This ensures the foliage stays a good size and a rich colour with a healthy shine.

The leaves appreciate occasional misting to increase humidity, and dusting to keep them looking their best. Sometimes, a sticky clear goo is seen near the stems. Quite why it is exuded, I'm not sure, but it seems to do no harm. This is a very easy plant for novice gardeners. Little in the way of pests and diseases bothers it. Propagation is from cuttings.

ABOVE
A big-leaved jungly plant for indoors.

Trachelospermum asiaticum

Trachelospermum asiaticum is a tough little evergreen climber, despite its fragile appearance. The delicate-looking stems wind around anything in their path. It is a perfect choice for a small garden, as growth is exceptionally slow. It can take several years for a small specimen to settle in and start to cover walls or fences. Its slowness makes it a good choice of plant for training up and over pergolas, as pruning is a chore that can be more or less ignored.

The dark green foliage is attractive enough on its own, but this plant has the added advantage of wonderfully fragrant flowers. They are small star-shaped blossoms and a rich deep cream in colour. Produced throughout summer, they have the fabulous scent of gardenias.

Trachelospermum asiaticum must be planted in lime-free soil to remain green and healthy-looking. Keep it sheltered from strong winds in a lightly shaded position. Full sun gives more flowers but the foliage can look a bit bleached; full shade keeps the foliage looking wonderful, but few flowers are produced. A carefully

chosen site somewhere in between these light levels would be about right.

The soil should be preferably fertile and fairly heavy. Clay or loam in the soil would stop it from being too free-draining. Although constant moisture is appreciated, never let the soil become waterlogged, as this would rot the roots. If using tap water, ensure that it is lime-free. Once the plants have become established, watering can be reduced considerably and, in fact, mature plants could be classed as almost drought-tolerant.

This native of Korea and Japan is amazingly hardy, taking seriously low temperatures in its stride. Feeding can be largely forgotten unless the soil is very poor. Keeping it hungry increases flower production. If the foliage needs a bit of a boost, give it a light dressing of blood, fish and bone at any time during the growing season.

Propagation is easiest and quickest from cuttings. Green aphids can be a nuisance on the new shoots, and regular inspections should be made for them. If cutting or pruning the stems, wear gloves, as milky white sap pours out from any cuts. This sap is messy but harmless.

Trachelospermum jasminoides
Star Jasmine

SYN. *Rhyncospermum jasminoides*

The main claim to fame of this evergreen climber is its wonderfully sweet scent. Clusters of white, star-shaped flowers are produced in profusion from late spring right through until early autumn. Its foliage is attractive too, forming a dense covering of small, glossy leaves against walls, trellis or fencing. Pruning is rarely required. Although it is not self-clinging, the shoots are capable of wrapping around whatever come their way, whether canes, wires or wooden posts. After ten years, it will have covered an area of only about 4m (13ft) in height and 2.5m (8ft) in width. After a hot summer, long green seedpods are produced in pairs.

Lime-free soil is essential and so is lots of moisture, until the plant becomes established enough to fend for itself. In hard-water areas, use only stored rainwater. Mature plants could be considered almost drought-resistant. Too much sun gives a bleached appearance to the leaves, while too much shade gives fewer flowers, so a planting position in light shade would be about right. Feed this plant only when it looks a bit jaded, and then apply just a light dressing of blood, fish and bone

during the growing season. Keeping it hungry increases flower production.

Although fairly hardy, *Trachelospermum jasminoides* is a popular choice for conservatories. It is not the easiest plant to grow indoors and should be given a massive pot and never be allowed to dry out. If it does, even for a short period of time, flower buds and leaves are shed in alarmingly high numbers. Under glass, red spider mite is a common visitor, and regular inspections are needed to ensure that any outbreaks are dealt with as early as possible.

Outdoors, the main pests are green aphids, which can gather on the new shoots in summer. Sometimes large numbers of leaves turn bright red. Pretty though this colouring is, it is a sign of stress that could be due to extreme cold or dry soil, or vine weevil, if it is grown in a pot. Propagation is easiest and quickest from cuttings. If a leaf or stem breaks, milky white sap can seep from the cut. This is messy, but harmless.

Vitis coignetiae
Crimson Glory Vine

The most spectacular of all vines, and its fine qualities more than make up for the fact that it is deciduous. This plant is very vigorous and needs plenty of space to romp across. It will wrap around anything in its way, whether it's along wires or trellis or soaring up through trees. The large jungly leaves can be up to 30cm (1ft) across on mature plants. They are a pretty sage-green, and produced in sufficient quantities to conceal walls or fences completely. A distance of 6m (20ft) could easily be covered within ten years.

In the autumn, the foliage takes on amazing shades of bright scarlet and crimson, which is very vibrant and extremely noticeable. The bare stems are brittle, and care should be taken when tidying up the plant for the winter. Any pruning can be done more easily when the leaves have disappeared. Sometimes, bunches of little black fruits appear on older plants. These are not good to eat and should be left on the plant.

Rich, fertile, well-drained soil is needed to support such energetic growth. Clay soil or loam would be perfect. Although it is not a lime-hating plant, shallow chalky soils would lack the food and water needed to produce really good results. During the growing season, lots of water is required, especially for young plants. Older, established plants can usually fend for themselves. During its winter dormancy, extra irrigation is rarely required, even if it hasn't rained for many weeks.

Enrich the soil annually in late spring with heaps of well-rotted manure or plenty of blood, fish and bone. Remove any brown leaves tangled in among the stems to keep it looking tidy.

Propagation is easiest in the winter when the plants are dormant and leafless. Either use hardwood cuttings or chop up the stems in sections, making sure there is a vine 'eye' in each segment for new growth to sprout from.

Green aphids can sometimes be a nuisance on new growth. In a cold wet season, grey fluffy mould (botrytis) can appear on the leaves. Don't bother spraying the plant if this is seen. Instead, just hand-pick off any affected foliage.

Trees

Where would we be without trees? Life just wouldn't be the same. Trees are such a brilliant invention that there should be at least one in every garden.

Trees add that extra dimension to any garden – they provide height and a much more natural, appealing look to a planting scheme. Using just low-growing plants gives a really flat, unfinished appearance. Trees come in all shapes and sizes to suit everywhere, from the largest country estate, the average suburban garden, right down to the tiniest courtyard.

They provide much needed shade from the hot summer sun. They attract all sorts of wildlife into the garden, providing accommodation for birds and insects. Some, such as *Pinus radiata*, can be used as coastal windbreaks, creating enough shelter to enable more delicate plants to grow successfully in an otherwise harsh environment. Some of the taller types of tree, such as *Eucalyptus aggregata* or *Quercus ilex*, can be grown as canopies over particularly cold gardens, giving a degree or two of extra frost protection during the winter months. Trees also add movement and life to any setting, and gardeners don't plant enough of them.

Even in the tiniest garden, there'll always be room somewhere for a tree.

The trees featured in this chapter are all architectural in some way. They have been carefully chosen for their special qualities. For example, there's the colourful bark of *Arbutus* x *andrachnoides*, the shapely outline of *Phillyrea latifolia*, the large leaves of *Paulownia tomentosa* or the evergreen presence of *Laurus nobilis angustifolia*. Some trees, such as *Pseudopanax crassifolius*, have been included because they are downright odd. Virtually all of them, however, are easy to maintain.

Many people ask what the ultimate height and spread of a particular tree will be before they decide whether or not it is a suitable purchase for their plot of land. This is never an easy question to answer because it depends on the location that the tree is destined for. For example, areas of high rainfall usually produce taller specimens than drier areas, while trees in inland gardens usually attain more height than those buffeted around on exposed cliff tops. What I can suggest, though, is that you try to learn as much about your preferred tree either from this book or by observing how the same kind of tree behaves in its intended locality.

Planting a tree is always seen as a special event for gardeners, and quite rightly so. If the correct tree has been selected for the proposed site, there is no reason why it should not live for many, many decades. Therefore, it makes sense to plant it correctly.

Years ago, tree nurseries grew their stock in the ground, then waited for the trees to become dormant in the autumn before lifting them to supply garden centres and other customers. Hence the tradition of autumn planting. Unfortunately, many people still believe that trees are best planted at this

time of the year, even though the modern practice of growing plants in containers means that this is no longer the case. Container-grown trees can be planted at any time, providing the ground is not frozen or waterlogged.

I would also avoid planting during the hottest summer months if rain hasn't been seen for a while. Late spring is the ideal time. Then the ground has warmed up a bit and the tree has the whole of the growing season to settle its roots in before experiencing autumn storms and winter cold.

To plant a tree, dig a hole measuring the same size as the container, so that the tree can be planted at the same level as it was in its pot. Planting too high might expose some of the roots, which can then dry out, whereas planting too deeply raises the level of compost around the trunk, which can lead to rotting. Throw a couple of handfuls of bonemeal into the bottom of the planting hole to get the roots off to a good start, and plant the tree carefully, making sure that it's straight.

Staking a newly planted tree is essential. Use a single stake for a young tree, and one on either side of the trunk for a larger tree. For a mature tree or a tree planted in an exposed position, use three stakes – one at every 120 degrees around the trunk (see photographs below). Hammer the stakes in hard using a sledgehammer, until one third of the length disappears into the ground. Insert the stakes vertically at the edge of the rootball, making sure they are long enough to support a good proportion of the trunk. Tie them in

ABOVE
Using the correct stretchy tying material ensures good support from all angles.

RIGHT
Staking and tying is an essential part of tree planting.

LEFT
Leave a wide
circle around
newly planted
trees and shrubs
to restrict
unwanted
competition
for water
and nutrients.

with rubber strips, which will stretch as the trunk grows in girth without causing any damage. Trees usually require staking for the first two years after planting. Check the ties every few months to ensure that a) they are still holding fast and b) they have not become too tight.

To finish the planting process, clear a large circle of any grass or weeds from the base of the tree to a diameter of at least 1.5m (5ft). Trees can become established at least ten times more quickly if they have no competition nearby for water and nutrients. Head gardeners in municipal parks know all about this, and a lot can be learned from them (see photograph, above).

Water new trees in well and, for the next couple of years, water whenever necessary to keep the ground moist until they are able to fend for themselves. Feeding with blood, fish and bone can take place each spring. Pruning is usually best done in the spring just as new growth is about to burst out. Any exceptions to spring pruning are referred to in the individual tree entries.

It is useful to remember that trees can be controlled by pruning. You can see that the tree in the photograph on the right has been shaped beautifully and, because it is never allowed to get any bigger, it is a perfect specimen tree for a small front garden. If it had been left to grow unchecked, it would have filled up much more of the available space, blocking out light and leaving little room for anything else to be planted.

BELOW
This tree has been lovingly clipped and shaped to ensure that it never gets too big for its allocated space in the garden.

Pruning also produces youthful vigour in tired old trees. For example, after a few years of steady growth, the foliage of a *Magnolia grandiflora* that has been trained in a large conical shape can become a bit sparse (see photograph, above left). However, ruthless hard pruning using a saw can be done just as the new growing season starts. By following the natural overall shape of the plant, cut back the branches so that all of the old foliage is removed.

Although this process is not for the faint-hearted, it works – trust me! At the end of the first growing season, new foliage will start to appear. By the end of the following year, the tree will be covered in luxuriant, healthy leaves (see photograph, above right).

If a tree has become too large for a small garden and is blocking the light, instead of having the whole plant removed, which would usually be very expensive, not to mention inconvenient, check out what other options there are first. Sometimes, crown-lifting the tree can be the solution to the problem. Crown-lifting is the term used for sawing off all the lower branches of the tree but leaving the top canopy untouched (see left). This technique can often remove enough volume to make the tree appear less threatening, as well as letting in more light.

I would *never* recommend sawing off the top of a tree (unless you are pruning a row of trees to create a giant hedge). Chopping off the top certainly allows in more light, but it is only a short-term solution. By pruning back this hard, the tree will be encouraged to grow even faster and the same problem will recur in a couple of years. Removing the top of a tree also completely ruins the shape, resulting in a rather sad spectacle.

The propagation of trees can be a rewarding experience, and for many of the plants described in this chapter it is quite an easy process. The best method to use for the trees described is given with each of the individual tree entries. Some can be propagated from seed, others from either root cuttings, hardwood cuttings, grafting or stem cuttings. Some trees are more difficult and need micropropagation in a laboratory. And one or two of them are just plain cantankerous – their propagation is best left to the experts.

Most of the trees that appear in this chapter are relatively free from pests and diseases, providing the plants have been properly planted and well cared for. Any particular problems to look out for will be referred to in the individual tree entries.

Over the last few years, there has been much hysteria about trees being planted near buildings. Tree roots are not roguish thugs and do not deserve such bad press. Most small to medium-sized trees with a maximum height not exceeding 7.5m (25ft) are quite safe to plant near houses and garden walls without any risk of them demolishing the entire neighbourhood. Rather than planting *fewer* trees in built-up areas, far *more* should be planted as they enhance our towns and cities and generally make life more pleasant.

RIGHT
Eucalyptus pauciflora 'Debeuzevillei', with its light open habit and beautiful snowy bark, is a fantastic choice for a small garden.

ABOVE
The foliage of
Acacia dealbata
has a delicate
appearance.

Acacia dealbata
Mimosa

A beautiful evergreen tree, perfect for smaller gardens, having an ultimate height of about 7.5m (25ft) in most climates. The foliage is a mass of ferny leaves that look far too delicate for coastal gardens, where these trees thrive, but they are more than capable of coping with the occasional blast of salty air. *Acacia dealbata* is also a good choice for milder, city gardens.

Lovely clusters of fluffy yellow flowers are produced in early spring. Deliciously fragrant, they are produced on plants raised from seed that are around five years old.

Native to Australia, *Acacia dealbata* can be seen growing wild throughout New South Wales, Victoria and Tasmania, thriving in the heat and sunshine. In cooler countries, it is best planted against a sunny wall, so that it can bask in plenty of heat. More heat and sun mean more flowers. Planting in too shady a spot won't do any harm, but it could become leggy and the flowers will be sparse.

Poor, sandy, well-drained soil suits this tree best. Avoid soil with high levels of chalk and lime. It rarely needs feeding. When newly planted, it will appreciate plenty of water, and then continuous watering in dry spells for the first couple of years, so that the soil doesn't dry out. After this time, the roots will have penetrated down deep enough for the tree to be classed as drought tolerant. To keep the foliage dense and bushy, clip lightly every year, sometime between the end of the flowering season and mid-summer. Flower buds start to form in late summer, so late pruning would sacrifice flowers for the following year.

This is a very easy tree to cultivate, and is rarely troubled by pests or diseases. It's a popular choice for conservatories because of the fragrance of the blooms. However, it's not a good candidate for containers due to its speed of growth. Savage pruning immediately after flowering, together with copious amounts of water, can help to prolong its life indoors. A shortage of water, plus being cramped in too small a pot, will result in considerable leaf drop. If grown indoors, keep a close watch for scale insects.

ABOVE
Bright yellow
fragrant flowers
are produced in
copious amounts
in early spring.

Acacia pravissima
Oven's Wattle

A pretty little weeping tree with unusual foliage quite unlike any other tree. The leaves on *Acacia pravissima* are hard-textured tiny triangles that run along the length of each stem. They are interesting, rather than beautiful, and not really proper leaves at all – they're grandly referred to as *phyllodes.* This evergreen tree is an Australian native that enjoys lots of sunshine. It is the best choice for gardens too cold to cultivate the more familiar ferny-leaved *Acacia* because *Acacia pravissima* is the hardiest of its type. Its ultimate height away from its native country is about 4m (13ft).

This is an easy tree to grow from seed, with rapid growth during the first few years. When a height of 1.8m (6ft) has been reached, start to remove the lower branches to encourage it to become tree-shaped, rather than an untidy bush. The top growth folds over as the tree ages, forming a weeping habit. Light pruning of the foliage produces a thick head more speedily.

Flower buds start to form at the end of the summer on trees over five years old. These stay closed right through the winter and open out in early spring. They take the form of large clusters of fragrant fluffy flowers that are bright yellow in colour.

Plant in a sunny position, sheltered from the wind, in soil that is poor, well drained and free from lime or chalk. Feeding is not usually necessary. Don't allow it to dry out for the first couple of years. Too little moisture can result in the leaves taking on a bronzed appearance, and at this stage full health is rarely regained. Once *Acacia pravissima* has become established, it can take care of finding its own water supply, coping well even in drought conditions.

This makes a good choice as a specimen tree for even the smallest garden. If it starts to outgrow its allotted space, heavy pruning along the top or sides will do no harm at all. In fact, the more it is pruned, the bushier and better it becomes. Cut it back using shears any time during late spring and mid-summer, when new flower buds will start to form for the following spring.

ABOVE
Unusual triangular foliage, together with masses of beautiful flowers, makes this evergreen weeping tree a spectacular choice for small gardens.

Ailanthus altissima
Tree of Heaven

This fast-growing deciduous tree from China has huge leaves, making it essential for a jungly garden. The leaves are made up of lots of leaflets radiating out from the main central section (this style of leaf is called pinnate). *Ailanthus altissima* can easily reach 12m (40ft) or more, and grows just about anywhere. Its lofty habit gives us its common name. It is best kept as a single-stemmed tree: remove any side growth, so that all its energy can go into achieving its height as quickly as possible.

The enormous leaves can be made even larger by chopping all of the previous year's growth back hard at the end of each season after they have been shed for autumn. This encourages fresh vigour each spring, producing leaves up to 1.2m (4ft) long. The sheer size of the foliage more than compensates for it being deciduous. The leaves also turn a nice buttery yellow for a couple of weeks before dropping. Don't handle them more than necessary – they give off a peculiar odour a bit like vomit!

Ailanthus altissima trees are perfect for planting as the first layer of a jungle garden. Put them at the back of the planting plan to give a fast-growing foil for smaller trees, palms and bamboos, finishing with a layer of ferns and groundcover plants at the front for a complete leafy look. *Ailanthus altissima* is very tough and copes with pollution well, making it an excellent choice as a street tree for inner cities.

Although tolerant of most conditions, best results will be gained from planting in a moist, rich soil in sun or light shade. Because of the size of the foliage, planting in a sheltered spot away from the wind will keep the leaves in perfect condition. Male and female flowers are usually found on separate trees. The female ones are rather unexciting; the male ones are both unexciting and unpleasantly smelly.

Propagation is easy from seed but, because the female trees are more desirable, taking root cuttings from a known female tree is a more suitable method – the gender of seed-grown plants is never known until the tree flowers. Because of the horrible pong from the leaves and the male flowers, a more imaginative alternative common name should perhaps be applied to this tree.

ABOVE
The luxuriant pinnate foliage of *Ailanthus altissima* makes a fine addition to any garden.

Albizia julibrissin
Silk Tree or **Pink Siris**

This stunning little deciduous tree is ideal for a small garden. Its large, ferny leaves give it a delicate look. Despite this, *Albizia julibrissin* is surprisingly hardy and can cope with some seriously low temperatures. The flowers are fluffy pink powder-puffs that give off a delicate fragrance in sunny weather.

In cooler climates, the maximum size is unlikely to be much more than 6m (20ft). There are also a couple of varieties often available: 'Rosea' and 'Ombrello'. These have deeper pink flowers and are much smaller, reaching no more than around 4m (13ft).

This tree has a relatively short season, so, although it is perfectly hardy, to extend its growing period as much as possible, choose a warm, sunny, sheltered planting position, preferably close to a sun-baked wall. The soil should be poor, well drained and slightly acid. Avoid planting where there is chalk or lime in the soil. Watering will be necessary to start with but, once the tree becomes established after a couple of years, this is usually unnecessary because *Albizia julibrissin* is extremely drought tolerant.

Albizia julibrissin is native to areas of Asia, from Afghanistan through to Korea, but it is well suited to Mediterranean-style gardens. Before purchasing, check that it is free from coral spot, a fungal infection to which this tree is prone. If it is found on trees already in the garden, cut back affected areas well beyond the visible damage and burn the sawn-off wood. Coral spot is more likely to be seen on very old trees or trees grown in waterlogged soil.

Flowers appear in mid-summer and last for six to eight weeks. After very hot summers, long, green seed pods are often produced. New plants can easily be raised from ripe seeds to produce *Albizia julibrissin*, but 'Rosea' and 'Ombrello' must be grafted to ensure consistent results.

Not much maintenance is required, apart from a bit of pruning to keep the head a tidy shape. Pruning should take place when the tree is dormant. This can be done in autumn or, in colder areas, it can be left until early spring.

ABOVE
Albizia julibrissin is surprisingly tough, despite the delicate appearance of the ferny foliage.

BELOW
The fluffy pink flowers are an added bonus in the summer.

■ ■ Albizia lophantha

A beautiful evergreen tree for conservatories or very mild areas outdoors. It grows quickly to produce a dense mass of ferny leaves. The mature trunks are attractively patterned and the flowers are delicate, fluffy puffs of pale lemon. If left unpruned, the eventual height could exceed 8m (26ft).

As it is so fast-growing, *Albizia lophantha* is not really suitable for growing in a pot, which causes rather a dilemma as to how it should be raised in a conservatory. Some clever gardeners have the forethought to allow for borders of soil inside their conservatories. That way, plants can be raised under glass, while their roots grow unrestricted as nature intended. But, hindsight being a wonderful thing, most conservatories can be used only for growing plants in pots. If this is the case, choose an enormous pot, the largest that you can transport through the door. Pot the tree up in a good-quality loam-based compost, such as John Innes no. 3, adding a bit of extra grit to help with the drainage. *Albizia lophantha* can then be left to grow happily for years. When it starts to outgrow even this generous

accommodation, it can be hacked back annually to keep it at a more manageable size.

Full sun or bright light is essential for this tree's well-being. Too much shade can cause considerable leaf drop and produce tall spindly growth. If it's grown in a border, drought resistance can develop within a couple of years.

If grown in a pot, constant moisture is vital, so that the compost never fully dries out – keeping the roots permanently moist, but not waterlogged, is the key to success. As soon as the compost dries out, displeasure is shown immediately by much shedding of leaves – a sort of horticultural flounce! Once this happens, it is difficult to get the balance right again. It is tempting to slosh a whole can of water at it in a panic, but this will probably lead to yellowing of the leaves and even more leaf drop.

It really is worth persevering with this tree's care, though, because a well-looked after *Albizia lophantha* is a fine sight indeed.

ABOVE
The exotic foliage of this beautiful evergreen makes it an essential plant for a large conservatory.

Aralia elata
Japanese Angelica Tree

A small and shapely tree from Japan and another essential addition to a jungly garden. It can be forgiven for being deciduous because of its fabulous foliage. The leaves are enormous and beautifully crafted into delicate leaflets along the length of each stem. Their fresh green colour turns an attractive shade of crimson in early autumn, just before the leaves drop.

The stem is an oddity, bearing lots of thorns all the way up the trunk, even into maturity. This becomes more noticeable in the winter when the tree is bare. Generous clusters of frothy cream flowers are produced in late summer.

Aralia elata is often left to grow naturally as a multi-stemmed tree, but it is far superior if grown on a single stem. To achieve this, clip off any suckers from the roots as soon as they appear. These can be used for propagation. Otherwise, raise new plants from fresh seed or root cuttings. This very hardy tree can cope with being cut back hard in its dormant winter period to control its size but, if left unpruned, it's unlikely to reach much more than 6m (20ft). Cut away any side shoots from the stem so that all the foliage creates a canopy at the top.

Although an unfussy tree to cultivate, the best results come from planting in rich, moist soil in light shade, sheltered from strong winds that could tear the leaves. Apply a light feed in late spring just before new leaves unfurl. A mix of blood, fish and bone is as good as anything.

Buy the biggest tree you can afford, as young plants are annoyingly slow to reach a decent size. Once planted out into the garden, growth often speeds up considerably. If cut back hard every year, at least 1.2m (4ft) of new growth can be produced the following season. Since the foliage is so delicate, buying one in full leaf is not a good idea, as transporting it home without doing any damage is quite tricky.

Aralia elata is usually without problems, but sometimes capsid bugs can be a nuisance, making enormous numbers of small unsightly holes in the foliage. Spray the leaves at the very first sign, checking underneath them, as this is where these rather timid green beasts lurk.

ABOVE
Aralia elata has some of the best foliage found on a fully hardy small tree.

ABOVE
The spiny thorns along the trunk and stems make an unusual feature on this lovely tree.

Araucaria araucana
Monkey Puzzle

People rarely have neutral feelings about *Araucaria araucana* – it's either loved or loathed. It's certainly different, and I think it's rather splendid. The leaves are sharp blades that cover each branch and the length of the trunk, making it impossible to climb, hence its common name. The branches are long and spidery.

Araucaria araucana is probably the slowest-growing plant in this book. It can eventually reach 18m (60ft) but will take about a century to do so. It was the height of fashion for Victorian gardens, but it's now planted much less often as few gardeners seem to have the patience to grow it. It used to be a familiar sight in its native Chile, but monkey puzzle forests are becoming scarce, and the diminishing numbers are starting to cause concern.

These trees always look best planted in groves, but they are most often seen as single specimen plants in the front garden. A lot of space is needed for even one plant to mature – a park would be required for large numbers – and some thought needs to go into where you position them. If a tree gets too big, transplanting it would be almost impossible.

It requires enough space for you to be able to walk around it and view it from all angles, as it really is a marvellous thing to own.

If planted in groves or avenues, a matching pair is seldom seen. They are all propagated from seed, and the resulting trees are widely assorted in shape, size and growth patterns. Cones containing edible seeds are sometimes produced on older specimens.

Lots of sunshine and moist, loamy soil are ideal for these trees. As they are so slow to grow, planting one less than 60cm (2ft) tall is not advised. Expect to pay an unusually high amount even for one of this size.

An annual feed of a blood, fish and bone mix would be beneficial, especially when the tree is young. Pests and diseases are rarely a problem.

ABOVE
A magnificent specimen of *Araucaria araucana*, which was probably planted at least sixty years ago.

BELOW
A close-up of the unusually sharp foliage.

Araucaria heterophylla
Norfolk Island Pine

SYN. *Araucaria excelsa*

This native of Norfolk Island, off the north-eastern coast of Australia, is used to a balmy climate, so unless your garden is blessed with similar weather patterns, consider *Araucaria heterophylla* as suitable for only frost-free conditions. It makes an ideal choice for conservatories and also for the interior of the house, where light levels are usually quite poor. It is a very easy and forgiving tree, tolerating practically all conditions except overwatering. If your track record of keeping indoor plants alive is not good, try this one. Kill this and your future attentions ought, perhaps, to turn to knitting or embroidery instead of horticulture.

Araucaria heterophylla is beautifully symmetrical, growing as an inverted 'V' shape, rather like a fancy Christmas tree. The branches are arranged in layers and covered with peculiar curly foliage, just like green wire wool. The tree top ends in a narrow point. It is fast-growing and can soon outgrow its allotted space in the conservatory. Don't worry, however, because when it touches the roof, cut it off wherever you wish with sharp

secateurs. It will look a bit flat on the top for a couple of months, but it will soon start to sprout new growth and regain its former glory within a season.

Plant it in the largest pot you possess in John Innes no. 3 compost. Make sure the tree is straight, move it into a cool but frost-free position and give it a good soaking. The only maintenance required after this is to keep a check on the watering, ensuring that the compost never dries out completely. Be careful not to overwater it either: too much water will turn the leaves a horrid yellow colour. An annual light dressing of a blood, fish and bone mix in spring will keep it looking healthy.

This tree tolerates shade very well, where it retains a better dark green colour than if planted in full sun. It is rarely bothered by pests or diseases. Propagation is easy from fresh seed.

Arbutus x andrachnoides
Red-barked Strawberry Tree

If your garden has room for only one specimen tree, *Arbutus* x *andrachnoides* is almost total perfection. It's evergreen, easy to cultivate and fast-growing when young. It has wonderful cinnamon-red bark that peels off in strips from the branches and trunk all year round. Large bunches of pretty, bell-shaped flowers appear all through autumn and most of the winter. Waxy in texture and of the palest creamy white, they look so delicate that they appear almost transparent. The evergreen foliage is bright green, with each leaf lightly serrated. The new growth in spring is a lovely emerald-green, with bright reddish tinges to the edges.

When young, *Arbutus* x *andrachnoides* can put on at least 60cm (2ft) of growth per year, but this rate gradually slows down as the tree ages, so that a thirty-year-old tree will probably be no more than 7.5m (25ft) tall. *Arbutus* x *andrachnoides* is a hybrid between two Strawberry Trees, namely *Arbutus unedo* and *Arbutus andrachne*, and is found growing naturally in parts of Greece. Being a hybrid, it rarely sets fruit, but sometimes bright red strawberry-like fruits appear on older plants.

The propagation of this tree is notoriously difficult with only a ten per cent success rate from cuttings. Large numbers can be produced only in a micropropagation laboratory. Very few nurseries stock the genuine article, even though many of them list it. Unfortunately, it can take some time before the mistake is discovered – the distinctive peeling bark doesn't appear until the plant is about five years old.

Arbutus x *andrachnoides* is a tough tree and can be planted almost anywhere, except severe frost pockets. When planting, choose a spot that's within easy reach. The bark is gorgeous all the time but, after a shower of rain, the cinnamon-red becomes an even deeper colour and takes on a glossy glow. It is impossible not to want to caress it.

This amazing tree performs best in full sun in any well-drained soil, even tolerating chalk or lime. Stake it very well, using three stakes unless it is really tiny. Trees shouldn't really be planted out until they are at least 90cm (3ft) tall and have started to turn woody. Buy one with the fattest trunk available. Sheltered sites out of the wind produce the fastest growth. However, if they're planted in exposed windy coastal sites, all their energy is put into the thickening of the trunk first, while the height stays more or less the same for several years.

Remove the lower branches as the tree grows, so that as much as possible of the red bark becomes visible. Pruning is not generally necessary, but regular trimming along the top and sides with a pair of shears makes an even denser crown. Do any pruning during late spring or early summer. Feed annually in spring by sprinkling a couple of handfuls of blood, fish and bone around the tree.

Keep newly planted trees well watered for the first two or three years until they are established. After this period, they will start to develop considerable drought tolerance. In early spring, just before the new growth starts, you will notice large numbers of existing leaves turn yellow and drop off. This can be rather alarming, but it's quite normal and lasts for only three or four weeks.

The only pests likely to visit *Arbutus* x *andrachnoides* regularly are green aphids, which enjoy feeding off the sap during summer. The only other problem to watch out for is black fungal spots on the leaves, which is usually caused by waterlogging in the soil. Pull off any affected leaves and improve the drainage. If the leaf spot becomes excessive after a really wet winter, then more drastic action might be required (see right).

1. If leaf spot has spread to all parts of the foliage, causing much of it to turn brown and die, then only the tips of the branches will look healthy.

2. Sometimes virtually nothing is left of the foliage at all.

3. In late spring, when new growth is expected to appear fairly soon, hack off all the stems and branches with a sharp saw, to leave a well-balanced shape to the crown. It doesn't matter if there is not a single leaf remaining on the whole tree.

4. Within just eight to ten weeks, new growth will start to sprout from all over the bare branches.

5. During the following weeks, this growth will develop quickly to produce a proper-looking tree once more.

Arbutus glandulosa
Mexican Strawberry Tree
or **Eastwood Manzanita**

SYN. *Arctostaphylos glandulosa*

A very rare evergreen tree from Mexico and, considering its exotic provenance, surprisingly hardy in colder climates. Its beautiful bark – reddish-bronze and very smooth – is the main attraction. The colour changes throughout the year, with the red peeling away to reveal pale grey or bright green patches. These are sometimes covered with a fine dusty coating, which gradually disappears to leave a smooth reddish-bronze colour once again.

The fresh green leaves are of generous proportions, and new spring growth has an attractive crimson tinge. New stems and branches are also bright red before turning woody. When young, this tree is fast-growing but it slows down considerably as it ages. It could reach 4m (13ft) in ten years, with the ultimate height in a cool climate unlikely to exceed 7.5m (25ft). The flowers are clusters of pearly white bells produced, as a rule, in late summer, but they sometimes crop up at other times of the year too.

Most well-drained soils will suit this tree, but avoid those containing excessive amounts of chalk or lime, as its tolerance to these isn't really known. Full sun is essential. Don't plant out very young trees; wait until they are at least 1.2m (4ft) tall. By then, they should have a reasonably sturdy trunk with some woody growth. Always stake new trees as soon as they are planted. The fibrous root system means that this tree will cause no structural damage even if planted right next to a house wall.

Very little maintenance is required. Water well until established, but never allow the soil to become waterlogged. A light feed with blood, fish and bone in spring would be beneficial. Prune occasionally with shears to keep the head bushy. Removing the lower branches as the tree matures will reveal more of the sumptuous bark. Green aphids, which feed on the sap of very young shoots, could be a problem in early summer. Black fungal spots on the leaves can also cause problems if allowed to spread. Propagation can be from seed or cuttings, but neither method has a high success rate.

ABOVE
The smooth red bark of *Arbutus glandulosa* is its main claim to fame.

BELOW
Lots of large, exotic leaves are produced on crimson stems.

Azara microphylla
Vanilla Tree

This pretty tree with a graceful weeping habit is from the border regions of Chile and Argentina, and was named in honour of a Spanish patron of science, J.N. Azara. The foliage consists of lots of small shiny leaves, and tiny yellow flowers appear in early spring. You have to look hard to see the flowers – there are lots of them spread along the stems, but they are so small as to be almost invisible. They don't need to be brash and showy, though, because their strong vanilla scent is so overpowering that it can be detected from many metres away – a small garden can easily be filled with the heady fragrance.

In an average cool climate, the overall height will be a maximum of only 4m (13ft). Growth from a young plant is fast for the first few years, then it slows down, barely putting on a few inches a year after that. *Azara microphylla* could be grown in even the smallest garden. As it ages, the foliage becomes less dense, creating a more open habit. To regain some of the bushiness, trim occasionally with a pair of shears during summer. Don't prune after this time, as the next season's flower buds could be chopped off by mistake.

Choose the planting position carefully. Too much sun will make the foliage turn a greenish-bronze; too much shade will make the crown rather thin. Light shade will keep the foliage glossy and a good shade of dark green. Any moist soil will do, although rich, fertile clay soil seems to produce the best results. It can tolerate chalk and lime in the soil, but enrich this annually in late autumn or early spring with a good helping of well-rotted manure. A sheltered position away from strong winds is recommended, but I once grew one on the coast and it seemed oblivious to the intermittent salty blasts from the sea.

Remove the lower branches as the tree gains height to reveal more of the trunk. This is pale grey in colour but becomes beautifully gnarled as it ages. Keep well watered, as *Azara microphylla* doesn't appreciate drought, but take care not to allow waterlogging.

Pests and diseases rarely cause any grief. Propagation is easy from ripe cuttings.

ABOVE
Masses of glossy leaves, combined with strongly vanilla-scented flowers, make this shapely tree irresistible.

Catalpa bignonioides
Indian Bean Tree

A very showy deciduous tree, native to eastern areas of the United States, with huge floppy leaves of a bright emerald-green. Mature trees can grow to 7.5–9m (25–30ft) in height with a width to match. A lot of growing space should be given to this splendid tree so that its whole shape can be seen.

The exotic white flowers are produced in large clusters, and these are followed by bunches of long dangly brown beans up to 45cm (18in) long.

Catalpa bignonioides makes an excellent specimen tree in the garden. Plant it in rich, moist soil and never let it dry out, although avoid waterlogging. Established trees can usually fend for themselves in finding water, but in periods of drought, they will appreciate a helping hand. To get the maximum size from the leaves, feed heavily during early spring and summer. Applications of well-rotted manure would be highly beneficial.

It can be grown in full sun or light shade in any soil. Plant somewhere away from strong winds – large leaves can shred and look tatty in a windy site.

Propagation is easy from fresh seed. Pests and diseases are rarely a problem, although, sometimes after a wet summer, the leaves can be affected by mildew. As these drop in the autumn, there is little point trying to treat them; the next season's crop of leaves will grow back fresh and healthy.

For smaller gardens, a more compact version – *Catalpa bignonioides* 'Nana' – is sometimes available. This will reach a height of only around 3.7m (12ft), and the crown stays a tight compact shape. It is fine as a single specimen, taking pride of place in the garden, and it is also a perfect choice for an exotic avenue – the longer, the better. A row of at least seven trees on either side would look most impressive. The planting distance should be about 3m (10ft) apart.

The cultivation for 'Nana' is exactly the same as for the type, although propagation can be done only from cuttings.

ABOVE
Catalpa bignonioides 'Nana' is a shapely version of this tree, and is becoming a very popular choice.

ABOVE
The gorgeous flowers are produced in copious amounts.

Cordyline australis
Cabbage Palm

Although neither a palm nor a cabbage, this
exotic-looking tree is an essential part of any
architectural garden. It is a fast-growing tree
that has become hugely popular over the
last ten years and it is now a familiar sight
everywhere. Despite its hardiness colour code
of red, this tree has survived many winters
growing outdoors in temperate climates
during recent years.

Cordyline australis comes from New Zealand
and is easily raised from seed. Its eventual
height away from its native country won't
be much more than about 4.5m (15ft).

On mature plants, the trunk is a lovely
corky stem, and the head is a dense mass
of long narrow leaves. Flowers appear in
giant lumps on long stalks in early summer.
They are highly fragrant, and the scent can
be enjoyed from a considerable distance.
After flowering, the head of the tree divides
into several clumps, eventually creating
a wide bushy mass.

This tree can tolerate most types of soil
and conditions except waterlogging, which
will lead to rotting and eventual death. Full
sun is best, but light shade is fine too. Any
well-drained soil is suitable, but loam would
be its number one choice. It is excellent for
windy seaside gardens, as it's capable of
coping with severe salty blasts. As a rule,
staking is not required, but if you're planting
a large tree more than 2.5m (8ft) tall in a very
exposed site, some support would be advised.

Small specimens are often seen planted
in summer bedding schemes in pots. They
are totally unsuitable for growing in a
container unless it's for a maximum of two
seasons. Fast-growing, they perform fifty
times better when planted directly into the
ground. Make sure there is a
wide circle of bare earth
around each newly planted
tree, as competition from
grass and weeds seriously
affects its success.

This is a variable tree,
which is best planted either
as a single specimen or in
groves where uniformity
doesn't matter. Some remain

as single-stemmed plants, while others grow as multi-stemmed trees. They are often planted in avenues along seafronts, where a matching pair would be hard to spot. I planted a pair of the same size and from the same batch within 1.8m (6ft) of each other eight years ago. Despite receiving exactly the same care, one is now tall and thin, while the other is fat and bushy.

There are many coloured varieties of *Cordyline australis* on the market. Most of them are quite hideous, though, and their bright colours usually fade to a horrid muddy brown after a couple of years. In addition, they are nowhere near as hardy. One exception is *Cordyline australis* 'Albertii', which, although not very hardy either, does at least retain its fine colours into maturity.

If planted in the ground, *Cordyline australis* is rarely troubled by pests and diseases, but if it's grown in a pot and under glass, red spider mites can be a nuisance.

This tree needs very little maintenance. A good helping of blood, fish and bone applied in the spring will keep it happy, and the removal of all old brown leaves should be done whenever necessary. This process is known in the trade as 'brown-bitting' (see right).

Brown-bitting is done for three reasons. Firstly, it improves the appearance, as brown leaves are not at all pretty to look at. Secondly, it allows the corky bark to be visible and, thirdly, a tree shape is more pleasing than an untidy blobby bush. The whole process can take a couple of hours, and huge piles of discarded foliage can build up.

For whatever reason, some cordylines never need this treatment because they shed their brown leaves all by themselves. Why this happens on some trees but not on the majority is a bit of a mystery.

If a hard winter is forecast, *Corydline australis* can be wrapped up for the coldest months quite easily (see opposite).

1. To begin brown-bitting, work from the lower level first, cutting off any brown leaves with a sharp pair of secateurs, and snipping as close to the trunk as possible. Never pull any leaves off; this can damage the inner layer of the bark.

2. Using a stepladder, trim off the leaves up to where some nice green growth starts. Also trim back any old flower stems.

3. The finished result with the trunks on view.

4. A close-up of the trunks.

1. To wrap a *Cordyline australis* for the winter, you will need a ball of string and some horticultural fleece or anything else porous, such as hessian. If wrapping a tall tree, you will also need a stepladder. Scoop up the head of leaves vertically and tie with string in several places. Tie firmly but not too tightly – just enough to protect the vulnerable new inner growth.

2. Take a large roll of fleece and completely encircle the whole plant several times .

3. Tie up the plant neatly at frequent intervals. Leave the plant wrapped like this only during the very coldest spells, untying it as soon as the weather warms up. If you find the fleece offensive to look at, cover the whole ensemble with some attractive bamboo sheeting.

Cordyline indivisa
Mountain Cabbage Tree

Cordyline indivisa reigns as king of all exotic trees. It really is a magnificent plant that's worth the effort of trying to grow successfully. Huge heads of foliage are produced with massive leaves over 1.5m (5ft) long and up to 20cm (8in) wide. They are matt olive-green with an orange midrib on the front, and pale blue-grey on the reverse side. They can grow either as single-stemmed trees or as multi-stemmed specimens. The trunks have a thick, corky bark.

In their native New Zealand, these trees reach lofty proportions, but in colder climates, they are unlikely to grow more than 3.7m (12ft). They are easy to propagate from seed, but after the seedling stage, cultivation can be difficult, so it helps to have some background information. These are mountain trees that hang off cliffs in a high rainfall area, and any excess water runs straight off them without collecting around the rootball. *Cordyline indivisa* should therefore be grown and nurtured as a giant alpine plant.

Constant water and exceptionally sharp drainage are essential requirements. They hate growing in pots because they are prone to drying out, but transplanting them into larger pots as they get bigger causes root disturbance, which they also hate. However, planting seedlings straight into the ground also presents problems because, until they reach a decent size, they are prone to rotting if rain gathers in the central crown of foliage. These plants are unbelievable fusspots.

Try putting a seedling into a plastic pot with a minimum capacity of three litres. Use loamy soil with at least 50 per cent of chipped bark stirred in. Water frequently from below the foliage, not above. Leave it in this size of pot until it is almost pot-bound and about 60cm (2ft) tall. Carefully cut away the pot using sharp secateurs, taking care not to disturb the roots. Gently plant it into the ground and firm the surrounding soil in lightly. If ten plants are treated this way, you might end up with one fantastic specimen.

Once the tree reaches 1.8m (6ft), the difficulties cease and it should live to a ripe old age. Mature trees produce large clusters of creamy white flowers annually. Pests and diseases are not a problem for older plants.

ABOVE
Growing *Cordyline indivisa* is a real challenge for even expert gardeners.

Cordyline kaspar
Three Kings Cabbage Tree

The delightful common name of this tree alludes to its native land. *Cordyline kaspar* is found only on the Three Kings Islands, which are situated off northern New Zealand. It has wide leaves of a lush dark green that can be 90cm (3ft) long and 8cm (3in) wide. Mature plants form a short, stout trunk and have wide heads of leaves bursting from the top. The maximum height away from their native habitats will be only about 4m (13ft). This tree is an upmarket version of *Cordyline australis* and much prettier. Although easy to propagate from seed, supplies of fresh seed always seem in short supply, so *Cordyline kaspar* can be hard to track down, even at specialist nurseries.

This tree is unusual in another respect too. It is marvellous for growing in a pot – something I don't recommend very often. It can sit in the same pot for years, while remaining in prime condition. I have a 2.5m (8ft) tall specimen, healthy and happy, that has been in the same pot for more than five years. Every year I think that I really ought to plant it in the ground, and somehow never get around to it, but still it carries on looking good.

It's remarkable. It does receive huge helpings of food and is kept well watered, though – plants cannot grow in pots all by themselves.

Plant *Cordyline kaspar* in a sunny spot in fertile loamy soil that drains freely. Waterlogging is about the only thing that will kill it. It will also cope well with windy coastal gardens. Feed annually in the spring with a blood, fish and bone mix. This tree looks good planted in a leafy garden scheme, and blends well with other cordylines, palms, eucalyptus and tree ferns.

If kept confined to a pot, use John Innes no. 3 compost and water regularly, but allow the pot to dry out between watering sessions, rather than keeping it moist. Heap on piles of rotted kitchen waste several times during the growing season to keep the soil fertile.

Trees planted in the ground rarely suffer from any pests or diseases. Plants grown in pots under glass in conservatories or greenhouses are prone to red spider mites. If the pot is of a manageable size, taking it outside for the hottest summer months will help to keep it free of these bugs.

ABOVE
Cordyline kaspar has shapely rich green foliage that always looks good, even if confined to a pot.

Cupressus sempervirens 'Pyramidalis'
Italian Cypress

This straight, formal tree is an essential ingredient for an Italian-style garden. Despite its association with a hot climate, *Cupressus sempervirens* 'Pyramidalis' is a very tough and hardy tree, coping easily with temperatures of -20°C (-4°F).

It is best grown in full sun and poor well-drained soil. Too much food in the soil produces long, lush side growth, which can spoil the compact shape of the tree. If this happens, clip the sides with a pair of shears. The more this tree is clipped, the more lush and splendid it looks, just like a well-kept hedge. To keep an avenue looking uniform, trim off the tops at any height. For a more natural-looking finish, use a slanting cut instead of slicing across horizontally. The wood and crushed foliage give off a lovely pungent aroma, which makes clipping a thoroughly enjoyable task.

Growth averages 30cm (1ft) per year, and a height of around 9m (30ft) can be reached after 30 years. These trees are a narrow form of the plain *Cupressus sempervirens*. They are often sold with other names such as 'Stricta', 'Green Pencil' or 'Totem Pole'. All of them are the narrow form with a width of no more than 45cm (18in), even when mature. Older trees can produce fruit similar to conkers. As the weight of these can also pull the tree out of shape, clip them off.

Newly planted trees will need irrigating for a couple of years but, after this, they develop outstanding drought resistance. Waterlogging around the roots will soon lead to certain death. Although *Cupressus sempervirens* 'Pyramidalis' can deal with fairly breezy weather, it cannot cope with the full brunt of coastal gales, so a sheltered site is preferred. On such a narrow tree, staking looks untidy and should be avoided.

Aphids are the bane of this tree's life. Keep a close watch for them and spray at the first sign. If not dealt with, their bodily excretions will soon attract black sooty mould, which is most unsightly.

The fungal disease coryneum used to affect this tree but, in recent years, coryneum-resistant plants have been developed, so this should be a thing of the past. Check with your supplier before purchasing.

Daphniphyllum macropodum

A small, handsome, evergreen tree, native to Japan, China and Korea. The glaucous-green leaves have a waxy appearance and look similar to some types of rhododendron but, unlike rhododendrons, *Daphniphyllum macropodum* is blissfully content to grow in alkaline soil.

The young stems are a deep crimson colour, adding to the tree's appeal immensely. The new spring growth is also highly attractive, with leaves emerging a bright apple-green.

In cooler climates, *Daphniphyllum macropodum* only just passes as a tree. The ultimate height is unlikely to exceed 3.7m (12ft), even after twenty years. Growth is tediously slow, and patience is needed to cultivate something of a respectable size. The wait is well worth it, though, as the end result is a highly attractive, unusual tree that looks like nothing else.

Plant it as a small specimen tree in a prominent position where it can be viewed easily. It can cope with sunshine but stays a better colour in light shade. Fertile, well-drained soil in a sheltered spot away from any strong winds is preferred. Refrain from planting trees that are very young – wait until some wood develops first. Its slow growth makes this plant a good contender for a pot. It can sit happily in the same pot for years, but must never be allowed to dry out. Check the compost regularly, even in the winter, and keep it almost permanently moist. Make sure the drainage is good, though, because it won't appreciate being waterlogged.

Apart from watering, maintenance is easy. Give a light feed in the spring – a small sprinkling of blood, fish and bone will suffice. Pruning is largely unnecessary, but if a side shoot grows out more quickly than the rest, cut it off to keep the head in a balanced shape. Mature plants have a nicely rounded outline without much help at all from the gardener.

Pests and diseases are rare. Occasionally, there is some die-back of the stems but this is usually the result of overwatering. Propagation is from semi-ripe cuttings taken in early summer.

ABOVE
Daphniphyllum macropodum is a seriously posh addition for a small garden.

BELOW
The bright green of the new foliage is especially attractive.

Drimys winteri
Winter's Bark

A fine, evergreen tree from South America, *Drimys winteri* is a perfect candidate as an unusual specimen tree for a small garden. The leaves are long and narrow, with a waxy texture to them. They are mid-green in colour and aromatic when crushed. The bark also gives off a pleasantly pungent aroma when sliced into. Flowers are produced in early summer. These are clusters of palest cream with a lovely fragrance. The tips of the new growth in the spring are curled up tightly into small balls of bright red that resemble berries.

Away from its native habitat, the maximum height will probably not exceed 6m (20ft), and this size is reached fairly quickly, usually within ten to fifteen years. *Drimys winteri* has a narrow habit and takes up little space in the garden. It is easy to cultivate and ideal for beginners.

It is happy in full sun or light shade, and appreciates rich, fertile, moist soil. Although adequate supplies of water are needed, it will not tolerate permanently boggy conditions. It can be left to grow as a large shrub or trained as a small tree by removing lower branches as it matures. Young trees can be trained as single-stemmed specimens. Older plants that have been left to grow unclipped for many years are best kept as multi-stemmed trees. Sometimes *Drimys winteri* is also seen trained as a wall shrub, which is a good method of growing it in colder areas, where it needs the protection of a warm wall. Keep it out of strong winds; a sheltered site will result in a better-looking plant.

A light feed in the spring is desirable. Give extra rations if the soil is poor or chalky. This tree is little troubled by pests and diseases. The easiest method of propagation is with semi-ripe cuttings taken in early summer.

The common name, Winter's Bark, has nothing to do with the season but with a Captain Winter, who sailed to South America with Francis Drake. While there, Winter was given a tea made of the tree's bark to cure a stomach ailment. When he returned to England in 1578, he took a piece of bark back with him.

ABOVE
Drimys winteri is a fine evergreen tree with handsome shiny foliage.

BELOW
The new buds in the spring resemble bright red berries.

Eriobotrya japonica
Loquat

This jungly evergreen plant will grow almost anywhere. It can develop leaves up to 60cm (2ft) long and 20cm (8in) wide. These are dark green, deeply crinkled and lightly dusted with a powdery coating. An exotic tree, *Eriobotrya japonica* is perfect for giving a tropical look to a leafy garden and looks good planted with palms, bamboos and other bold and leafy extravaganza.

It can be grown as a large shrub or small tree, reaching up to 4m (13ft) tall with the same width. Removing the lower growth and training as a single-stemmed tree while the plant is very young is easy to do. In warmer areas, or after a long hot summer in cooler ones, luscious edible fruits, the size and colour of apricots, can form in early autumn. The new spring growth is especially attractive, imitating shuttlecocks of the palest green. Scented cream flowers form in late summer.

To get the largest leaves, choose a planting position in shade with a rich clay soil. Water copiously throughout spring and summer, even when established. Feed with hefty dollops of well-rotted manure in mid-spring and again in early summer.

Just before the new growth starts in spring, *Eriobotrya japonica* has the alarming habit of shedding up to half of its old foliage in just a few weeks. Because the leaves are so large, this is very noticeable. New leaves quickly take their place, though, and the whole ghastly experience is soon forgotten. Any pruning should be done in early spring. Autumn pruning causes the plant to go into a sulk for the entire winter, and it will recover only very reluctantly the following year.

Aphids are regular visitors and should be sprayed at the first sign. Capsid bugs can also wreak havoc on the new shoots. A more serious threat is a fungal disease related to apple scab. This begins as brown circles on the leaves, usually after a cold, wet spring, but can spread rapidly to the stems unless treated promptly. Pick off all affected leaves and spray every six weeks with a copper-based fungicide. Plants grown from seed are more prone to this problem than those grafted onto a more resistant type of rootstock.

ABOVE
Pale green new growth forms 'shuttlecocks' in early spring.

ABOVE
Masses of fragrant cream flowers are produced in late summer and early autumn.

Eucalyptus aggregata
Black Gum

A fast-growing evergreen tree with masses of greeny-grey leaves that shimmer in the sunshine. This Australian tree is brilliant for hiding the next-door neighbour's latest building project. Its speed of growth and dense canopy of foliage make it perfect for rendering ugly views a distant memory, without blocking the natural light. It can grow at a rate of 1.8m (6ft) per year for the first five years, then growth slows right down to around 60cm (2ft) per year.

The leaves are long and narrow, and when crushed emit the familiar aromatic *Eucalyptus* scent. The bark is constantly changing its appearance as small areas peel away throughout the year, leaving patches of different shades of brown and grey.

Eucalyptus aggregata often grows as a multi-stemmed tree, and its spread can almost equal its height. As this can be up to 12m (40ft), a large garden is needed for it to grow unrestricted. For smaller gardens, remove all side growth and lower branches as the tree matures, so that all growth is above head height. The only space then taken up in the garden is by the diameter of one single trunk.

A sunny position is best, although partial shade is fine too. Poor, sandy soil is ideal to produce slower top growth while the roots are settling in. If the soil is too rich, all the energy goes into the foliage, making a top-heavy tree. This is okay until there's a strong storm, which could easily blow it over. To avoid this, stake all trees heavily with three stakes, so they are supported from all angles. In sheltered areas, large specimens can be used to provide instant screening. In exposed coastal areas, smaller juvenile trees are a more sensible choice.

Unlike most *Eucalyptus* trees, *Eucalyptus aggregata* is happy to receive constant and copious amounts of water. It could virtually grow in a permanent bog. Another of its characteristics, not shared with many other *Eucalyptus*, is its ability to tolerate some lime in the soil, although excessive amounts of lime or chalk should be avoided. Propagation is easy from seed as long as it is fresh. Pests and diseases are not usually a problem.

Eucalyptus glaucescens
Tingiringi Gum

A fast-growing gum tree ideal for giving height to the back of the garden in double-quick time. *Eucalyptus glaucescens* rockets straight up, without giving any thought at all to developing dense side growth. These trees can be planted almost side by side without getting in each other's way, just like a grove of giant bamboo.

Because all the growth is at the top, they do not make good screening trees, but smaller, bushier trees or shrubs can be planted directly in front of them as a second layer to the garden's planting plan. All *Eucalyptus* are bad contenders for growing in containers, but *Eucalyptus glaucescens* is probably the worst of them all – don't even think about it!

The common name is so good that it's almost worth buying a specimen for that alone. Tall and dead straight, the trunk peels and sheds bark in strips throughout the year. The juvenile foliage in gum trees always differs quite considerably from adult foliage, but with *Eucalyptus glaucescens*, the difference is even more of a contrast. The elongated adult leaves bear no resemblance at all to the dainty, circular, blue foliage of the young growth,

which is coveted by flower arrangers. The aromatic oils contained in these leaves are the most pungent of all the hardy *Eucalyptus*; after handling the foliage, the wonderful smell can stay on the hands for quite some time.

Plant in very well-drained soil that does not contain lime or chalk. Stake trees heavily as soon as they are planted. Poor, sandy soil is ideal for the root system and for slowing down the growth slightly. Fertile clay increases the height by a minimum of 1.8m (6ft) per year until it reaches 9m (30ft). After this time, growth is slower until 12m (40ft) is attained. Full sun is essential. Usually the only way *Eucalyptus glaucescens* can be killed is if the soil becomes excessively waterlogged.

As a rule, pests and diseases are not a problem. Propagation is easy from fresh seed.

Eucalyptus nitens
Shining Gum or **Silver Top**

Eucalyptus nitens has the distinction of producing the largest, longest foliage of any hardy gum tree. Masses of tropical-looking leaves hang down to give an exotic addition to any garden. It looks as if it just cannot be hardy enough to grow in cooler climates away from its Australian habitat, but appearances are deceptive: this tree can tolerate some surprisingly low temperatures.

The leaves are blue-grey with a leathery texture. The trunks are tall and straight, and strips peel off in layers throughout the year, revealing patches and stripes of greenish-brown, fawn and pale yellow. The new shoots and young branches have a square, angular look to them, adding to this tree's appeal.

Eucalyptus nitens makes an excellent screening tree, blotting out ugly views speedily. However, it is such a beautiful plant that it also makes a good choice as a single specimen tree for a prominent place in the garden. Young trees can put on as much 1.8m (6ft) of new growth per year. The overall height in an average temperate climate could be 12m (40ft) within ten years.

Plant in full sun, avoiding frost pockets, and in a sheltered position away from strong winds, which would spoil the leaves. Any soil is suitable, except one containing lime or chalk. Stake heavily, immediately after planting. Water in well and keep irrigated for the first couple of years until established. After this period, it develops exceptionally good drought tolerance.

This is a very easy tree to cultivate, and pests and diseases are rarely a problem. Excessive waterlogging would eventually lead to its death, as would being planted where cold winter winds can race through it. Planting this tree in a container would be a really bad idea – don't even think about it for a nano-second. The only place *Eucalyptus nitens* belongs is in the ground.

Propagation is easy from fresh seed. All *Eucalyptus* are grown from seed, which leads to the variation seen between each plant. They are impossible to grow from cuttings – it is a process that would challenge even the most experienced gardener.

Eucalyptus pauciflora 'Debeuzevillei'
Jounama Snow Gum

A manageable-sized *Eucalyptus*, with a stunning bark, ideal as a specimen tree for a small garden. The trunk and branches peel off in layers throughout the year, revealing attractive coloured patches of white, cream, palest grey and delicate tints of beige and fawn. The evergreen foliage consists of large steely blue leaves that smell delicious when crushed between the fingers. Of all the beautiful hardy gum trees to choose from, this is easily the best.

It can be grown as a single-stemmed or multi-stemmed tree, depending on its intended space in the garden. If a single-stemmed tree is preferred, simply remove any unwanted lower branches as it matures. The height after ten years will be no more than 5m (16ft) which, for a *Eucalyptus*, is tiny. It has a ridiculously long name, but mentioning just the final word 'Debeuzevillei' is usually enough for specialist nurseries to know which tree is meant.

This tree deserves pride of place in the garden and, because of its striking colour, looks particularly effective if it has a dark background behind it to show it off as much as possible. The older and bigger this tree gets, the more good-looking it becomes.

Full sun is essential, and sandy, well-drained, neutral to acid soil is best. Don't plant into soil that contains lime or chalk. If the site has rich, fertile soil, stake the tree heavily as soon as it has been planted. Rich soil promotes rapid top growth before the root system has developed enough to support it. Until the roots have had time to burrow down deep enough, it has no chance of staying anchored in storms or gales.

This is an easy tree to cultivate, and the only thing likely to kill it is an excessively waterlogged soil. Pests and diseases are not usually a problem. Propagation is easy from fresh seed. Its natural distribution is in only a small area of south-eastern New South Wales.

Ficus carica
Common Fig

Although usually grown just for its lovely juicy fruit, this tree deserves to be grown as a foliage plant in its own right. Strongly architectural, it fits into all types of exotic planting schemes. The bark is pale silvery grey, and the leaves are huge, jungly and deeply lobed. It is deciduous, but this fact can be forgiven not only because of the size and shape of the foliage, but also because of its bright yellow autumn colouring.

Figs are often seen forced to grow spread-eagled against a sunny wall or shoved into a tiny pot – this is to increase fruit production. But forget about the fruit and concentrate on the well-being of the plant as a proper tree. Plant it as a free-standing, single-stemmed specimen in a shady, moist part of the garden. The more shade and moisture it receives, the larger the leaves become. Choose a sheltered spot, as the large leaves can be torn and shredded by strong winds.

It is slow-growing, taking many years to develop into a fat, stocky tree. It is also very greedy, thriving on regular doses of well-rotted manure throughout the growing season. The ultimate height will be no more than around 5m (16ft), but if a more compact tree is required, pruning is easy. Old, unwanted branches can be cut back really hard to less than 30cm (1ft) of the main framework. This is usually done in the spring, just before the new season's shoots appear. In mild gardens, however, it can be done quite safely in the autumn just after the leaves have dropped.

Pruning also increases the plant's vigour and helps the crown to keep a balanced shape. Cut out any twisted or overlapping branches to stop the crown from looking overcrowded.

Water regularly, even when established, during spring and summer. Make sure the soil is well drained – the roots do not like waterlogged conditions. A healthy, well-fed and well-watered tree is unlikely to be troubled by diseases. Capsid bugs can sometimes be a nuisance, disfiguring the large leaves with their familiar trademark of tiny holes. Propagation is easy from hardwood cuttings taken in the autumn.

Genista aetnensis
Mount Etna Broom

A small evergreen tree with a beautiful cascading habit. The foliage is delicate and sparse, and the branches are light and feathery. The whole tree appears as though it's made up of green wispy grass. Much tougher than it looks, it is excellent for exposed windy gardens on the coast or on hilltops, coping well with strong gales and sea breezes. The trunks are usually gnarled and twisted, giving it character. In mid-summer, the whole canopy is covered with masses of small, bright yellow flowers, which are highly fragrant on a still, sunny day.

Fairly fast-growing, it puts all its energy initially into its height rather than its bulk. This makes young specimens top-heavy, so staking is essential when planting. To assist with producing some strength and girth to the tree, trim the head with shears every year until the trunk is chunky enough to support some weight. Remove any lower branches as the tree develops, keeping it as a single-stemmed tree rather than as a large shrub.

Genista aetnensis can look a little uninspiring until it is at least five years old, so buying a tree that is old enough to look interesting is advised. Once it matures, it becomes better and better with each year.

Choose a spot in the garden that has full sun. Poor soil that is sharply drained works best. Once established, watering is not required. Another good reason for buying this tree is its superb drought resistance. Boggy soil is just about the only thing that will kill it. Maintenance is almost non-existent, and even annual feeding can be dispensed with.

Genista aetnensis can look fine on its own as a single specimen, but it's even more splendid planted in small groves. It is perfect in any Mediterranean planting scheme, blending in well with other small ornamental trees or with lower companion plants such as dwarf palms, ground-covering succulents or spiky *Agave*.

Older branches may become too twisted and heavy to hold their own weight. As it would be a pity to cut them off, give them a helping hand with a forked wooden prop for support. Pests and diseases are not often a problem. Propagation is easy from fresh seed. Cuttings can be taken too, but these tend to produce inferior trees that can be short-lived.

Ilex crenata
Japanese Holly

Japanese sculptured trees such as *Ilex crenata* are currently enjoying immense popularity. These amazing evergreen trees can take well over fifty years to create. And, as with all things fashionable, they have been given a wealth of different names, including pom-poms, cloud-pruned trees, *niwaki*, even big bonsai. All of the larger sculptured trees are seriously expensive due to the time and work that has gone into them. Some of the smaller ones have more manageable price tags, but they are always a special purchase that needs a great deal of thought beforehand.

Ilex crenata is one of the best choices of plant for sculpting. It is fully hardy, and the small leaves are easy to keep clipped into shape. As it is slow-growing, clipping is normally necessary only a couple of times a year. Usually, any rogue leaves spoiling the alignment are snipped off at once, rather than waiting for when a full coiffure is needed. Not a single leaf or new stem should be allowed to encroach outside of its rigidly strict silhouette. Buy a pair of super-sharp Japanese clippers made especially for this purpose.

These plants look fantastic in a Japanese-style garden and also in an English-style topiary garden. They can sit in pride of place on the terrace or, for those gardeners feeling a really extravagant moment approaching, one either side of a large front door.

These trees are usually left in the pots they were bought in. The welfare of the plant would be hugely improved, however, if they were planted directly into the ground. They are happy in sun or light shade in a sheltered position away from strong winds or salty breezes. Keep the soil moist, and feed annually with a couple of handfuls of blood, fish and bone. If it is to spend its life growing in a pot, check the watering regularly. Even after it has rained, the soil can remain dry because the rounded tops of these trees act as large umbrellas, keeping the rain away from the roots.

Pests and diseases are rare, but red spider mites can be a problem in hot dry summers if the tree has not been watered enough. Propagation is easy from cuttings, but to grow a finished sculptured shape from a cutting would take decades.

Ilex perado platyphylla
Canary Island Holly

A sensible little evergreen tree, despite its
rather daft name. Although it grows fast from
the seedling stage, it takes years to reach
a decent size, which makes it perfect for even
the tiniest gardens. After ten years, it will
probably still be no more than 3.7m (12ft) tall.
Its tough leathery leaves are mid-green in
colour. Each leaf has very small barbs around
the perimeter, reminding us that it is a holly,
even if it doesn't immediately look like one.

The bark and stems on older plants can
take on an ebony appearance, making it look
black and glossy. The berries produced in the
autumn are as red and shiny as you would
expect from a holly.

Native to the Canary Islands and the Azores,
this tree copes well with sea breezes, making
a lovely decorative plant for small coastal
gardens. Because of its slowness of growth,
together with its tolerance of a windy position,
this tree has the rare qualities of not only
being able to spend much of its early life in
a container, but also being able to cope with
a high-storey roof terrace. Even roof terraces
tucked away in inner cities seem to have wind

funnelling around them as it whooshes through
narrow streets and bounces off large buildings.

Ilex perado platyphylla used to be thought of
as a rather tender plant, but experience has
shown that it is capable of coping with very low
temperatures for prolonged periods. Although
happy growing in full sun, light shade gives it
a stronger colour. It isn't fussy about
soil, but well-drained loam is
recommended. Water in well
to start with until established.

If planting in a container,
use John Innes no. 3 compost.
Keep the soil constantly
moist. *Ilex perado platyphylla*
doesn't like to dry out or to have
its roots standing in pools of water.
When it has outgrown its pot, transplant
it carefully in late spring or early summer, just
as it is about to commence the new season's
growth. It hates root disturbance, so has
a better chance of recovery if moved then.

Pests and diseases are not usually a problem.
Propagation can be from seed or semi-ripe
cuttings taken in summer.

Laurus nobilis angustifolia
Narrow-leaved Bay

Although the Common Bay Tree (*Laurus nobilis*) is very well known, *Laurus nobilis angustifolia* remains largely unheard of. This is a pity because it is prettier, more graceful, hardier and more salt-tolerant. The foliage is narrower, longer and slightly serrated, with the familiar pungent aroma, and can be used in cooking in the same way as ordinary bay leaves. Cream flowers form in clusters in summer, sometimes followed by large black berries.

If left to grow naturally, it forms a small bushy tree that will grow to a maximum of only about 4m (13ft). It forms a layered conical shape with the lower width spreading to about 2m (6½ft). The whole tree tapers off nicely at the top. It can also be grown in other ways just like ordinary evergreen bay trees: clipped and trained into a hedge or shaped into the more traditional style of lollipop to add height to a herb garden.

Laurus nobilis angustifolia can be planted in full sun or light shade. It is unfussy about soil, but fertile and well-drained would be its preference. Water regularly during spring and summer for a couple of years until established.

It will then be able to look after itself, developing remarkable drought tolerance. If these trees are kept in pots, drought tolerance never develops, as the root system cannot spread out to find its own water supply, so watering needs to be done regularly for its entire life.

Feed annually in spring and again in mid-summer using something like a mix of blood, fish and bone. Clipping can be done throughout the year, to keep the hedge or lollipop in shape. There's no need for secateurs – this plant is quite happy to be set upon with a pair of shears.

Scale insects can be a problem. Inspect the leaves frequently and if you spot any, scrape them off immediately. These creatures suck into the sap causing the foliage to distort. If left to build up in large numbers, they are almost impossible to deal with and the plant will be gradually covered in black sooty mould as a result of their sticky secretions. Propagation is easy from semi-ripe cuttings taken in summer.

ABOVE
The leaves of *Laurus nobilis angustifolia* are much prettier than those of the more familiar bay tree.

ABOVE
Clusters of pretty cream flowers appear during the summer.

Ligustrum lucidum
Chinese Cloud Tree or
Chinese Glossy Privet

A fantastic evergreen tree with a shapely rounded head. The leaves are large and glossy, the trunks straight and sturdy. It's the perfect tree for forming avenues, and excellent for inner city streets because of its tolerance of pollution. It makes a handsome choice for a single specimen tree in the garden. It is also useful for screening unwanted views: its broad head blots out the offending vista speedily, while the space taken up by its trunk is minimal. Fast-growing, it quickly reaches 3.7m (12ft), then slows down considerably until it reaches its maximum height of about 7.5m (25ft).

In late summer, trees are covered in frothy masses of cream flowers, which give off a pleasant scent. These are followed by large clusters of blue-black fruits, which hang on the tree for months. Buy this tree from a reputable nursery, as it is often confused with *Ligustrum japonicum* and labelled incorrectly.

Plant in sun or shade. This is one of the few trees that prefers chalk. *Ligustrum lucidum* can cope with low temperatures and also a windy, exposed position in a mild area. However, it cannot cope with strong winds and very cold

weather at the same time: it can go into a sulk and shed copious amounts of foliage. However, recovery is quick and, by the end of the following spring, lush verdancy is once more in evidence. Keep the soil moist for at least two seasons after planting. It is almost impossible to overwater this tree. Stake heavily to support the trunk and keep it straight. After a couple of years, it will have produced enough girth to hold it steady.

If planting as a single specimen, leave plenty of room around the tree so that you can admire its strong shape. For screening purposes, plant one tree every 2m (6½ft). For longer avenues, one tree per 3m (10ft) is usually sufficient.

Clipping is not usually needed as it forms its rounded shape naturally. Feed once a year with a generous amount of blood, fish and bone around the base of the trunk in late spring. Pests and diseases are rarely a problem. Propagation is easy from ripe seed.

■ Lomatia ferruginea

For anyone who likes a challenge, try growing this lovely evergreen tree. It's a real beast of a plant at all stages, from propagation to maturity, but a successful gardener will be rewarded with one of the rarest and most beautiful trees around. Many special plants have been introduced to our gardens from Chile but *Lomatia ferruginea* is one of the finest.

The leaves are wonderfully crafted into giant ferny fronds, each one with an underside covered in russet-brown 'velvet'. In the high rainfall areas of Chile, this tree grows to around 9m (30ft), but in an average temperate climate, don't expect it to reach much more than 4.5m (15ft) even after many years. Flowers are sometimes produced, followed by odd-shaped seed pods, but the main reason for owning one of these trees is the foliage.

The problem, though, is how to grow it well. Good light is required, but not full sun or too much shade. It likes to be constantly moist, but just enough to strike a balance. Too much water can kill it virtually overnight; too little and it will shrivel and turn brown. It hates being in a pot and detests root disturbance

when it's taken out. If this isn't bad enough, its soil requirements are the most challenging of all. It likes poor, acid, well-drained soil that never receives any food containing phosphates. If you look on a packet of any brand of fertilizer at the garden centre, you will see that this ingredient appears on nearly all of them. *Lomatia ferruginea* belongs to the *Proteaceae* family of plants, which means that any phosphate will kill it stone dead. Some food is appreciated, though; small amounts of nitrogen are highly beneficial. Occasionally phosphate-free plant food is sold in specialist horticultural premises, so it is always worth searching around.

Once this tree reaches 1.5m (5ft), the worst problems are over, and there is no reason why it shouldn't reach maturity, providing it continues to receive the same care and attention it has been used to.

Pests and diseases are not usually a problem. Propagation is best left to the experts.

Lyonothamnus floribundus asplenifolius
Santa Cruz Ironwood Tree

An irresistibly beautiful evergreen tree that is almost perfect, despite its ludicrous name. The lush ferny foliage ranges in colour from the emerald-green of the young growth through to the deep dark green of the adult leaves. The foliage has a soft delicate appearance but it is much tougher than it looks. During hot sunny days, or very cold frosty ones, the leaves exude a pleasant marshmallow fragrance, which can be detected from some distance away. The trunks of mature trees have a gnarled and craggy look, and the bark peels off in cinnamon-red strips throughout the year. Long clusters of white flowers sometimes appear on mature trees after a long hot summer but, although produced in copious amounts, they are not terribly exciting to look at.

This tree needs a sunny spot in a sheltered garden – strong winds can leave it looking tatty and the leaves can become scorched. Very, very well-drained soil is essential. Avoid soil containing large amounts of chalk.

For the first few years, it puts all of its energy into its height, instead of its bulk, and can become top-heavy. It needs the support of a strong stake when planted. Regular pruning of the head also increases its sturdiness. Use shears to clip the crown – the more it's clipped, the bushier the plant becomes.

Water well for its first season, but drought resistance builds up quickly, so irrigation is not usually necessary once established. A light feed can be given in early spring – use a half dose of blood, fish and bone sprinkled around the trunk.

Although found in the areas around California, this tree looks quite at home in Mediterranean-style gardens. It also makes a fantastic specimen tree for small gardens. Away from its native habitats, it is unlikely to grow taller than 4.5m (15ft).

This is a fairly easy tree to cultivate as long as waterlogged soil is avoided. Aphids can be a problem on the new shoots in summer. Propagation isn't too difficult if fresh seed can be obtained.

ABOVE
The new growth of *Lyonothamnus floribundus asplenifolius* is bright emerald-green.

BELOW
Mature trees have cinnamon-red peeling bark.

Magnolia delavayi

Enormous leaves are the main attraction of this wonderful Chinese tree. They are among the largest of any hardy evergreen tree, with each leaf 30cm (1ft) long and 20cm (8in) wide. Caterpillar-green on top and pale glaucous-green underneath, they have a solid texture and are heavily veined. This tree is fairly fast to gain height, but can take years to put on bulk. It is well worth the wait, though, to experience the result in maturity. It is a wide-spreading tree and, after about forty years or so, the height and spread could both be around 7.5m (25ft).

Huge flowers appear in late summer. Few and far between, they last for only a couple of days but are spectacular. They are a deep rich cream, lightly fragrant and easily 20cm (8in) across.

The really remarkable thing about *Magnolia delavayi*, though, is its ability to withstand chalk. Most *Magnolia* refuse to grow anywhere near it. This one not only tolerates a chalky soil, but positively thrives in it.

In a mild garden, it can be grown as a large shrub or as a free-standing specimen tree. In colder districts, grow it near a wall for added protection against cold winds. The heat reflected from a sunny wall will also increase its vigour. These trees prefer full sun, but can cope with light shade. They are happy in coastal areas, as long as they are not bearing the full brunt of any salty gales. Stake them well when planting and keep them watered, but not soggy, for their first couple of seasons. Any well-drained soil will suit, but they are particularly fond of a bit of added loam.

Magnolia delavayi is not seen in many nurseries probably because propagation is difficult. Layering is the most common method used, which in itself is not too tricky. It is the lack of material that is the problem.

Very young trees can take a while to get going, which makes the purchase of a semi-mature plant a safer option. Once established, it is easy to maintain and usually refreshingly free from pests and diseases. Feed annually with a light dressing of blood, fish and bone in late spring.

ABOVE
This tree is very rare but well worth searching for at specialist nurseries.

BELOW
Rich cream-coloured flowers appear in late summer.

LEFT
A mature specimen of *Magnolia grandiflora* is a wonderful sight.

Magnolia grandiflora
Bull Bay

Traditionally grown as a large wall shrub but far superior as a free-standing tree, *Magnolia grandiflora* looks far too exotic to be hardy. This explains why early introductions were planted against sunny walls – nobody would believe it could survive away from a hot climate.

This splendid evergreen tree has large, waxy leaves that are dark green and glossy on top and dusted reddish-brown underneath. The flowers are everything that could be hoped for from a magnolia: huge waxy cups of palest ivory that smell delicious. The strong spicy aroma can waft around the whole garden. Individual flowers don't last more than a couple of days, but mature trees produce lots of them over a period of several weeks at the end of summer. Each bloom can be up to 30cm (1ft) across.

This tree will grow to 6m (20ft) in twenty-five years, so is suitable for a small garden. It can form a rounded head 4.5m (15ft) across, which could be clipped to reduce its size. It prefers full sun, but light shade is fine. Rich, fertile, well-drained soil produces the best results, but this adaptable tree can cope with most conditions, even chalk as long as it is not present to excess.

If the soil is very alkaline, the leaves will take on a yellowish tinge, which can be helped by administering sequestered iron.

Adequate moisture is required, especially in the early years after planting. Once established, it develops an ability to tolerate almost drought-like conditions. Feed well with generous doses of blood, fish and bone in late spring. Just before new growth starts and sometimes during the flowering season too, large amounts of leaves turn yellow or brown, before dropping off and piling up in alarming heaps on the ground. Providing this process lasts for only a short time, there is nothing to worry about – new leaves will soon appear.

Various named forms, such as 'Exmouth', 'Goliath' and 'Samuel Somer', are sometimes offered for sale. Delightful as they are for their variations of leaf or flower size, the straight form of *Magnolia grandiflora* is the most widely available, the fastest-growing and the easiest to cultivate.

ABOVE
Huge fragrant blooms appear at the end of the summer.

Magnolia macrophylla
Big Leaf Magnolia

Magnolia macrophylla has the biggest leaves of any hardy deciduous tree, reaching 90cm (3ft) long and 30cm (1ft) wide on mature trees. The incredible foliage conjures up images of the tropics, and exotic jungle animals are half expected to hurtle through them at any minute. The leaves are beautifully textured, soft to the touch, fresh matt green on the upper surface and silvery white underneath.

After a very slow start, the overall height could reach 9m (30ft) in 30 years. Although grown chiefly for its foliage, the flowers are also spectacular: they are white with a purple base, wonderfully fragrant and more than 30cm (1ft) across.

This beautiful tree is extremely fussy as a youngster, but worth all the grief because of what can be achieved in its adulthood. Buying the most mature tree available will help enormously as, once *Magnolia macrophylla* has become woody, half the battle is over, as it is fully hardy. Small, immature plants are very susceptible to cold weather. Small trees are also intolerant of damp winters, which makes them vulnerable to fungal diseases.

Finding the right planting position can be difficult. Rich, fertile, moist but well-drained soil is preferred, and a low pH is essential. Chalk or lime won't be tolerated at all. Getting the correct amount of light can be tricky. Sunny conditions ripen the wood more quickly but produce smaller leaves. Too much shade makes for a very unhappy plant. Light woodland shade with an overhead canopy of very large, broad-leaved, evergreen trees would be perfect. Shelter from wind is another essential requirement, otherwise the large foliage quickly becomes shredded and tatty. It is best for young trees to be planted out in late spring, so that all new growth will be out of danger from late frosts.

Pests and diseases are not generally a problem for older trees, but capsid bugs are occasional visitors. Propagation is a nightmare for this tree. Fresh seed is difficult to acquire, cuttings are usually unsuccessful, and grafting is a slow and lengthy process, all of which explains its rarity in cultivation. *Magnolia macrophylla* could perhaps be considered for micropropagation in the future.

ABOVE
Massive leaves up to 90cm (3ft) long are produced on mature trees.

Maytenus boaria
Maiten Tree

A fast-growing tree from Chile, similar to a willow but evergreen. The foliage is a mass of bright green leaves that shimmer in the sunlight. The overall height could easily be 7.5m (25ft) within ten years. Tiny, insignificant flowers are produced in late spring.

The fast growth of this tree makes it ideal for screening. The crown is bushy enough to obscure any unwanted views, without being oppressive and blocking the light. It's also a good choice as a specimen tree for a large garden. For really spacious gardens, these trees look fantastic planted in large groves.

If your garden is small but you feel that life can't be lived without a *Maytenus boaria*, it is possible to train them from a young age into informal lollipop shapes, almost like topiary. The trunks can be stopped at 1.5m (5ft) and the heads kept rounded into diameters of 90cm (3ft) – smaller dimensions would be difficult to keep in shape. Once the desired size has been attained, clip frequently with shears. Give them a severe cut in spring and trim little and often throughout the growing season to keep them bushy. This could involve at least six sessions per year. Don't try to keep these in pots – unlike most topiary, which is relatively happy in containers, this tree will not tolerate being confined in this way.

Maytenus boaria is happiest in full sun, but a bit of shade won't cause any harm. Any type of soil will do, even chalk, but it must be very well drained. Boggy conditions around the roots will not be tolerated. It is excellent for exposed hilltops or coastal gardens where the breeze can swish through it. Even the occasional salty gale can be shrugged off.

An easy tree to maintain, it requires just a light feed once a year with a small helping of blood, fish and bone in late spring. Unwanted top growth can easily be trimmed with a pair of shears at any time of year. Pests and diseases aren't usually a problem. The easiest method of propagation is from root cuttings.

Myrtus luma
Orange-bark Myrtle

SYN. *Luma apiculata*
Myrtus apiculata

The soft suede-like orange bark makes this tree irresistible to the touch. Its colour varies in intensity throughout the year. In summer, the bark splits and peels to reveal patches of creamy white, which gradually darken and change back to orange. Young plants do not have the characteristic orange bark – this will start to appear after five years. As the colour of the bark is so striking, removing lower branches as the tree grows is a good idea, to allow more of the sumptuous orange to be on view.

This tree has many different names attached to it. I've given the shortest and easiest here, but there are at least two more synonyms.

Myrtus luma can reach heady heights in its native countries of Chile and Argentina. In colder and drier climates, expect little more than 4.5m (15ft). Extra height can be gained in high rainfall areas. It is almost impossible to overwater this tree, and the more rain it receives, the better the results. In its native habitats, it is frequently seen growing in bogs.

The foliage is a dense mass of tiny evergreen leaves that are aromatic when crushed. Fragrant white flowers appear in late summer. They can last for several months, and are followed by large fat fruits. These are black, juicy and edible and can be made into jam – I'm told it produces a decent result.

Myrtus luma is extremely intolerant of drought, and copious amounts of water are essential for it to look its best. A dense, compact head of foliage is produced if grown in full sun. In the shade, it will have a much more open habit. Too much food can easily scorch the leaves, so keep this to a minimum. Feed just enough to keep the foliage a good dark green, which is usually only necessary on very chalky soil. Pests and diseases are rare. Propagation is easy from seed or cuttings.

Apart from its use as a beautiful specimen tree, it can be left to grow as a bush or even as a rather smart hedge. Its small leaves respond well to frequent clipping, and it is easy to keep in shape. Use a sharp pair of shears for trimming whenever necessary. The best time to do this is between late spring and early autumn. If the flowers are more important than a neat shape, wait until just after flowering.

Their suitability for pruning, together with their fast-growing habit, makes these trees excellent candidates for formal topiary. Try turning them into Japanese pom-poms. A reasonable result can be achieved in about a quarter of the time it takes with more traditionally used plants. You will need a pair of secateurs or Japanese pruning scissors (*hasami*) plus a ball of hessian string and some slender bamboo canes. Also essential is the artistic vision to look at the tree, imagine what can be created and see the finished result in your mind, before you even start. See below for instructions.

In creating the pom-pom topiary, the foliage is drastically reduced, meaning that the tree needs much less water. However, never let it dry out completely – further leaf loss at this stage would be disastrous! Throughout the following growing season, regularly trim each pom-pom. The more they are clipped, the faster and denser they grow. Check the canes and string occasionally to see if the branches have been 'set' into shape, although this is unlikely to take place within two years.

As the tree ages, the trunk should gain girth and more orange colouring. Any unwanted growth sprouting from the trunk or from the roots should be removed at once. What the poor thing is trying to do is to turn back into a bush.

LEFT
This photograph shows a 'finished' tree about eight years after it was started. These pom-pom trees are never really considered finished, though, as they improve with every passing year.

1. Select a tree that is about 1.8m (6ft) in height and fairly bushy.
2. Ruthlessly thin out any unwanted branches, keeping only the basic skeleton of trunk, crown and seven or eight well-spaced branches with tufts of foliage left at the ends – these will become the individual pom-poms. Shape the crown of the tree into a well-rounded head.

3. Spread out the remaining branches to make an evenly balanced shape, tying them down with hessian string attached to the pot. If any branches need lifting instead, attach them along the length of bamboo canes with hessian string.
4. Chop off any unwanted lengths of bamboo for a neat appearance. Cut back hard each individual pom-pom.

Nerium oleander
Oleander

A familiar sight in all parts of the Mediterranean, where it is commonly used as a street tree. It can reach 4.5m (15ft) and is perfect for planting in avenues in sunny locations. As it is not reliably hardy, in colder climates it will need to be kept in a conservatory in winter to protect it from damaging frosts. It can be trained as a half-standard tree and kept to a height of 1.8m (6ft), or clipped into a large shrub to make it more manageable for overwintering under glass.

Nerium oleander is an evergreen tree, and older specimens develop a lovely gnarled trunk. But it is for the flowers that they are usually grown. These are produced in large quantities, and the flowering season seems to last for months. The beautiful blooms come in pure white and all shades of pink through to deepest rose-red. In recent years, cultivars of pale lemon and apricot have been produced. Each flower is usually around 5cm (2in) across. Most have no fragrance but, occasionally, some varieties carry an appealing almond scent.

Grow *Nerium oleander* in the largest pot possible. Although plants have to be overwintered indoors, they are much happier and healthier spending the summer out of doors on a terrace. Pots, therefore, have to be moved around, and the size and weight of the container has to be balanced with what can physically be transported.

Use a soil-based compost such as John Innes no. 3, with some extra grit stirred in for good drainage. Stand the plants in full sun to maximize flower production. Keep very well watered during the growing season. If planted in the ground, they can fend for themselves and become almost drought-tolerant but, in pots, they are totally reliant on the gardener for their water supply.

Feed well in early spring and mid-summer with a general purpose fertilizer. Clip savagely after flowering to encourage new bushy growth the following year. Take care when handling this plant as all parts of it are poisonous.

A well-cared for plant can remain trouble-free, but those forced to spend all their lives in pots under glass during the full heat of the summer can suffer from mealy bugs, red spider mites, scale insects and just about everything else horrid. Propagation is easy from cuttings.

ABOVE
The showy flowers of *Nerium oleander* bring a touch of the Mediterranean to conservatories and greenhouses.

Nothofagus dombeyi
Dombey's Southern Beech

This is a splendid evergreen tree for large gardens. It is tall and wide-spreading with the overall shape presented in graceful layers right down to ground level. The foliage consists of a mass of tiny leaves that are dark green and shiny. Native to Argentina and Chile, mature trees in Chile can have a girth of 9m (30ft) and are widely used for timber. *Nothofagus* trees are closely related to the common beech found in the northern hemisphere.

Away from its natural habitat, a mature tree is unlikely to exceed 9m (30ft) in height even after thirty years. Its spread after this time could be 6m (20ft). Although evergreen, if really cold winters are experienced, it becomes deciduous, recovering fully the following spring.

Because of its beautiful shape, it deserves to be planted with thought for its future. Make sure there is plenty of space around it so that it can be viewed with appreciation in years to come. A large grove of them in a public park would be a fine sight.

Propagation can be from seed, but cuttings are usually much more successful. Growing these plants in containers is something of a challenge, but it is an easy tree to cultivate once it is of a decent size and planted directly into the ground.

Position it in full sun or light shade in good quality loamy soil. Although moist soil is preferred, boggy ground is not at all suitable. Chalky soil should also be avoided, not because it hates lime, but because chalk tends to dry out quickly and is much less fertile. Feed with just a light dressing of nitrogen-based food in late spring. A mix of blood, fish and bone is fine, but use half measures. Much more success will be gained from planting in rich soil to start with, rather than relying on artificial means.

Choose a planting position that is sheltered from cold northerly winds. This will not only help to ensure the foliage does not drop in the winter, but will also keep the leaves a fresh bright green.

Pruning should be unnecessary, and pests and diseases are not usually a problem.

ABOVE
The branches and foliage of *Nothofagus dombeyi* hang down in elegant layers.

Olea europea
Olive Tree

Although usually associated with warm Mediterranean climates, this evergreen tree is tougher than it seems and can adapt to much cooler surroundings. It copes well with inner city gardens and sheltered coastal gardens. Suburban gardens inland can also be considered if the tree is given the protection of a warm wall. The older the tree, the hardier it becomes.

The trunks are rarely straight, becoming gnarled and twisted with age. *Olea europea* has an open habit, and the foliage is just dense enough to give some privacy, without blocking the light. The leaves are grey-green and shimmer in the breeze, while the flowers are small insignificant clusters of pale yellow, followed by large fruits, which are unlikely to ripen except after a really hot summer.

Olea europea has a spreading habit; after twenty years it could be 3.7m (12ft) high and almost the same wide. Its size is easy to control by trimming regularly with a pair of shears – this can be done any time during the spring and summer. Give adequate moisture for the first couple of years only. Once established, it is one of the most drought-resistant trees around.

Plant in full sun and feed lightly with blood, fish and bone in the spring. Any type of soil will do. Very little maintenance is required. This is a really easy tree to cultivate – the only ways to kill it are by watering far too much or far too little.

Olea europea makes an excellent conservatory plant. Plant it in the largest container possible and pot into loamy compost, such as John Innes no. 3, with some grit stirred in for extra drainage. Plants grown in containers must never be allowed to dry out and need watering several times a week during spring and summer. They can cope better than most plants with the hot, dry atmosphere found in many conservatories. If kept clipped into shape to control its size, it can live in the same pot for years.

Pests and diseases are rarely a problem if grown outdoors. Under glass, make occasional inspections for scale insects. Propagation is easy from cuttings.

Osmanthus yunnanensis

Osmanthus yunnanensis is a little-known evergreen tree from China. It forms a distinctive shape and can be spotted immediately from some distance away. The crown is a beautifully formed dome, and it looks as if many years of clipping have been lavished upon it to create its curved top. However, no help has been given by the gardener – it has managed all by itself.

The large leaves are matt olive-green and attractively crinkled around the edges. Small, creamy white, fragrant flowers are usually produced in late winter. This was a popular tree when first introduced into cultivation, but fell out of favour because the flowers weren't showy enough. According *to Hillier's Manual of Trees and Shrubs* 'its magnificent leaves conjure up thoughts of spectacular flowers which fail to materialise'. Fortunately, these days, more gardeners are beginning to realize that the shape and presence of a tree are more important than its blooms.

Mature trees can have a height and spread of 6m (20ft). Young trees grow fairly fast but, unfortunately, all the early energy is put into its height. Its spread takes much longer to achieve, and the curved, finished effect of the crown takes several decades. This is not a tree for an impatient gardener.

Choosing a planting position needs careful consideration. Although the span of a mature tree is not huge, it needs plenty of space around it so that its shape can be appreciated fully. A sunny spot is preferred, but light shade is acceptable. Although not a lime-hating tree, better results would be gained from a rich, loamy soil, rather than a thin chalky one. Drainage needs to be good, but the soil should contain enough organic matter to retain moisture, so that the roots do not dry out. Site away from strong winds.

Feed annually in spring, preferably with a small heap of well-rotted manure, and irrigate regularly throughout the growing season for the first couple of years after planting. Once the tree has settled in and become established, watering becomes necessary only in a really hot, dry summer. Pests and diseases are not a particular problem. Propagation can be from cuttings taken when fully ripe at the end of summer.

ABOVE
Osmanthus yunnanensis is one of the rarest evergreen trees that can be grown in cooler climates.

Paulownia tomentosa
Foxglove Tree

A fabulous Chinese tree with huge leaves and an essential plant for a jungly garden. *Paulownia tomentosa* can have two very different looks, depending on how it is grown. If left to grow naturally, it will develop into a small tree reaching no more than around 7.5m (25ft) in an average temperate garden. The bark is attractively spotted and speckled. Branches form a neat open canopy, and flowers are produced in late spring, before the leaves appear. They are fragrant, pinkish-purple and shaped like a foxglove (*Digitalis*) flower. The leaves start to unfurl in late spring. These are large and soft, heart-shaped and very exotic. Although this tree is totally hardy, flowers are reliable only in warmer areas.

The alternative method of growing this tree is much more dramatic and jolly good fun. Chop it back hard to within a few inches of old wood each year in early spring. Although this stops the tree maturing enough to flower, compensation comes in the form of leaves that can reach preposterous proportions of almost 90cm (3ft) across. The whole plant can grow to a height of 3m (10ft) each year before being cut back

down to start the process over again. When the leaves fall in autumn, their size makes them hit the ground with an audible thud.

To get the largest, fastest and jungliest growth, copious amounts of water are vital, and the soil must be rich and fertile, especially if the second method of cultivation is chosen. Feed heavily every four weeks from early spring to mid-summer with piles of well-rotted manure or lashings of blood, fish and bone. Plant in a sheltered spot. The large foliage can become torn and shredded if planted in the wind. Choose a position with good light but not full sun, as the leaves can become a bit bleached. Light shade ensures they remain a rich emerald-green.

This tree is best purchased when dormant, as transporting it in full leaf can be tricky. Choose one with the straightest stem. It is fairly trouble-free, but keep a watch for capsid bugs, which can leave hundreds of tiny holes across the foliage. Propagation is easy from fresh seed.

ABOVE
Massive leaves up to 90cm (3ft) across are produced on *Paulownia tomentosa*.

ABOVE
Trees covered in these early blooms look almost tropical.

LEFT
This beautiful shapely tree is one of the finest evergreens in the world.

Phillyrea latifolia
Green Olive

Phillyrea latifolia is a wonderfully architectural little evergreen tree. The trunk is rarely straight, but twisted and gnarled like its cousin, the European olive. The foliage is a series of tightly packed heads, sculpted into domes and billowing cloud shapes. It is very slow-growing and does not start to develop its characteristic shape for at least five years, so planting a semi-mature specimen is advisable for impatient gardeners. The overall height after twenty years will be no more than 4.5m (15ft) with a width of perhaps 3m (10ft). Although small, it needs to be planted with enough space left around it so its perfect shape can be appreciated.

This tree is often seen in churchyards planted as a single specimen; most of these older examples were planted around the 1900s when they were especially popular. Although it has the appearance of a miniature holm oak, *Phillyrea latifolia* is much more suitable for small gardens. It looks fantastic in Japanese-style gardens and is a good candidate for 'cloud pruning'. It looks equally at home in Mediterranean-style gardens and is also excellent for planting as an evergreen avenue.

In late spring, insignificant clusters of small yellowish flowers appear. These are followed by spherical blue-black fruits if the season is very warm. A native of south-east Europe, it has been grown in colder climates for centuries.

Plant in sun or light shade in any soil that is well drained. Once established, this is one of the most drought-resistant trees around. Unless the soil is very poor, there is no need for feeding. If grown on very thin, chalky soil, a couple of handfuls of blood, fish and bone can be sprinkled around the trunk each spring. It is very tolerant of windy, exposed positions, and the occasional salty gale seems to do no harm, making it a good choice for coastal gardens.

It responds very well to clipping, which is largely unnecessary if it is grown as a proper tree, but it does mean that it can be grown successfully as a hedge or shaped into topiary.

Generally, it remains free from pests and diseases. However, when buying one of these trees, check that it is free from whitefly: specimens reared under glass are prone to attacks from these beasts. Propagation is easy from cuttings.

Photinia serrulata
Chinese Hawthorn

SYN. *Photinia serratifolia*

Photinia serrulata is one of the very best lime-tolerant evergreen trees that can be grown in colder gardens. The leaves are large, glossy and slightly serrated, as its name would suggest. The new growth in the spring is very striking. Instead of the loud red colour that some of its relatives possess, the spring colouring of this tree is much more subtle. The copper-coloured new leaves are not only highly attractive, but also resistant to late spring frosts. However cold the weather, they remain unscathed.

This Chinese tree can either be left to grow naturally as a huge shrub or trained as a small tree. As a shrub, it needs lots of space but, as a tree, it is not at all intrusive. The height after ten years will be no more than 3.7m (12ft). The tall, straight trunk is topped with a rounded, compact head that keeps its tidy shape without assistance. It looks beautiful as a specimen tree in a small garden. In larger gardens, groups planted together look good, and they are also marvellous for creating an unusual avenue.

The tints of the spring growth last for several months, from late winter until late spring, then gradually disappear as the leaves age.

Adult leaves are a very lustrous shade of dark green. Huge clusters of white, frothy flowers appear in great profusion in late spring or early summer. They are followed by red berries.

This tree is just as happy grown in full sun or light shade. Plant in a sheltered spot away from strong winds. Best results would be gained from fertile, moist soil, but just about any soil can be coped with. Good drainage is important, and young trees need support from staking when being transplanted. Keep the trunks free from new growth, which sometimes sprouts from along its length. Feed annually in late spring with a good helping of something like a blood, fish and bone mix. Any pruning required should take place immediately after flowering.

Plants are rarely troubled by pests and diseases, although various leaf spots sometimes appear if the tree is stressed or waterlogged. Propagation is reasonably easy from fresh seed or ripe cuttings.

Pinus montezumae
Montezuma Pine

There is no pine tree more beautiful than *Pinus montezumae*. It's a magnificent, evergreen coniferous tree from Mexico. Although not very hardy, it just about slides into the orange hardiness colour code. The main feature of this lovely tree is its abundance of long and graceful needles that few people can resist running their hands through. These are bright emerald-green and up to 45cm (18in) long. The colour darkens a little as they age, but this in no way lessens their appeal – the softness of the foliage remains just as irresistible.

In colder climates *Pinus montezumae* won't reach more than about 6m (20ft) in height, even after twenty-five years. It is very slow-growing, and a decent-sized specimen should be obtained if it is to be a main focal point in the garden. Plenty of room should be left around it when planting out because its width can be at least half that of its height. Since it would be a pity to have to prune this tree, it is unsuitable for a very small garden.

Small specimens are very fuzzy and appealing, and it is tempting to buy one on impulse. If your garden is tiny, an ideal solution would be to keep one in a large container for about five years and then pass it on to a chum who has more space in which to grow it on.

Full sun is essential, as is shelter from cold, damaging winds. The soil should be light and sharply drained. Too much moisture around the roots will turn the foliage a sickly yellow before killing it off completely. These trees are a bit top-heavy when young, so staking must be done immediately they have been planted.

If the correct spot has been selected, it should be an easy tree to grow. No pruning is required, and only a light feeding once a year in late spring is necessary. A light dose of any well-balanced fertilizer can be applied. Pests and diseases aren't usually a problem. Propagation is easy from fresh seed, but seedlings take many years before they are large enough to be planted outside.

ABOVE
Pinus montezumae has irresistible shaggy foliage.

Pinus patula
Mexican Pine

Another lovely Mexican evergreen tree, which is surprisingly tough considering its provenance. Fast-growing, it can reach 9m (30ft) in height within about ten years, with an ultimate height of 15m (50ft), even in colder climates. It has long, spreading branches that drape gracefully to the ground in a candelabra shape. Long, soft needles hang down like curtains from each part of the tree. These are a vivid green and can be up to 30cm (1ft) long. *Pinus patula* makes a wonderful specimen tree for a large garden. Enough space should be left around it so that it can be admired from all angles.

In smaller gardens, the lower branches can be removed so that more space is left at ground level. This reveals the trunk, which is a fine feature in itself. It thickens up quickly, becoming rough and craggy. It is a lovely reddish-brown colour, and worth sacrificing a few branches for.

Experiments have shown that it is possible to keep this tree pruned Japanese-style for really tiny gardens. The tips to the ends of the branches and the top leader can be pinched out frequently as they grow. This encourages two or three sprigs of new growth from where there was previously just one. If this treatment is maintained throughout each growing season, a new shape of tree will very soon emerge. It is shorter, denser, shaggier and has a definite look of the Orient about it.

Plant in full sun and in a sheltered spot away from cold winds, which tend to turn the ends of the needles an unattractive shade of brown. Neutral to acid loamy soil is preferred, but it can cope with very small traces of chalk or lime. Excessively alkaline soils won't be tolerated at all. Good drainage is vital so that water doesn't gather around the roots. Water well for the first couple of years until it becomes established.

Feed *Pinus patula* just occasionally with a light dressing of blood, fish and bone in late spring. Feed only when the tree is actively growing. Pests and diseases are not usually a problem. Propagation is easy from fresh seed.

ABOVE
The graceful elegance of *Pinus patula* makes it an excellent choice as a specimen tree.

Pinus pinea
Umbrella Pine or **Stone Pine**

A shapely, round-headed evergreen tree, ideal for medium-sized gardens requiring more than a hint of the Mediterranean. Its height will eventually match the width of its head – around 5m (16ft) after fifteen years. The rough and craggy trunk can become fairly stocky after just a few years. The head of foliage is a mass of soft, feathery pine needles. Large cones are regularly produced, which contain edible seeds sold as pine kernels.

This tree is perfect for a wide range of environments, even hostile ones. It grows well on clay, flint, chalk or loam; even poor, dry, sandy soil is not a problem. It copes marvellously with strong coastal breezes. It is suitable for planting as a single specimen or in a small grove. Trees also make splendid avenues. Strong tree stakes, preferably three per tree, are required when planting mature specimens. These should be kept in place for at least three years.

Don't feed for several years unless the soil is really poor, so that all the energy can be concentrated on the root system. The roots need to be strong to support the wide crown of foliage. To give the roots the best possible start, throw a couple of handfuls of bonemeal into the bottom of the planting hole before positioning the tree on top. If planting large container-grown trees, expect considerable leaf drop during the first year. This is all as a result of the tree being transplanted and going into shock. By the following season, growth should once more be lush and plentiful.

Pinus pinea must have full sun; too much shade results in a sparse, open habit. It will never thrive in boggy conditions, although it should be watered regularly for the first two seasons until it's established. After this, the roots should have penetrated the soil far enough to find their own water supply. Once established, it has excellent drought tolerance.

To make the tree an even better shape, saw off the lower branches as the tree gains height to raise the crown. In mature trees, this creates a flatter and more spreading shape, rather than a rounded one. Propagation is easy from seed, but growth is very slow – expect a tree of no more than 60cm (2ft) after four years. Pests and diseases are not usually a problem.

ABOVE
Leave plenty of space around *Pinus pinea* when planting so that its spherical symmetry can be appreciated.

Pinus radiata
Monterey Pine

This is one of the fastest and toughest evergreen trees around and an essential part of a coastal garden. It is native to the hillside areas of Monterey on the Californian coast. The foliage is dark green with the needles tightly massed together. Large, handsome cones are produced on mature trees.

This tree will take all the salty winds and howling gales that are a familiar part of life if you have a seaside garden. It positively thrives in these hostile conditions that would turn most plants into a brown and crispy mess – unless an adequate windbreak can be established, a normal garden is virtually impossible to create in a position right on the seafront or cliff top.

Pinus radiata can be used as a single specimen conifer or be planted in large groups to provide windbreaks for more sizeable gardens. A row of them is ideal for screening purposes. They can also be planted and kept trimmed as a huge hedge through which even the fiercest sea storms would fail to penetrate. A coastal garden is not essential, however, and these trees can live happily in any inland garden too. They can cope with exposed hilltops or be quite happy just planted wherever a large tree is required.

Trees can easily put on up to 1.8m (6ft) of growth per season in their early years, although after about five years, annual growth slows down to about 90cm (3ft) or less per year. The ultimate height in an average garden could be 18m (60ft) after twenty-five years. If the height is wanted but not the bulk, remove the lower branches so that the foliage starts from much higher up. The only space taken up then is from the trunk.

Pinus radiata needs full sun, and well-drained soil is vital. The larger the tree and the windier the site, the stronger the staking should be. Support it from all directions with three stout stakes. Any type of soil will do, and feeding is not usually important. Pests and diseases do not generally appear to be much of a problem. Propagation is easy from fresh seed.

Pittosporum tenuifolium

A charming little evergreen tree from New Zealand. It has masses of pretty leaves, which are pale green, glossy and attractively crinkled around the edges. The black stems create a striking contrast to the foliage, making it popular with flower arrangers.

The tiny flowers are chocolate-brown and appear in the spring. According to *Hillier's Manual of Trees and Shrubs*, they have 'an exquisite honey-like fragrance', but I can't say that I've ever noticed much of a scent at all. *Pittosporum tenuifolium* is reasonably fast-growing and could be 4.5m (15ft) tall in about fifteen years. The ultimate height of a mature tree would be no more than 9m (30ft). The crown of the tree has a beautifully curved, almost sculptural, appearance.

It is very well suited to coastal gardens, where it is commonly seen as a specimen tree, because of its tolerance to salty winds. A very versatile tree, it can be grown in all shapes and sizes. Young plants can be trained as trees in the normal way. However, if left to grow as a shrub, it responds well to clipping and can easily be converted to a shapely rounded dome, or be clipped formally into an angular hedge. It can also be left to grow in a pot if its size is kept manageable.

This tree is very easy to grow. Full sun would be preferred, but I've seen them planted in light shade and they look fine. Light, crumbly soil with perfect drainage would be best, but they can adapt to most types, including chalk or clay. Water well to start with but, unless the summer is exceptionally hot and dry, they can usually fend for themselves. Annual feeding can mostly be dispensed with, but a light feed in late spring is fine. The only conditions that would not be acceptable are cold, winter winds or prolonged waterlogging.

There is a rather nice variegated form called 'Silver Queen' that has lovely silvery cream variegation to the foliage. Smaller than the green form and a little less hardy, it still makes a good choice for a mild garden. There is also a ghastly purple form, but the less said about that, the better.

Propagation is easy from ripe cuttings taken in late summer. *Pittosporum tenuifolium* is not usually plagued by any particular pest or disease.

Podocarpus macrophyllus
Maki

This unusual small evergreen tree, native to Japan and China, is actually a conifer, although it doesn't look like one. Instead of conifer-like needles, it has proper leaves that spiral all the way along each branch. Bright green, about 20cm (8in) long and very slender, they have a thick, leathery texture and stand vertically all over the tree, giving it a bristly appearance.

Podocarpus macrophyllus is incredibly slow-growing, taking many years to become large enough to plant out, but its distinctive look is worth waiting for. Buy the biggest you can find. A twenty-year-old tree will be only about 1.8m (6ft) tall and 90cm (3ft) wide. It will fit into the tiniest garden, as even mature trees are unlikely to exceed 3.7m (12ft) in an average temperate climate. For really patient gardeners, it can also be used as a hedge; it will need very little clipping once it has formed the basic shape.

This tree must have a shady spot, as too much sun gives the leaves a yellowish tinge; in shade, they remain a rich, dark colour. The soil must be neutral to acid, and contain no chalk or lime. It also needs to be rich enough to hold some moisture, while managing to be well drained enough not to become boggy. Light soil is preferred so that the roots don't have to work too hard finding their way through. It needs to be tucked away from any winds to stop the edges of the leaves scorching. If you have a quiet, sheltered, woodland garden or a shady courtyard, this tree is essential.

Perfectly hardy and related to the yew, this tree is slow enough to be considered for growing in a large container. Use compost with some peat (or peat substitute) in it, and never let it dry out. It will be years before it needs repotting.

A light dressing of blood, fish and bone can be applied during early summer. Sometimes, after a wet summer, the leaves become a little less green. A 'quick fix' in the autumn with some potash food will green them up again. Pruning is unlikely to be needed, apart from the removal of an occasional shoot that has grown in a way to upset the tree's basic outline. Chop this off with secateurs right back into the tree, so that the cut end is hidden from view.

Propagation is from seed. The seeds will need a light sandy soil to get them started. Pests and diseases are uncommon.

Podocarpus salignus
Willow Podocarp

An irresistible little tree from Chile with luscious emerald-green, willow-like foliage positively dripping from every branch. Go out and buy one now!

Hardy, evergreen and coniferous, *Podocarpus salignus* is related to the yew, although little resemblance can be seen until familiar red berries are produced on older trees. It is the ultimate specimen tree. For larger areas, plant in groups, where they will produce more berries. They can be planted as an unusual but extravagant hedge. *Podocarpus salignus* also fits in beautifully with any exotic style of garden, contrasting and complementing palms, ferns and large-leaved trees.

In its native Chile, it is a sizeable tree, but elsewhere expect only a maximum of 7.5m (25ft) in height and 3m (10ft) in width after twenty-five years. The branches drape right down to the ground, concealing the trunk. It is always a bit of a dilemma whether to leave the branches growing naturally or to remove some of the lower ones, to reveal part of the trunk. Attractive in its own right, the trunk is reddish-brown, fibrous and peels off in strips.

Plant a decent-sized tree, as it can take several years for the roots to become settled enough for the foliage to resume growing. Once new leaves start to appear, the growth rate is 15–20cm (6–8in) per year.

Choose a spot that has light shade, moist soil and is completely sheltered from cold winter winds. Neutral to acid soil is preferred, but slightly alkaline conditions can be tolerated. The soil needs to be rich enough to hold onto some moisture, without water gathering around the roots, so good drainage is required. Feed only light doses of blood, fish and bone annually in late spring; too much food can scorch the ends of the leaves.

Pruning is rarely required unless a hedge is being formed. Avoid cutting into old wood; clipping should be done little and often so that only the new growth is trimmed.

Pests and diseases aren't usually a problem. Propagation is best from seed; trees produced from cuttings do not seem to be of good quality.

ABOVE
Podocarpus salignus is one of the world's most beautiful trees, deserving the most visible spot in the garden.

ABOVE
Lovely vivid green, soft foliage hangs off each branch, forming a graceful mass.

Prunus laurocerasus
Cherry Laurel

'What is *Prunus laurocerasus* doing in a chapter on trees?' you may ask. Cherry laurel is normally seen growing as a shrub or a hedge, but look at the picture and see what can be achieved with a bit of pruning and sawing. It is quite easy to turn this plant into a really sculptural little tree that is not only fully hardy but evergreen as well.

Prunus laurocerasus makes a fine hedge or screen because it is fast-growing and has large glossy leaves. It can reach 6m (20ft) tall and 3m (10ft) across within twenty years. For spacious gardens, this is all well and good, but such dimensions can be overpowering for tiny gardens. The tree illustrated encroached on someone's driveway, and the owner was faced with the choice of either chopping it down, parking the car elsewhere or getting busy with the saw and a pair of shears. The third option was taken, and there is now room for cars to be driven underneath the foliage, and a lovely new tree has been formed.

Whether this plant becomes a hedge, a tree or a shaped shrub, it will need regular clipping Bossy garden 'experts' insist that large leaves are cut with secateurs at their base so as not to cut them in half. That's fine if you have nothing better to do. I find that by using shears, a perfectly good result can be accomplished if you have a good eye for a straight line.

Planting in sun is OK but the leathery foliage takes on a richer colour in the shade. Fertile, moist soil is preferred; clay soil is perfect. Although not a lime-hater, thin chalky soil just doesn't hold on to the moisture and nutrients required. In late spring, creamy white flowers appear, followed by lots of berries that ripen to a deep, shiny black.

Young plants can be trained into single-stemmed plants as they grow, making them into trees from the start. They are also good candidates for creating half-standard trees, i.e., with a stem of 90cm (3ft) and foliage formed as an 'umbrella' on the top. Grown this way, they can live in large pots for years. Feed well annually with well-rotted manure or blood, fish and bone. Keep well irrigated for the first five years of life. Propagation is easy from cuttings. No particular pests or diseases are a regular nuisance.

Pseudopanax chathamicus
Chatham Island Lancewood

This distinctive evergreen tree is native to the Chatham Islands, off New Zealand. A small tree and very slow-growing, its height after ten years will be no more than about 1.8m (6ft), topped with a compact crown. The leaves are long and tapered, with a leathery texture and slightly serrated edges. They are upright and spreading. The colour is dark olive-green on the top and paler beneath. As with many *Pseudopanax*, the leaves become shorter and wider as the tree matures.

This tree is perfect for very small gardens. It can look effective when planted in number throughout the garden and under-planted with low-growing, clipped plants such as *Buxus sempervirens*, *Hebe rakaiensis* or *Pittosporum tobira* 'Nanum'. For larger gardens, plant it with groups of other New Zealand native plants such as *Cordyline australis* and *Phormium tenax*.

Full sun is desirable for faster growth. The soil type can be almost anything, as long as it is free-draining, but the roots prefer to work through a light, loamy soil, rather than a heavy clay one. Water sparingly to keep it just moist.

Occasional dry spells do no harm at all. A light feed of blood, fish and bone can be given in late spring if the soil is particularly poor.

This tree can sit in a pot for years, as the root system is very slow to develop. If it is to spend some of its early life cultivated in this way, use a soil-based compost such as John Innes no. 3. It tends to grow straight up without any bushiness for many years. To encourage more growth lower down, the growing point can be chopped off at any level. Several new shoots will sprout from wherever it has been cut.

Although the hardiness colour code is orange, it only just fits into this category, and care should be taken when choosing a site. Keep sheltered from cold winter winds and avoid planting in frost pockets. It would be happy in a heavily built-up area of an inner city, where frosts are rare. It would also be blissfully content in a mild coastal garden.

The new spring growth seems to be a magnet for aphids but, otherwise, pests and diseases generally do not give cause for concern. Propagation is usually from fresh seed.

ABOVE
An unusual tree from New Zealand and definitely one your neighbours won't have.

Pseudopanax crassifolius
Lancewood

A really weird New Zealand tree that is pure horticultural fantasy. It is for the foliage that *Pseudopanax crassifolius* is considered peculiar. The leaves undergo metamorphosis through several stages, the second stage being the oddest. The seedling leaves start out small, black and shiny, then mature into the next phase, ending up 60cm (2ft) long, only 1cm (½in) wide, brownish-black and plastic-looking. Sometimes they have an orange or red stripe running down the centre. The edges are sharply serrated. Even odder than their appearance is the way the leaves hang downwards at a 45-degree angle, giving an upside-down look to the tree. Either loved passionately or disliked intensely, this tree certainly draws a lot of attention from next-door neighbours.

After this phase, the leaves go through several stages until they reach adulthood. Each season's new growth becomes shorter, wider and greener until the leaves look almost normal. They also stop hanging downwards and gradually lift up. A mature tree can reach 6m (20ft) with a crown of evergreen foliage spreading to around 2.5m (8ft).

The trunk and branches are craggy but dead straight, and the trees get their common name, supposedly, because the New Zealand Maoris used them to make lances and spear handles.

With an almost non-existent root system, this tree is exceptionally good for growing in a large pot, where it can sit happily for years, but the best results will be had from planting directly into the soil. It needs a quiet, sheltered spot in a sunny position. Salty sea air can be coped with very well, but avoid planting where there would be continuous buffeting by strong winds.

Almost any soil would be suitable, but heavy soil that becomes waterlogged would soon rot the roots. Keep well watered if grown in a pot. If planted in the ground, dry conditions seem perfectly acceptable. No special care is needed, and annual feeding is not that important.

Propagation can be either from fresh seed, which will produce variable results, or from cuttings, which can behave very oddly, producing new leaves that launch straight into the strange adult phase. Aphids can be a nuisance on new growth, but few other problems seem to afflict this plant.

Pseudopanax ferox
Toothed Lancewood

A crazy-looking evergreen tree from New Zealand that's like no other tree you've ever seen. If the tree described on the previous page sounded odd, this one is even more abnormal to look at.

The leaves of *Pseudopanax ferox* also metamorphose through several stages from juvenile to adult, with the second phase again being the most peculiar. They are 45cm (18in) long and just 1cm (½in) wide. Dark brownish-black, they often have a red, yellow or orange stripe running down the centre. The edges are very sharply serrated, and the whole leaf looks like a large hacksaw blade. The leaves hang down the tree at a 45-degree angle, and it would be easy to convince yourself that the tree had been planted the wrong way up. It is thought that the leaves evolved this way to make them unappetizing to passing animals, thereby assuring the plant's survival into maturity. It's certainly an interesting theory.

Pseudopanax ferox is very slow-growing and, after five years, might still be only 60cm (2ft) tall. Away from its native New Zealand, its ultimate height is unlikely to exceed 4m (13ft).

There is room in even the tiniest garden for one of these. It will sit in a container for years without getting root-bound. It needs very little food; an occasional handful of blood, fish and bone every few years will be enough. The only way to kill it is by overwatering.

Neighbours will take great delight in poking fun at this wonderfully unusual tree; it's so peculiar-looking that it could be mistaken for something no longer alive. But learning to love it and appreciate its quirky qualities is not difficult.

Unless your garden is very mild, don't plant out very young specimens. They need to age for a while before they become hardy. The warmest and sunniest planting position possible is advised. Water sparingly, just enough to keep the soil moist.

Aphids can be a problem on young shoots, otherwise this is a very easy tree to cultivate. Propagation is best from fresh seed, although very variable plants are likely to be produced.

▪ Pseudopanax laetus

This lush and leafy small tree or large shrub from New Zealand is slow-growing, taking years to reach its maximum size of 3m (10ft) tall and 1.8m (6ft) wide. The leaves are large, jungly, dark and glossy with a leathery texture, but the new young growth is a fresh bright green. The buds emerge as tightly curled-up knots, which gradually open up as twisted bunches of foliage before finally unrolling out into normal-looking leaves up to 30cm (1ft) long.

The stems of the evergreen *Pseudopanax laetus* have a striped look before maturing into woody trunks. It grows naturally as a large, bushy mound but can be trained as a tree quite easily. Removing the lower stems as it grows changes it into a more conventional tree shape and reveals its attractive bark. The foliage left on top makes a dense rounded crown.

This plant is useful as well as beautiful. It adores shade, which makes it ideal for jungly garden schemes, for filling dark corners or under-planting beneath tall canopies of palms, bamboos, eucalyptus and acacias. It contrasts well with other New Zealand plants such as *Cordyline australis* and *Dicksonia squarrosa*.

In a cold winter, the leaves can react badly. If they become seriously frosted, there is nothing to be done, but if temperatures dip to only about –4°C (25°F), the leaves droop and give the impression they are past the point of no return. Ignore this completely. If the temperature rises a little in the next couple of days, they will recover fully and you are left wondering what all the fuss was about.

Its slow growth and tough constitution make it a excellent choice for a large terracotta pot. It can live in a container for years, as long as it is never allowed to dry out. Choose it for a shady courtyard or roof terrace. It is so robust that it will even cope as a houseplant or in a shady conservatory. As it appreciates a bit of humidity, a position around an indoor swimming pool is another option. Use a soil-based compost, such as John Innes no. 3, water regularly and feed in spring and again in summer with any balanced food containing high amounts of nitrogen.

Pests and diseases are nothing to worry about. Propagation is quite easy from seed or cuttings. Both methods are slow to produce anything substantial.

Quercus ilex
Holm Oak

As one of the hardiest, toughest and most versatile trees available, *Quercus ilex* has many virtues. From a distance, it looks like a large olive tree. A mature plant has a thick, sturdy trunk topped with a dense head of grey-green leaves that catch the light beautifully. This is a large tree, but very slow-growing, taking at least fifty years to reach 15m (50ft).

These evergreen trees can be used in a number of ways. They are an essential windbreak for large coastal gardens, where they create good shelter, allowing more delicate plants to be grown near the sea without being blasted by salty gales. For smaller gardens, they can be kept clipped as a tall hedge, which would still act as a buffer against sea winds. Single specimens look very stately as pride of place in good-sized plots, while groups planted together create a imposing presence on a large estate or park. They can also make the most marvellous avenues, clipped formally as large 'lollipop' shapes.

In a large, cold garden, if trees are planted fairly close together and regularly crown-lifted (see pages 138–9), the canopies of foliage can act as a frost barrier, protecting anything planted underneath; a few degrees of extra warmth can make a big difference in the horticultural world.

Quercus ilex can grow virtually anywhere. It prefers sun or light shade, but almost full shade can be tolerated. Any soil will do, even heavy chalk, but loamy soil would be its first choice. It can be planted on any site, from sheltered woodland to exposed hilltops. It is astonishingly drought resistant, although irrigation should take place frequently during the first couple of seasons until it becomes established. Just about the only thing it would hate is a waterlogged position. It really is a very easy tree to grow.

Newly planted trees should be heavily staked. If any hedges or shaped trees need pruning, clip annually in summer. A good feed of blood, fish and bone can be given in early spring. Aphids, sooty mould and powdery mildew should all be checked for occasionally.

Propagation is easiest from seed (acorns) but this method will produce wide variations of leaf form, not only in size, but also in shape. Leaves can range from being smooth edged, slightly serrated or even heavily serrated.

ABOVE
Quercus ilex is a perfect choice for a formal evergreen avenue.

Quercus myrsinifolia
Bamboo-leafed Oak

SYN. *Quercus bambusifolia*

Quercus myrsinifolia is a delicate-looking evergreen oak, native to China and Japan. The leaves are a fresh green and finely tapered. Its spring growth is an unusual shade of dark purple, which is very striking against the rest of the tree. The leaves gradually unfurl before maturing to their normal green colouring.

This is a small tree with a spreading habit. Growth is painfully slow: it takes years for it to become anything worth looking at. It's worth the wait, though, because after fifteen years you could be looking at the most beautiful tree in the neighbourhood. Its height will then still be no more than around 3.7m (12ft). The short, shapely trunk will be topped with a gracefully spreading canopy, almost as wide as the tree is tall, and the crown will be densely packed with masses of shining leaves. The maximum height in an average temperate climate, even after fifty years, is unlikely to be more than 9m (30ft).

Propagation is not difficult, providing some fresh material can be tracked down, though this can be a feat in itself. Small seedlings are not easy to persuade into putting on any bulk. If you're lucky, about 30 per cent of a batch might produce little trees. They are difficult to cultivate and still risky until they are at least 1.8m (6ft). Once they reach this size, they are much more reliable and ready to plant out into their permanent site. They are fully hardy at this stage and have usually started to become more woody. Because of the temperamental nature of this tree in the juvenile stages, it is worth hunting around to buy a larger specimen.

Plant this tree in a semi-shady, sheltered site and stake well. The soil should be rich and heavy enough to hold onto some moisture without waterlogging. Loamy, lime-free soil would be best. Give it enough room to mature without crowding into nearby shrubs or other trees – this splendid tree deserves to be seen. Single specimen trees look wonderful in small or medium gardens; in large gardens, small groups of trees could be planted. Feed small amounts of any balanced organic fertilizer in late spring. Pruning is not really necessary, but a light clipping over the top of the crown into a more rounded shape can emphasize the tree's curves. Aphids might be occasional visitors but, generally, this tree remains trouble-free.

ABOVE
Quercus myrsinifolia is nothing like the immense trees of the more common species of oak. The leaves are similar to those of a small-leaved bamboo.

Quercus suber
Cork Oak

Grown for its stunning bark, *Quercus suber* is a familiar sight throughout Spain and Portugal, where it is a commercial crop, having provided the wine industry with the material for many millions of corks over the last few centuries. The corky covering of the trunk and branches takes at least twenty years to mature enough for the first crop. When it has been stripped, it replenishes enough for further crops to be taken every seven or eight years.

Unless you have your own vineyard, keep *Quercus suber* purely as an ornamental tree. Its thick, craggy bark makes a fine feature in the garden. It is evergreen and reasonably hardy. Compared with the trunk, the foliage is almost irrelevant, but the large amounts of little, shiny leaves are pleasantly attractive. In hot climates, this can become a sizeable tree. In cooler climates, expect a maximum height of only 7.5m (25ft) after thirty years.

These trees are very variable. Some grow naturally as almost multi-stemmed bushes; others are a definite tree shape, having a sturdy trunk topped with a dense crown. They look best planted in large numbers, but if you have room for only a single specimen, choose a fairly mature tree with an interesting and almost straight trunk. This can then be planted as a central focal point in the garden. Plant it where it can be seen easily and where it can be reached, as touching the corky bark is irresistible.

Plant in a sunny spot. *Quercus suber* can cope with almost any soil. In dry, poor soils, water regularly until established. Rich, moist and fertile soil will give the best results. Avoid very heavy clay soil that retains too much water, as waterlogging will cause problems. These trees can cope with windy or exposed gardens very well, which makes them ideal for planting by the coast. Salty sea breezes do no harm at all.

Propagating from acorns is not difficult, but a lot of patience is required to produce trees of a rewarding size. They gain height quite quickly, but take years to develop much bulk. Pests and diseases are not really a problem.

Rhus typhina
Stag's-horn Sumach

A small, deciduous hardy tree native to eastern areas of North America. It has many fine features, compensating for the fact that it is not evergreen. The leaves, which are huge, 60cm (2ft) long, and exceptionally architectural, are made up of leaflets running all along the central rib. They look like the fronds of an exotic fern. The stems of new foliage are bright pink. Older stems and branches are covered in fuzzy brown 'velvet', which is wonderfully soft to the touch. These have the look and feel of deer antlers, hence the tree's common name. Male and female flowers appear on separate trees, followed by fat conical fruits covered in dark red bristles. The fruits are very noticeable, as they appear late in the autumn after the leaves have dropped. They sit upright among the branches and can be 15–20cm (6–8in) long.

Autumn colour is a special feature of *Rhus typhina*. The intense colours range through the spectrum from green to yellowish-green to bright yellow to orange and, finally, to a vivid bright scarlet. The change of hue takes many weeks to complete. Female trees tend to have the best colouring.

This plant grows naturally as a multi-stemmed, suckering shrub. It is, however, much prettier trained on a single stem from a young age, with all the other branches removed as it grows. You will be left with a shapely little tree with a wide-spreading canopy. The ultimate height will be only about 4.5m (15ft) with a width almost to match.

Plant in sun or light shade in any well-drained soil, although fertile soil gives the best results. Feed annually with a mix of blood, fish and bone. Remove any unwanted suckers that come up from around the base. If grown as a large shrub, keep a tidy shape by cutting back hard every year, almost to ground level. This will encourage new vigorous growth the following season. This is a very easy tree for beginners. It is best planted away from other plants so that its shape can be appreciated.

Propagation is easiest from root cuttings taken in the autumn when the tree is dormant. Pests and diseases are not common.

Tamarix gallica
Tamarisk

The sight of these wonderful feathery trees blowing in the breeze acts as a reminder of childhood holidays on sandy beaches. They are nearly always found planted near the seafront because of their unequalled salt resistance. They can shrug off the fiercest coastal gales and remain totally unscathed. The light, wispy foliage filters the wind brilliantly, acting as a windbreak to whatever is planted behind.

These trees are most noticeable during the summer, when huge quantities of sugary pink flowers appear. These last for weeks and are a lovely frothy sight. Trees can be left as big bushes for coastal windbreaks in large spaces. For smaller gardens, they can be bought and planted as proper trees. They have gnarled and craggy trunks topped with unruly masses of branches and smaller stems. The sparse foliage acts as a wonderful screen without blocking out the light.

To keep these trees tidy, they can be pruned savagely at the end of the year. To keep their size under control, they can be hacked back hard, right to the top of the trunk. This will encourage lots of new growth for the following season. Up to 1.8m (6ft) per year could be expected. If pruning is not done, this fast-growing tree will slow right down producing less and less height each year until a maximum of only around 6m (20ft) is reached. *Tamarix gallica* is neither fully evergreen nor fully deciduous, but somewhere in between, depending on the weather and the site. During the winter, it can therefore look a bit tatty, so the untidiest bits can be removed if required.

Their associations with the sea doesn't mean these trees cannot be planted anywhere else. They are extremely hardy and could live almost anywhere, but the soil requirements are different if planted inland. By the coast, they can live on very poor soil. The salty air is absorbed by the plant, which somehow reduces transpiration (water loss through the leaves). If planted inland, where salty air is non-existent, richer loamy soil that retains moisture will give much better results. Full sun is vital.

Pests and diseases are rarely a problem. Propagation is usually done by taking cuttings of the previous year's growth.

ABOVE
The feathery foliage of *Tamarix gallica* is a fine sight in a breezy coastal garden.

Trochodendron aralioides
Cartwheel Tree

This unusual Japanese tree is the only member of its family, although it is vaguely related to magnolias. It could be classed either as a small multi-stemmed tree or as a very large shrub. It is evergreen and exceptionally hardy. Away from its native climate, its height is unlikely to exceed 6m (20ft). The branches are wide-spreading and their span could reach the same dimensions as the tree's height. The apple-green leaves are waxy with scalloped edges. The new buds produced in spring are an unexpected shade of bright rose-pink. The flowers are also unusual with an air of 'Jurassic Park' about them: they are a vivid sulphur-green.

These trees are slow to get started and can be tricky to cultivate when very young. Once they reach about 90cm (3ft), though, the worst of the problems are over.

This is a difficult plant to site in the garden. It is very slow-growing and could take ten years to reach just 1.8m (6ft), but it needs plenty of space left around it for when it matures, as the root system will not appreciate being disturbed if it's relocated. If kept moist, it could live in a large pot for a number of years. Then, once it

becomes too big for a container, a permanent planting site could be found in the garden.

Shelter from wind is its main requirement, not only from coastal winds, but also from cold easterly winter winds in exposed inland gardens. This tree is happy in sun or shade, but light shade seems to suit it best. Most types of soil are acceptable, but those containing large amounts of chalk are best avoided. It is not a lime-hating tree, but chalky soil drains too quickly, and *Trochodendron aralioides* likes to be kept moist. As long as it is frequently irrigated, it is happy in clay, peat or loam.

This tree is virtually maintenance free. If the soil is alkaline, occasional doses of sequestered iron would be beneficial and would help to keep the foliage a good colour. During the winter, the leaves can become speckled. These dark brown bits seem to cause no lasting harm, and when the plant starts to grow again in spring, it always comes through its usual apple-green colour. Propagation is best and easiest from seed. An annual dose of blood, fish and bone can be applied in spring. No particular pests or diseases are a problem.

ABOVE
This prehistoric tree has tough leathery foliage preceded by bright pink buds.

Viburnum tinus
Laurustinus

A reliable and easy evergreen tree, more often seen as a large shrub, but much prettier when grown on a single stem. It is suitable for just about any garden, however small; after many years, the ultimate height is little more than 3.7m (12ft). The trunks are often twisted and shapely, topped with a dense rounded crown of foliage. The leaves are dark green and not very exciting; the shapely silhouette is a much more interesting reason for growing this tree.

The white flowers are an attractive feature. Produced in generous clusters, they cover most of the tree all through the winter. There are some very good forms of *Viburnum tinus* – the most popular is 'Eve Price', a pink-flowering form. Blue-black berries follow the flowers in spring.

This tree is best grown in light shade to keep the foliage dark and healthy but, in sun, more flowers are produced. It will grow in almost any type of soil, but fertile loamy soil is best. It should be kept just moist at all times. A feed of blood, fish and bone in late spring will keep the whole plant looking good.

This versatile tree can be grown in almost any garden. It is especially suitable for seaside gardens, as salty winds do not present a problem. It responds well to pruning, and any clipping should be done as soon as the berries have dropped but before the following year's flower buds start to form.

The lower growth of this plant can be left on so that it can be grown as a large shrub. Trim with shears to keep the shape tidy. It also makes a good hedging plant, and can be trimmed in a formal shape with straight sides and a level top. It is particularly effective as a windbreak in coastal gardens. These plants are sometimes seen shaped as 'lollipops' with a total height of only about 1.5m (5ft). Grown in pots, they make a change from the usual pair of bay trees placed either side of a front door.

Pests and diseases are not a major problem, but aphids can be a nuisance on new shoots. If seen, spray at once before large colonies build up. The sticky substance they excrete will attract fungal spores and lead to sooty mould. Propagation is usually from semi-ripe cuttings.

ABOVE
With careful pruning, a shapely little tree can be created.

BELOW
Profuse amounts of flowers are produced in late winter, followed by blue-black berries.

Other leafy exotics

This exciting group represents some of the more outrageous architectural plants. Plants such as bamboos and climbers are easy to define, but this section deals with a wide range of 'extras'. All are special in their own way, even though they don't fit into any particular category.

The plants featured in this chapter include those with giant-sized leaves such as *Gunnera manicata*, *Viburnum cinnamomifolium* and *Tetrapanax papyrifera*, all of which can add drama to a jungly garden where foliage is more important than flowers.

Loud, brightly coloured flowers are represented too, with the tropical-looking lemon and orange *Hedychium gardnerianum*, the large bright yellow *Telanthophora grandifolia* with flower heads the size of dinner plates, the majestic purple of *Tibouchina urvilleana*, the massive red spikes of *Lobelia tupa* and the brilliant blue of *Agapanthus africanus*.

Some of the plants described here have a strong presence with both their leaves and their flowers, making them an almost essential addition to any planting scheme. The absurd hardy banana *Musa basjoo* is often top of the list as a choice for adventurous gardeners. The New Zealand flax *Phormium tenax* consists of a huge mass of leaves, with ridiculous flower spikes that tower above, making them another popular plant for almost any type of garden. *Melianthus major* is currently enjoying a wave of popularity with its large bluish leaves and strange red flowers. And for unrivalled flamboyance, there are the massive leaves and shocking pink blooms of *Canna iridiflora*, which are a truly awesome sight.

BELOW
The huge leaves of *Gunnera manicata* dwarf most other plants in the garden.

Many of the plants described are useful as well as beautiful. There are some that can romp across the ground such as *Rosmarinus repens*, *Euphorbia myrsinites* and *Ephedra*, creating a foil to taller trees or spiky plants, as well as acting as a mulch to keep down the weeds. There are shapely rounded plants such as *Hebe rakaiensis*, *Hebe parviflora angustifolia*, *Baccharis patagonica* and *Corokia* x *virgata* to act as a contrast to some of the more brutal designs. There are also unusual plants for salty seaside gardens. Tough, evergreen plants such as *Olearia macrodonta*, *Spartium junceum* and *Griselinia littoralis* are not only architectural, but also vital ingredients of coastal planting schemes.

Some plants such as *Prunus lusitanicus*, *Buxus sempervirens* and *Camellia japonica* become architectural only with a helping hand from the gardener. Left to their own devices, these evergreen shrubs are quite shapeless. However, with some expert clipping and pruning, they are immediately transformed and promoted into the architectural class. Just think of box (*Buxus*) cones and balls and what striking features they are in gardens of any size.

Finally, there are those plants that are just plain weird and the sort of horticultural oddities that keep gardening really exhilarating. Plants such as *Cynara cardunculus*, *Poncirus trifoliata*, *Echium pininiana* and *Eryngium pandanifolium* are exactly the kind of things that make life worth living.

ABOVE LEFT
Mahonia lomariifolia has winter flowers that could brighten up the shadiest corner.

BELOW
Canna iridiflora has large exotic foliage with the added bonus of shocking-pink flowers.

ABOVE RIGHT
The fabulous foliage of *Euphorbia mellifera* looks just as good in the winter as it does during the warmer months of the year.

All the plants featured in this chapter have different requirements and preferences in the garden. Some will only grow well in the shade, some must have full sun. Some appreciate almost drought-like conditions, some almost need to live in bogs. Poor soil suits some, others must have rich, fertile conditions. As a very general rule, plants with large dark green leaves such as *Fatsia japonica* and *Mahonia lomariifolia* prefer shade. Small-leaved plants, especially those with grey foliage such as *Euphorbia myrsinites* and *Corokia* x *virgata*, need lots of sun. Slow-growing plants with little leaves such as *Ephedra* and *Rosmarinus repens* can cope with dry conditions. And fast-growing plants with enormous leaves such as *Musa basjoo* and *Canna iridiflora* need lots of water. The individual cultivation needs of all the plants described are fully explained on the following pages.

Most of these leafy exotics can be planted as special additions to otherwise fairly pedestrian gardens, just to add a bit of glamour here or some excitement there. However, it would be easy to have nothing else but these wonderful plants to create something truly stunning and quite unlike anything else in the neighbourhood. With these types of architectural plants, it is possible to have something of interest in the garden for the entire year, long after the roses and summer bedding plants have finished their annual performance.

Virtually all the plants in this chapter are evergreen, but there are some that are deciduous and so lose their leaves every autumn, or herbaceous and so die back to nothing every winter. These plants have been included either for their extraordinary lush verdancy or for their gigantic size or for their exotic floral contribution to the garden. They are still architectural plants, even if their presence is only temporary.

Every plant in this chapter has something special to offer. The only difficulty is which specimens to choose, as all of them are so irresistible.

LEFT
Musa basjoo
is one of the
most outrageous
plants featured
in this chapter –
every garden
should have one.

BELOW
Fatsia japonica
has large, leathery,
evergreen foliage
that is fully hardy
everywhere.

What these
leafy exotics
share is a strong
architectural
quality.

Acanthus mollis
Bear's Breeches or **Big Spinach**

The huge, soft leaves of *Acanthus mollis*, 60cm (2ft) long and 30cm (1ft) across, make enormous clumps of foliage and are always glossy, as if they have experienced a fresh shower of rain. The flower spikes are very stately, towering above the foliage in large numbers during summer. Resembling large pink and white lupins, they can reach up to 1.5m (5ft) in height, and are made up of long-lasting flowers and bracts. They make excellent cut flowers and are suitable candidates for drying. Although sometimes classed as herbaceous, the classic behaviour of dying down each winter occurs only in very cold gardens. In an average temperate climate, *Acanthus mollis* remains beautifully green all year round. The word *mollis* means soft or velvety in Latin.

The planting position needs some thought. Clumps can become large after five or six years, so plenty of space should be given to allow for expansion each year. *Acanthus mollis* hates root disturbance and will not usually survive being dug up and moved.

Plant in either full sun or light shade in a spot sheltered from strong winds, which can shred the leaves. Rich loamy soil is preferred, and this needs to be kept moist at all times in order to achieve the best results. After a very harsh winter, the plants can look very tired. If this happens, cut all the leaves down to the base. They will quickly reshoot and provide masses of fresh new growth for the forthcoming season.

Annual feeding is important to keep the foliage lush and healthy. Either give generous helpings of well-rotted manure or sprinkle a few handfuls of blood, fish and bone around the base of each plant in spring. Remove any older leaves that have turned yellow or brown, cutting them right back to ground level.

This plant is an absolute martyr to slugs. Prevention is essential, and a slug deterrent that is harmless to other wildlife should be used regularly. Propagation is easiest from fresh seed sown in early spring.

ABOVE
The large glossy foliage is the main reason for growing this beautiful plant.

BELOW
The pretty flowers are an excellent added bonus.

Agapanthus africanus
African Lily

A spectacular acquisition, not only for its large, leathery foliage, but also for its amazing flowers. The leaves are glossy, strap-like and produced in copious amounts to form thick clumps. The flower spikes tower above the foliage on long, straight stems up to 1.5m (5ft) in length, and open up into large balls 30cm (1ft) in diameter, balanced on the top of every stem. Each flower head comprises dozens of individual blossoms usually either pure white or bright blue – they are truly stunning. Each year, as plants mature and increase in bulk, more and more flower heads are produced. There are many other types of *Agapanthus* on the market that are far hardier than this one. However, it is worth foregoing the hardiness in exchange for the size and shape of this plant's blooms, which are far superior to any of the others.

This plant actually does better in a large terracotta pot than it would in the ground. The reason for this is that if grown in a container, it is easy to move under cover if the weather becomes too wet and cold. Even in mild areas, these plants have been known not to reappear in the spring if left in the ground during a particularly soggy winter – they just rot away. If you are planting in the ground, *Agapanthus africanus* looks good in large drifts.

To get the best from these plants, give them rich, well-drained soil. Use John Innes no. 3 compost for containers. They are just as happy in full sun as they are in light shade. Keep sheltered from strong winds. Water regularly during the growing season but allow to dry out in the winter. Feed from early spring onwards with weekly doses of tomato food. This provides the potash needed to persuade the plant to put its energy into flower production. After flowering, enjoy the seed heads while they last, then cut each stem back as low into the plant as you can reach. Although evergreen, the foliage can become a bit tired and yellow at the end of the season. If this happens, cut it right back to the ground – it will soon produce new growth.

These plants are generally trouble-free except for the occasional visit by a rogue slug. Propagation is best done by division. Avoid growing from seed as the colours will vary enormously. Plants need to be at least four years old before they flower.

Alocasia macrorrhiza
Taro

This big, leafy plant from Sri Lanka immediately brings to mind images of jungles and elephants. The leaves are huge, each with a thick midrib and fleshy veins, but there will be only five or six on the plant at any one time. Away from its native habitat, the overall size will be diminished, but could still reach 2.5m (8ft) in height with a spread of 1.8m (6ft) within a few years. The spathes appear on older plants as pale green lumps rising out of the centre. These are fairly long-lasting, then start to peel back to reveal the seed heads.

Alocasia macrorrhiza can cope with full sun in a sunny conservatory, a brightly lit spot in a shady porch or almost full shade inside a house. Lots of sun produces more flowers and seed heads but can make the foliage more of a yellowish-green. Lots of shade gives healthy-looking dark green leaves, but the flowers and seed heads are usually absent. A position somewhere between these two sites will keep the foliage a beautiful colour without sacrificing the extras.

These leafy giants need massive pots – the bigger, the better. The soil should be rich and fertile, and never be allowed to dry out. Feed throughout the growing season with liquid food at every watering. During spring and summer it is almost impossible to overfeed or overwater. Drainage must be good, though – the roots won't tolerate sitting in pools of water. Keep the leaves as humid as possible, especially in hot weather. Spray with water a couple of times a day at least.

When growth has finished for the year at the start of autumn, ease up on the watering, keeping the soil only just moist. Remove any old brown leaves and flower stems, cutting them right back to their base. These plants need to be kept frost-free, so artificial heating in winter may be necessary if the conservatory is separated from the house. Ideally, 5–6°C (41–43°F) would be preferred.

Make regular checks for red spider mites. Propagation is easy from fresh seed.

ABOVE
The bright emerald-green leaves are supported by fat, juicy stems.

BELOW
The seeds are spectacular scarlet versions of corn-on-the-cob and last for many weeks.

Aspidistra elatior
Cast-iron Plant

During Victorian times, this was probably the most popular choice of plant available. It was the perfect houseplant for dark, smoky parlours, where it could grow happily for years, thriving on almost total neglect. Although it is still popular as a houseplant because of its tough constitution, it is rarely seen in the garden. Because of its success indoors, it is usually assumed that it cannot be hardy but, in mild coastal gardens or warm inner cities, *Aspidistra elatior* is quite content, growing into bigger and bigger clumps each year.

The foliage is dark green and looks like some sort of vegetable sprouting up. Clumps take many years to form a decent size. During very cold winters, the leaves may be scorched by the frost, and the whole plant is best cut down to ground level to start again the following year. The roots, though, are completely hardy and will survive much lower temperatures.

Flowers are rarely seen, but that doesn't mean that they are non-existent. They are not held high on the usual flower stems, but appear at ground level among the leaf stalks. They look like waxy primroses with pale lemon centres and dusky pink edges. Pollination of the flowers used to be attributed to slugs, which love to rootle around these plants, but this is now known not to be true.

The common name refers to its robust nature and its ability to survive without much attention. But to get the best from this plant, a bit of love and care will pay dividends. Plant in full shade to keep the foliage a rich colour. Make sure the soil is fertile and permanently moist. Feed well in spring with a few handfuls of blood, fish and bone. Slugs love to nibble the leaves, so some sort of slug repellent will usually be necessary.

Their slow speed of growth makes them ideal for growing in a large pot; this can either be kept in a shady part of the garden or indoors. Use John Innes no. 3 compost. Indoors, slugs won't be much of a problem, although red spider mites or scale insects could be a nuisance.

Propagation is easiest by division. They are found growing naturally in parts of China, Japan and the Himalayas.

Astelia chathamica
Silver Spear

A pretty plant from the Chatham Islands, which lie off the eastern coast of New Zealand, that can survive on almost total neglect. The leaves are long and sword-shaped, and look as if they have been sprayed with metallic silver paint. Their remarkable colouring really glints in the sunlight. Each leaf gently curves outwards and can reach a length of 1.5m (5ft). Large, densely packed clumps can fill 1sq m (4sq ft) within five years of planting out if conditions are right.

The flowers are disappointingly dull after the spectacular display of the foliage. Bunches of yellow bristly things sprout out of the centre of the plant and poke through the foliage in an apologetic manner. The stem and flower spike are about 30cm (1ft) long in total and add nothing to the plant's appearance; if you wish, remove them as soon as they appear. If their dullness can be tolerated, though, patience will be rewarded by a rather colourful show of bright orange berries afterwards.

In its native habitat, *Astelia chathamica* is seen growing as an epiphyte, encircling large trees and seemingly living off nothing but fresh air. The roots cling onto the trunk, and large

plants hang off in great bunches. Observing how they grow in nature gives some excellent clues as to how much neglect they can cope with. They can survive quite well in containers that are infrequently watered, but they are ten times better planted in the ground.

Plants prefer to be in a shady spot in any well-drained soil. Once planted, leave them alone. Make sure that the chosen planting position can be its permanent home, as they cannot cope with being transplanted. Feeding is unnecessary, so is watering, except during severe drought. Overwatering will cause the whole clump to rot very speedily. Once this happens, the roots cannot support the leaves and the plant collapses. Recovery is unlikely, as new roots do not regenerate.

Although happiest in shade, a sunny spot can be tolerated but the silver colour tends to be less strong and takes on a bleached look. They are virtually maintenance-free, except for the occasional removal of an old brown leaf. Pests and diseases aren't generally a problem. Propagation is best done by division but, as it hates root disturbance, this can be tricky.

Astelia nervosa

Yet more wonderful foliage from New Zealand, this time with leaves that have a metallic bronzy sheen to them and glisten in the sunlight. This variable plant produces leaves of all different hues, from silvery green, bronze and even some with metallic reddish tints. The flowers are irrelevant, so treat this plant as a foliage plant only. The evergreen leaves can be more than 90cm (3ft) long and arch outward at the tips. Clumps are densely packed and can reach 90 x 90cm (3 x 3ft) after five years, providing the growing conditions are suitable.

Astelia nervosa is an epiphyte, which means that it prefers the high life, hanging onto trees in great clumps. However, it can also live quite happily on the ground given the right conditions. If it can survive up in the air, this gives us a clue as to how little it can tolerate being planted in soggy ground. The soil must be exceptionally well drained, so that any rain can run off immediately – planting on a sloping bank would help to meet this requirement. A shady spot gives the best colouring to the leaves, keeping them richer and darker. In bright sunlight, they can take on a paler, more bleached appearance.

A fairly rich soil also gives better results, but annual feeding is not that important.

Astelia nervosa is most useful in those shady, dry spots of the garden where little else seems to thrive. These plants can be tucked away by a shady wall or planted beneath a canopy of large trees whose roots tend to suck up all the surrounding moisture. They look much more effective in large numbers to create natural-looking drifts rather than just one or two specimens. In smaller gardens, this is obviously not possible, but even a group of three looks better than one solitary plant.

After planting, unless the following summer is exceptionally hot and dry, there is no need to water at all. In fact, the only thing likely to kill these tough plants is overwatering: the roots can't cope with even temporary waterlogging and the whole plant can collapse very quickly.

Pests and diseases aren't much of a problem, although aphids can gather around the new growth as it appears. Propagation can be done from seed, but the method of division is better, as a parent plant can be carefully selected for its colouring.

ABOVE
Astelia nervosa is the perfect choice for cold gardens.

◼ Aucuba japonica longifolia

A fine evergreen shrub from Japan, perfect for that dark, shady spot in the garden where little else will grow. The leaves are beautifully tapered and so glossy they look as if they have been treated with a leafshine spray. They have a leathery texture and are a nice shade of racing-green. The flowers are flattened clusters of dark red, and it is quite difficult to get terribly enthused about them, but they are followed by bright, oval-shaped scarlet berries, which are much more attractive.

The plant itself grows into a rounded mound without having to be clipped into shape. It fills large gaps in the garden very well, and after eight years will probably have a height and spread of about 1.5m (5ft). Its circular shape can be further enhanced by just a few snips here and there with secateurs to keep any straying shoots within its main profile.

Give *Aucuba japonica longifolia* as much shade as possible. The more shade it receives, the darker and glossier the foliage becomes. It will grow in any soil, but rich and fertile conditions give the best results. Mature shrubs can be drought tolerant, but they need a few years of being well watered first. Once they have become established, watering is rarely necessary.

These plants can be used in many different styles of garden. They blend in well with traditional planting schemes, but look just as good in jungly gardens, where they make a fine contrast with plants that have large, soft foliage such as *Paulownia tomentosa* or with palms such as *Trachycarpus fortunei*. They have a strong-enough presence to be planted as a focal feature in a shady front garden. As they can reach 2.5m (8ft), they could be used for subtle screening against a boundary wall or fence. In larger gardens they can be planted in any woodland area underneath the canopies of tall trees.

This is a low-maintenance plant that can be left to get on with life without much assistance, although it does appreciate generous feeding with blood fish and bone, which should be applied in late spring. This plant does not perform well in a pot, and the foliage is difficult to keep a good colour without feeding heavily at least twice per year.

Pests and diseases are not usually a problem. Propagation is easily done from cuttings.

ABOVE
The large, lustrous berries are produced in copious amounts, and can stay on the plant for many weeks.

Azorina vidalii

SYN. *Campanula vidalii*

A shrubby perennial plant from the Azores that consists of lots of artistically arranged long, glossy leaves. It is slow-growing and ideal for a container, where it can live happily for years. In mild gardens, it can live outside all year, either in a large pot or planted directly into the ground. In colder areas, it makes a fine addition to the conservatory or greenhouse.

Flower spikes appear during the summer, opening up into dozens of large waxy bells of the palest china-pink. They have a delicate appearance but, unfortunately, not a delicate fragrance to match. In fact, they have the aroma of unwashed socks about them. The flowers are long-lived, lasting for several months. Their unattractive scent can only be detected from very close up, so there is nothing unpleasant about having them in the conservatory.

Azorina vidalii is a manageable plant, growing to not much more than 60cm (2ft) tall and 60cm (2ft) across, although the flower stems are held well above the foliage. It is easy to look after, too, requiring little attention. Any older lower leaves that have turned brown remain on the plant, instead of conveniently falling off. These can gather in large numbers, but pulling them off improves the plant's appearance enormously. It also helps to keep the plant healthy – if kept under glass during the winter, poor ventilation can cause botrytis, and the fluffy grey mould that accompanies this is most likely to affect the older lower leaves.

Any soil is suitable, providing it is free-draining because too much water retained around the roots can be fatal. If grown in a terracotta pot, use John Innes no. 3 compost. Lots of regular irrigation is necessary during the growing season, with just an occasional watering in winter. Feed well with blood, fish and bone annually in spring.

It is happy in full sun or partial shade, but needs to be sheltered from cold winds. Outdoors, the only problem is likely to be from green aphids, which find the new shoots appealing. Cut the flower stems off as low as possible into the plant immediately after flowering has finished. Propagation is easy from fresh seed.

ABOVE
The glossy rosettes of *Azorina vidalii* make a wonderful addition to the conservatory.

ABOVE
The sugar-pink waxy bells last for many weeks.

Baccharis patagonica
Magellan's Daisy Bush

This tough little evergreen shrub has a gently rounded shape and masses of tiny glossy leaves. Although it will grow almost anywhere, it is in coastal gardens that its character is most appreciated. In its native habitats of southern Chile, it copes brilliantly with being buffeted by the sort of howling, icy, salt-laden gales that would make almost any other climate in the world seem good-natured.

Baccharis patagonica grows slowly into a dense mound no more than 1.5m (5ft) both in height and width, and this will take at least ten years to achieve. It forms its dome shape naturally, but this can be helped further by regular light clipping. This will make the shape even tighter and the foliage even thicker.

The pale lemon daisy flowers are delightful, appearing in summer in copious amounts. Their best feature is their marvellous fragrance – the whole garden can be filled with the aroma of freshly baked fairy cakes as the scent wafts around on the summer breeze.

This plant is just as happy in full sun as it is in deep shade, and can grow in most soils except in very dry or very boggy conditions. It prefers to be kept just moist all year round. It is a useful shape and size for filling in gaps in borders or shrubberies, and also seems quite happy under trees where the soil is often lacking in nutrients because of greedy tree roots. And it is an essential addition to the most exposed, windy positions either on the coast or on hilltops.

Pruning can take place either in early spring or immediately after flowering. Don't cut into the old wood, as not all branches recover from such brutal treatment. Feeding isn't essential, but a small amount of blood, fish and bone can be given in the spring if the soil is very poor.

Propagation can be done at almost any time of year from cuttings. The most common unwanted guests are likely to be aphids, especially if the summer is excessively hot. The name *Baccharis* is thought to be derived from Bacchus, the god of wine, a reference to the spicy aroma of the roots, which were sometimes added during winemaking.

Tough this plant may be, but it tends to be quite short-lived. So, if yours has been growing well for twelve years and then dies for no apparent reason, it isn't necessarily your fault.

ABOVE
Baccharis patagonica is the toughest possible choice for gardens regularly battered by salt-laden gales.

Billbergia nutans
Queen's Tears

An exotic-looking plant, related to the pineapple, with shiny, strap-like leaves surrounding an urn-shaped centre – a clever structure designed to catch every drop of rainwater, a feature that's much more necessary in its native Brazil than in soggy, more temperate climates. Large flamingo-pink spears emerge from between the foliage and open up into pretty pink and green blossoms.

This clump-forming plant, which can eventually spread to about 90cm (3ft) across, will grow almost anywhere, and looks most effective planted in small groups, rather than as individual plants. Waiting for single plants to become decent-sized drifts takes years.

Although hardy outside in mild gardens, it makes an excellent houseplant and seems to thrive on neglect indoors. It is also ideal for growing in containers outside, and can sit in the same pot for years. It makes an interesting groundcover plant for spreading around under trees where the soil is often dry and poor. All conditions can be tolerated, from full sun to deep shade, but taking care to get the position absolutely perfect gives rewarding results. In full sun, masses more flower stems are produced, but the foliage can take on a yellowish tinge; in deep shade, the leaves stay a deep rich glossy green but there are fewer flowers. Getting a balance between the two will give healthy-looking leaves and a good crop of blooms too.

Lots of moisture is appreciated, but the drainage must be sharp to ensure that water doesn't gather around the roots. These plants can be grown as epiphytes, hanging off trees, and can give a Caribbean look to planting schemes if they are tied onto hardy palm trees: either wedge them between branches or place them on a bed of moss and tie them onto the trunk. Try adding a really jungly flavour to the garden by forcing them inside the hairy bits on the trunks of the *Trachycarpus fortunei* palm. They thrive when grown this way and, when established, can actually start to climb further up into the tree.

Billbergia nutans is almost maintenance-free. It needs little water and virtually no food. Even pests and diseases are a rare occurrence. The easiest way to propagate is by separating rooted suckers away from the parent plant.

ABOVE
The pretty blossoms of *Billbergia nutans* are very showy and tropical, and nod gently in the breeze. (*Nutans* is Latin for nodding.)

Brachyglottis repanda x greyi

An inspired piece of hybridizing between two New Zealand plants has produced huge floppy leaves up to 25cm (10in) long and 13cm (5in) across. They have a beautifully soft texture and are pale grey on the top and an unusual silvery white underneath. Their remarkable colouring makes them very noticeable in the garden.

Lots of yellow daisy flowers are produced in the summer, but try to be hardhearted about these and cut them off as soon as they appear. They are not especially attractive, but their appearance isn't the reason for removing them. By chopping them off, all the plant's energy will be diverted from flower production into making the leaves even bigger and better.

The overall size of mature plants is unlikely to exceed 1.8m (6ft) in height with a 1.2m (4ft) spread in an average temperate garden. Older plants can become leggy, but an occasional light pruning will keep the plant more compact. Prune gently with secateurs, not shears, by carefully cutting across the stems so that the leaves are left intact and not sliced in half.

These plants need full sun as well as lots of space around them to create a good airflow through the foliage. A coastal garden with a gentle breeze blowing would be a suitable spot for them. Damp, still, shady conditions can make these plants susceptible to botrytis, which produces lots of fluffy mould, particularly on the lower leaves. This is not only harmful, but also unsightly.

The soil must be very well drained and preferably quite rich, as fertile conditions also contribute to the leaf size. Mulching underneath with slate chippings or pea shingle helps to stop rain splashing wet mud onto the lower leaves, which is not only unsightly across such pale foliage, but can also accelerate botrytis. This plant is excellent in gravel gardens, where everything is mulched, and also good planted on a slight slope so that all excess rain drains away quickly.

Feed well every year during the spring with generous helpings of blood, fish and bone. Water regularly when first planted, but after the first season this chore isn't usually necessary. Apart from botrytis, pests and diseases aren't often a problem. Propagation is done by taking cuttings.

ABOVE
The leaves are large, soft and floppy, like lambs' ears, with snowy white undersides.

Buxus sempervirens
Box

Although a perfectly nice evergreen shrub or small tree, *Buxus sempervirens* is rarely seen growing in its natural form. The small leaves and slow speed of growth make it ideal for clipping. As it takes years for plants to become a decent size, it is usual to buy them at the size required. Shaping very young plants into full-size balls or cones is best left to the experts. Then, all there is to worry about is maintaining its current structure. The only exception to this would be miniature box hedging, so popular in traditional gardens, herb gardens and parterres. To buy enough mature plants for an instant effect would cost a small fortune.

Cones, balls or even cubes can be used in a variety of ways. They are ideal for lining walkways, or for either side of doors and gates. They are brilliant for growing in pots, as they can sit in the same container for years. Grown this way, they can be used singly or in long rows along paved areas. Different shapes also look effective grouped together. Occasionally oblong blocks are available for impatient and extravagant gardeners to make instant dividing boundaries between different sections of the

garden, or they can be placed in pots along a roof terrace to create some privacy.

Clipping should be done little and often. Try using good-quality lightweight shears. Shears need a bit of practice, especially on curved shapes, but it is worth persevering, as the result is far superior to anything that could ever be achieved with secateurs. Avoid clipping in bright sunshine or when it is frosty: both conditions can scorch the cut ends of the leaves. By cutting little and often, it remains easy to follow the exact shape. For gardeners who are especially fussy, clip the whole plant once, then do it all again immediately afterwards for a really fine finish. If you could stand doing it a third time, lovely velvety green surfaces will result.

Buxus sempervirens will grow almost anywhere and can tolerate most light levels and any type of soil. For best results, though, grow in bright conditions in fertile well-drained soil. Feed with blood, fish and bone in spring. Plants grown permanently in pots would also benefit from a helping of potash food in autumn to keep them a good colour in winter. Keep plants moist to prevent red spider mites becoming a problem.

ABOVE
Box is usually seen trimmed into all different shapes and sizes. Its foliage is very dense, and the more it is clipped, the bushier it becomes.

Callistemon subulatus
Bottle Brush

An Australian shrubby plant grown mostly for its spectacular 'bottle-brush' flowers. There are lots of *Callistemon* plants available but this one is the hardiest – it can be grown in cold inland gardens where most of the other types would fail. It's an untidy, sprawling shrub that benefits from the occasional hack with a pair of shears to keep it looking groomed. Mature plants can have a height and spread of around 2.5m (8ft) after fifteen years.

The flowers are large, cylinder-shaped and fluffy. They are bright red and produced in prolific quantities during the summer. The evergreen foliage is small and narrow, and surprisingly prickly. If this plant is left to grow naturally as a shrub, it must be planted directly into the ground. Plants trained as small trees can be grown in pots, providing the containers are huge and the crown of foliage is kept clipped into a controlled shape.

The planting position must be in full sun. The soil type can be peat, loam or clay, and either neutral to acid; chalky, alkaline soils must be avoided. For containers, use an ericaceous compost.

The small, sparse foliage makes *Callistemon subulatus* perfect for coastal gardens, where sea breezes filter through the plants without causing any harm. They look good as single specimens, or they can be planted wherever a softer look is required to contrast with larger-leaved architectural plants. They are also well suited to Mediterranean-style gardens, coping admirably with the poor, dry conditions often associated with such planting schemes.

Newly planted specimens must be well watered until established. After their first season, irrigation is rarely necessary and they become very drought-tolerant. If grown in pots, they must be watered throughout spring and summer when they are actively growing and during the flowering season. Any pruning should be done immediately after the flowers have finished. Pests and diseases are rarely a nuisance. Propagation is easy from seed, which can remain viable for many years after harvesting.

ABOVE
The dense foliage of *Callistemon subulatus* copes brilliantly with coastal winds.

BELOW
Vibrant red 'bottle-brush' flowers appear in summer.

Camellia japonica

With its large, glossy leaves and beautifully exotic flowers, this lovely evergreen plant has all the basic ingredients of an architectural plant. But, to make it a full member of this exclusive horticultural club, some pruning and shaping is necessary. By training it as a young plant into a small half-standard tree, it takes on a completely new identity. As a proper mini tree, it becomes better and better with age. The trunk gnarls and thickens, and the mop-head crown of foliage becomes more and more dense with each season's new growth.

This tough Japanese tree is the hardiest of all the camellias, and can survive in almost any climate. It has many named varieties to its credit, which come in a range of colours from pure white, all kinds of pink, through to various shades of red.

Trees that are kept clipped into shape can live for years in a large container. Pot them up in a mixture of peat-based compost and loam. This provides a rich-enough soil to support both the foliage and a good crop of flowers. The compost must never be allowed to dry out, especially while the flower buds are forming.

Otherwise, instead of turning into lovely blooms, they will shrivel and fall off. Plants cannot stand waterlogging either, so aim for a good moisture balance. Regular helpings of cold tea keep the foliage a deep glossy green.

Whether trained as a tree or left as a shrub, *Camellia japonica* will be much happier planted directly into the ground. Shrubs don't have to be shapeless and can be pruned into nicely curved mounds. Pruning should be done immediately after flowering, usually in early summer. Plant in a shady spot, sheltered from strong cold winds, in moist soil that is neutral to acid. Chalky soil will turn the leaves a sickly yellow colour. Feed annually with either large helpings of well-rotted manure or blood, fish and bone.

The main pests of this plant are various types of scale insects, but these affect plants in pots more than those in the ground. Scraping them off at the first sign is preferable to spraying them with chemicals. Keep a regular check for these beasts, as their population can increase massively once they take hold. Propagation is best from cuttings, but it will take years to produce a decent-sized plant.

ABOVE
The large exotic blooms come in many colours, but this rich red colouring is a personal favourite.

Canna indica
Indian Shot or **Canna Lily**

A splendid leafy addition to exotic planting schemes, having large, banana-type leaves and bright yellow and red flowers in the summer. It is an herbaceous plant, dying back to the rootstock every winter. Fast-growing, it can produce 1.5m (5ft) of new growth every year. Plants become bulkier as they age, eventually forming substantial clumps about 90cm (3ft) across. *Canna indica* is one the hardiest canna lilies available – its large leaves even seem to cope well with sea breezes and salty gales.

As *Canna indica* puts on serious amounts of growth during each season, give plants the best possible start by providing rich soil and applying copious amounts of water for the entire growing season. Enrich the soil with heaps of well-rotted manure and use a foliar feed as a top-up with every watering. Full sun is best but light shade gives good results too.

Plant in reasonable-sized groups for maximum impact. They look good with all types of architectural planting, adding splashes of colour here and there throughout planting schemes of palms, bamboos and anything big-leaved and jungly. In milder areas these plants can be left outside all year. In cold, wet areas, they are best dug up every winter and stored in dry peat in a greenhouse in exactly the same way that dahlias are treated. Alternatively, grow them in large pots that can be moved under the shelter of a carport or inside a cool shed for the winter months. Another option is to leave them where they are in the garden, wait until they have been blackened by the frost, cut them down to ground level with secateurs and mulch heavily with straw or bracken.

Apart from feeding and watering, very little maintenance is required. At the end of the season, as the leaves start to turn yellow, gradually cut them off. After flowering, don't be in too much of a hurry to chop down the stems as large crinkly seed capsules form. These are attractive in their own right, eventually splitting open to reveal large spherical seeds that are black and glossy. Use these fresh seeds for any propagation.

The main pests of this plant are slugs. The tender juicy leaves are a magnet for them, and repellent should be applied routinely.

Canna iridiflora
Giant Canna Lily

The very best *Canna* lily of them all, consisting of a huge mass of giant leaves topped with the most outrageous shocking pink flowers. *Canna iridiflora* can easily put on 2.5m (8ft) of growth per season before dying back for the winter and re-emerging the following year with even more vim and vigour. Although not very hardy, it can just about cope with temperatures down to –4°C (25°F). This plant is essential for making a seasonal leafy statement with other exotic plants. Its loud colouring looks perfectly in place with palms, bamboos, bananas, paulownias and other jungly plants. Don't try to grow these in containers – they are too large and energetic.

Plant them in a sheltered position away from strong winds. Because of their enormous leaves, they perform less well than other *Canna* in a windy spot. Full sun or light shade, as well as very rich, moist soil, are required. Apply well-rotted manure annually in early spring, and use a foliar feed as an extra boost with each watering. Copious amounts of water will be necessary for the whole growing season to get the very best from these astonishing plants. If lots of lush leafy foliage is produced every year but no flowers, try adding tomato food to their diet once a week from mid-spring to mid-summer. This will provide the extra potash needed to induce flower production.

In mild gardens, plants can be left outside all winter, cutting back the old foliage to ground level as soon as it has become frosted or yellowed. For colder areas, when the foliage has been chopped back, dig up the clumps and overwinter in a greenhouse. Store each clump in dry peat under the greenhouse bench in just the same way as dahlias.

Buy these plants from specialist nurseries, which pride themselves on accurate labelling, or when they are in flower so you can see what you are getting.

The easiest method of propagation is by division, splitting up the clumps just as they start to send up new buds for the spring. Make sure each divided section has at least one new bud on it. Use slug repellent as a matter of routine.

Cistus lusitanicus 'Decumbens'
Rock Rose

Lovely blobby mounds of fuzzy grey-green foliage give off a pleasantly pungent aroma in sunny, hot weather, reminding us of lazy, summer holidays spent in the south of France. The evergreen, rounded heaps can spread 1.2m (4ft) across while keeping to a height of only 90cm (3ft). Their curved shape requires no assistance from gardeners once it is planted out.

In early summer, the whole plant is covered with flowers as delicate as crêpe paper. They are pure white with just a few perfectly placed maroon blotches circling the centre. Each flower lasts for only a few hours, but they are so plentiful that a constant display is provided for many weeks.

Full sun is essential, and plants thrive in the kind of poor, dry conditions that most plants loathe. Plant into soil that has sharp drainage – even shallow chalky soils would be okay. Planting on a slope or bank would also be beneficial, so that all surplus rain runs off immediately. Water in new plants until they become established and their roots are well settled in. After this, watering is rarely required. They are among the most drought-tolerant plants on the market.

Position them towards the front of the border, so their flowers can be fully appreciated. In spacious gardens, they look good in large groups, but they also look fine as single specimens if space is limited. Perfect for Mediterranean-style planting schemes, they also make a soft and fluffy contrast to spiky desert plants that require similar conditions. They look wonderful cascading over dry walls or interspersed throughout large rockeries. They can be grown in coastal gardens and seem to thrive in the salty seaside air.

Don't bother with annual feeding. The poorer the soil, the more plentiful the flowers. If the overall shape needs tidying up, clip lightly with shears as soon as flowering has finished. Take care not to cut back into old wood.

In cold, wet conditions, botrytis (grey fluffy mould) might be a problem, and in hot summers, a few aphids might give some grief. Generally, though, most pests keep away. Propagation is easy from semi-ripe cuttings taken in late summer.

ABOVE
The flowers open fully only on sunny days. They are of such a fine texture that no cutting is required to remove the spent ones – they just curl up and fall off in a flutter.

LEFT
Growing your own lemons in the conservatory is a tempting idea.

Citrus
Lemon, Orange, Kumquat or Clementine

All types of *Citrus* are beautiful, and everybody loves them. The fabulous smell of *Citrus* blossom is irresistible, and the idea of being able to pick your own home-grown lemons or oranges is very tempting. Unfortunately, they are an absolute devil to grow in conservatories, and probably at least 90 per cent of all plants meet with a slow and horrible death. They have all the problems associated with growing plants in containers, and a whole lot more besides. But if their fussy cultivation requirements can be met, having a thriving, healthy plant is a rewarding experience.

Although growing little trees from fruit pips is a popular idea, the chance of them growing into mature plants, dripping with home-grown fruit, is more or less nil. Start by buying a decent-sized one from a specialist nursery, preferably choosing it yourself – that way, you know exactly what you are getting. Most *Citrus* plants are sold as ready-formed little trees. They are usually on display in various stages of flowering or fruiting. Their luscious fruits, heavily scented flowers and lovely glossy leaves are almost impossible to ignore.

As *Citrus* are not hardy, the conservatory is usually the only option for a permanent home. Position them in a well-lit spot that offers a bit of light shade, so that the scorching heat of the sun is filtered – the full heat of the summer sunshine under glass is too severe. *Citrus* prefer to live in even temperatures, and this in itself is quite a challenge. Conservatories can be boiling hot by day and rather chilly at night, especially during the winter. Try to aim for a level temperature of around 20–25°C (68–77°F) during the summer and about 10°C (50°F) during the winter. Plants can adjust gradually – it's the sudden fluctuation of temperatures that causes problems. A *Citrus* plant is the 'prima donna' of the plant world and can drop all its leaves in a fit of pique without any warning. Transferring it outside for the summer months and back inside for the winter would be a useful thing to do.

ABOVE
Citrus japonica (kumquat) produces little fruits that have a sweet edible outer peel surrounding a tangy juicy interior.

The type of heating used indoors needs to be considered too. Underfloor heating should be avoided. *Citrus* hate this and can shed their leaves within a couple of days of being subjected to it. Hot air heating won't do the plant much good either. Gentle heat from warm pipes or radiators is fine as long as the plant isn't in direct contact with them. Old-fashioned portable gas heaters are quite good, as these dry out the atmosphere less than most heaters would – it's the hot, dry air that we are trying to avoid. At any time of year, humidity is important. The leaves like moist air around them, and regular misting is preferred, especially in the summer. The flower buds also enjoy this treatment, as they can shed in large numbers before they get the chance to fruit if the air is too dry.

Grow these plants in large terracotta pots, using John Innes no. 3 compost with extra grit stirred in for impeccable drainage. Watering is also a tricky business. The compost likes to be soaked, then allowed to dry out slightly before the next watering. Don't allow it to dry out totally, though, otherwise that's another load of dropped leaves to clear up. Boggy conditions cannot be tolerated either.

Feeding is another important issue, and there are some excellent *Citrus* food products on the market. They come ready prepared in tubs, with one formula for winter and a different one for summer. These should be added during every single watering. The effect this has on the plants is amazing and, if the heating, watering and light levels are being monitored too, there starts to be more than a sporting chance of cultivating a fine-looking specimen.

Plants that are healthy and thriving can shrug off pests and diseases much better than plants that are stressed and neglected. *Citrus* can experience just about every problem known to man, and very regular checks need to be carried out for scale insects, aphids, mealy bugs, red spider mites and whitefly.

Various mildews and moulds can appear as well, just to keep things interesting. It's all a bit of a challenge.

It's worth bearing in mind that large, mature *Citrus* plants seem to be easier to look after than small plants. After all, they've been around a long time and have learned to cope with life. The snag with large specimens, though, is their cost. To pay lots of money for a fusspot of a tree would seem to be rather a gamble. One solution would be to seek out a maintenance contract with a conservatory plant specialist. These marvellous people visit your house regularly throughout the year and keep the plants in beautiful condition, leaving you just to enjoy them and pretend that you've done all the hard work yourself.

Corokia x virgata
Wire Netting Plant

A pretty, evergreen shrub from New Zealand with unusual colouring. The tiny leaves are dark green with a metallic bronzy sheen on the upper surface and powdery white underneath. The sparse foliage can be encouraged to become denser and bushier by regular clipping. Masses of little yellow daisy flowers appear in summer on the previous year's growth, followed by lots of bright orange berries.

The plant is a naturally occurring hybrid between two plants (*Corokia cotoneaster* and *Corokia buddleioides*), and it is one of my favourite New Zealand plants. It should be much more widely grown, as it is not only attractive but useful, too. It is very easy to cultivate and copes well with harsh conditions.

The height of a mature plant outside its native habitat, even after many years, is unlikely to exceed 2.5m (8ft). This makes it an ideal specimen plant for any sunny border. Its open habit and light colouring are a good contrast to plants with large green leaves. It looks perfectly in place whether planted in a Mediterranean-style garden or a traditional border. Its salt resistance is excellent, making it an essential addition to any coastal garden, and its wind resistance means that not only can it cope with strong sea winds, but it can also tolerate windy conditions inland, such as those experienced on exposed hilltops.

Its tiny leaves make it a suitable candidate for clipping. It makes an brilliant hedge, and the more it is trimmed, the thicker the foliage becomes. It can also be shaped in the same way as box plants and used in containers as cones, balls or domes. *Corokia* x *virgata* should be trimmed little and often, while taking care not to remove any flower buds or berries.

Apart from requiring a sunny position, it can grow almost anywhere. Soil can be chalk, clay, peat, sand or loam, as long as it does not become boggy. Good drainage is important, so even poor flinty soil would be suitable. Once established, irrigation is largely unnecessary, unless it is being confined to a pot, in which case regular watering will always be needed.

Feed every spring with a few handfuls of blood, fish and bone sprinkled around the base. Pests and diseases are virtually unknown to this plant. Propagation is easy from cuttings.

Crocosmia 'Lucifer'
Montbretia

Most *Crocosmia* plants have bright orange or vermilion flowers, but the variety 'Lucifer' has the loudest red of all. The fiery scarlet flowers are produced in copious amounts on the ends of long, wiry stems. They are long-lasting and a popular choice for flower arrangers. However, as they add such strong splashes of colour to a garden, it's probably better to leave them on the plant to enjoy outdoors.

They are grown from corms and die back each autumn. Growth starts during the spring, sending up lots of grassy leaves that open out into narrow sword shapes. The foliage can be up to 90cm (3ft) tall, with the flower spikes adding another 60cm (2ft) on top of that. *Crocosmia* 'Lucifer' starts to flower in late summer and carries on through the autumn, when most other plants have stopped flowering for the year.

These plants are best grown in large drifts for dramatic effect. They bulk up quickly and can gradually spread over a fairly wide area. A small woodland garden, where they can naturalize without having their wanderlust curbed, would be perfect. If they outgrow their allocated space in the garden, dig up chunks with a spade and either replant them elsewhere or give them away to appreciative gardening chums.

They are hardy almost anywhere, but in exceptionally cold gardens, the corms are best lifted and stored in trays of dryish peat under a greenhouse bench for the winter. They can be grown in full sun or light shade, sheltered from strong winds. The soil, which should be light, free-draining and fertile, must be kept moist throughout the growing season.

Generous quantities of rich food such as well-rotted manure can be applied each spring – they are surprisingly greedy for such fragile-looking plants. In late autumn, after the foliage has turned brown, cut it back to slightly above ground level, leaving just enough stem as a marker for where the plants are. The only other maintenance often required is to support each clump using canes and twine to keep them upright – the combined weight of foliage and flowers can make everything top-heavy.

Pests and diseases are not usually a problem, and propagation is easily done by dividing the clumps with a spade.

ABOVE
The flowers of *Crocosmia* 'Lucifer' are so bright that they are almost fluorescent.

Cynara cardunculus
Cardoon

Cynara cardunculus is great fun to grow. It's a huge brute of a plant that grows with amazing speed after its winter dormancy, putting on noticeable new growth every day during spring. The deeply cut leaves are soft to the touch, pale greenish-grey in colour and achieve enormous dimensions. An established plant that has been overwintered in the ground can easily put on 2.5m (8ft) in height and over 1.8m (6ft) in width during the growing season. It looks just like a giant vegetable, which, in a way, is exactly what it is. In France it is commonly grown for its edible stems, but in most gardens it is used as an ornamental plant, perfect for the back of planting schemes or as a special focal feature where all of it is fully on view.

Rising above the foliage in late summer, the flower stems become visible. The flower heads start off looking like mini artichokes, then open up into large thistles of the most astonishing electric-blue.

After flowering, the leaves look good for several months, but in winter they can start to look a bit tired and yellow, and are best cut down to the ground. Within a short time, even in the depths of winter, new buds start to form at the base of the old stalks and a small amount of growth is produced. With the onset of warmer weather, growth accelerates rapidly to begin the whole process over again. New plants should be planted in late spring or early summer and left in the ground permanently.

The soil must be rich and fertile to achieve maximum growth, and masses of water is required during the first season until plants become established. In subsequent years, watering is usually necessary only in exceptionally hot dry summers, although extra top-ups of water during any growing season are beneficial. Feed heavily with lots of well-rotted manure or several handfuls of blood, fish and bone annually each spring. Propagation is easy from seed, which can produce variable plants, some with much more deeply cut leaves than others.

Slugs and snails adore these plants, and black aphids love to congregate all over the flowers.

Danae racemosa
Alexandrian Laurel

Describing *Danae racemosa* is not easy, as it falls somewhere between a miniature bamboo and a bunch of asparagus. It is a fascinating plant and deserves a much more interesting description than its usual 'medium-sized shrub'. (Surely there can be no greater insult to a plant than this disparaging term?) It was named after Danae, a daughter of the splendidly named King Acrisius of Argos.

The new shoots are the start of its 'asparagus' phase, poking up through the ground in spring. These grow to about 60–90cm (2–3ft) and open out into wiry steams with leaves along the length. The leaves are not proper leaves at all and are blessed with the delightful name of 'cladode', which is horti-speak for a sort of flattened branch. Many shoots are sent out each spring, and remain all year round. As the plant matures, larger clumps of it begin to form, hence its 'bamboo' phase.

Danae racemosa is evergreen and very slow to spread. Even after ten years, it will probably extend to only around a metre (yard). After a hot summer, masses of bright scarlet berries smother the whole plant. They last for months

– all through the autumn and most of the winter too. Apart from its desirable appearance, this plant is extremely useful for difficult places in the garden where little else will grow. Deep, dark shade can be tolerated and so can dry conditions, making *Danae racemosa* especially valuable for growing beneath evergreen trees. Given a choice, though, this plant would always opt for light shade in moist soil to give the best and fastest results.

It can be grown in a pot with a fair amount of success due to its slow growth – use John Innes no. 3 compost, and never let it dry out.

This plant is a great favourite with flower arrangers, as it still looks fresh after several weeks in a vase. Propagation is easy by dividing up existing clumps. It is virtually maintenance-free, although a light feed in spring with blood, fish and bone would be appreciated. Pests and diseases are rarely a problem for plants growing directly in the ground. However, if they're grown in a container, vine weevils are almost guaranteed to be a nuisance. Always use soil-based compost for containers, not peat-based, as this helps to keep these vile creatures at bay.

ABOVE
Danae racemosa is one of the best plants for difficult areas of the garden. It thrives in dry shade where little else will grow.

Daphne odora 'Aureomarginata'

A beautiful little evergreen that grows into a nice blobby shape without the assistance of any clipping. These lovely mounds grow very slowly, and after ten years they're unlikely to be any bigger than 60cm (2ft) tall and 90cm (3ft) across. The shiny leaves are fresh green, subtly edged with pale cream variegation. The flowers open up during the winter and last for a couple of months. These small, flattened clusters of rose-pink blossoms give out the most heavenly perfume.

This is one of the best possible choices for a chalky garden. Unusually for a variegated plant, it is hardier and more robust than the straight green version. The only slight drawback is that it can be a bit short-lived and may have to be replaced occasionally. It is rare to see a mature clump more than 1.2m (4ft) wide.

Choose the planting position carefully because, once planted, *Daphne odora* 'Aureomarginata' is unlikely to survive being moved at a later date. A spot in full sun or light shade will give good results. The soil should be neutral to alkaline, and kept just moist. Never allow it to dry out or become too boggy. Good drainage is essential.

Plant towards the front of a sunny border, either singly or in small groups. Underneath windows or near doors are also good planting spots, so that their winter colour can be frequently viewed and their scent inhaled. At this time of year they are especially valuable, as little else in the garden is putting on much of a performance. Don't try to confine these plants to containers; they are short-lived enough as it is without subjecting them to the stress of living in a pot.

Give a light helping of blood, fish and bone in late spring. No other maintenance is generally needed. Small sprigs can be cut off for use indoors – the perfume is very strong and one cutting at a time is enough. Cuttings can also be used for propagation, although *Daphne odora* 'Aureomarginata' is such a slow-growing plant, there is never very much spare material to propagate from.

The only pests likely to give any grief are green aphids, which love to feast on the new growing tips.

ABOVE
The heavenly scent from the flowers lasts for many weeks during late winter.

LEFT
The bright
purple berries of
Dianella tasmanica
last for months.

Dianella tasmanica
Tasmanian Flax Lily

A slow-growing plant like a miniature *Phormium* that can sit in a pot for years. The evergreen flax-like leaves form a clump that spreads gradually to fill a space of only 60cm (2ft) square after ten years. The height at this age will be around 60–90cm (2–3ft). It's a very tidy, upright plant that needs no support and little maintenance.

The foliage is pleasant enough, but it's the flowers and berries that are the really attractive features. Long flower stems rise above the leaves during summer and open up into lots of tiny purple and yellow flowers, which last for many weeks. These are followed by berries of an extraordinary dark purplish-blue, which hang onto the plant for several months.

These plants are easy to cultivate. Use John Innes no. 3 compost for container-grown specimens, and water regularly throughout the growing season. They are happy in sun or shade. Feed annually in spring with a small handful of blood, fish and bone. Remove older leaves that have gone yellow or brown, and cut off spent flower stems as low into the plant as you can.

Although suitable for pots, these plants are much happier in the ground, where they can naturalize and give a better display. Any soil will suffice, but rich fertile loam is preferred, as it holds onto moisture without becoming waterlogged, which is exactly what *Dianella tasmanica* requires. Plants are fine in full sun but even better in shade, where their foliage stays a stronger colour, and the flowers and berries are more noticeable. They look effective planted in larger groups in the garden or near ponds, and are particularly striking used as groundcover under the canopies of evergreen trees, but more irrigation might be necessary, as large tree roots tend to guzzle up all available water. They associate well with tree ferns such as *Dicksonia antarctica*, but also look quite at home next to more ordinary plants in herbaceous borders.

Pests and diseases aren't usually a problem. Propagation is easy, either from fresh seed or by dividing the plant into sections by slicing through it with a spade. Blood, fish and bone can be used to feed large clumps in the garden by sprinkling it through the plants. Take care to hose it in afterwards so that none is left touching the leaves, which could scorch if rain doesn't appear for several days.

Echium fastuosum
Pride of Madeira

SYN. *Echium candicans*

Echium fastuosum has everything an exotic shrub should have. It is evergreen and remains a compact size, making it suitable for even the smallest mild garden. The foliage is large and tapered, forming rosettes on the ends of each stem. The soft and felty leaves can be blue-grey on some plants, grey-green on others. It is a variable plant and usually grown from seed, which can produce leaves of all different shapes and sizes because of its promiscuous nature.

The stems are long and untidy but attractive in their own right because of the tiny white bristly hairs that cover them. In twilight they form ghostly silhouettes. *Echium fastuosum* is reasonably fast-growing, reaching a height and width of about 90cm (3ft) after five or six years. It doesn't like being pruned, so its sprawling nature can't be tidied up. Mature plants can take on a long, leggy look and are best replaced every few years.

The flowers are produced in late spring or early summer. The spikes emerge from the centre of each rosette and are the most amazing shade of royal blue. It is at this stage that these plants are at their most irresistible –

there really is very little else like them in the garden. Because of their tendency to hybridize, though, sometimes a blend of other colours creeps in. The flowers last for many weeks and can be carefully cut back low into each leafy rosette when finished.

It is tricky to accommodate these plants in gardens – although they are not remotely hardy, they need to be planted directly in the ground outdoors. They hate being confined to pots unless they are really enormous ones. They love the indoor atmosphere of conservatories but don't like having their roots restricted. Indoors, they are best grown for a couple of seasons only and then disposed of.

Outdoors, find a spot in full sun. These plants are fine in exposed coastal gardens or sheltered inner city ones. The soil must be poor and exceptionally well drained – waterlogging will kill them in double-quick time. Choose the planting position carefully as they won't survive being transplanted later on. Water new plants frequently until established, then ignore them. Even feeding is not necessary. Pests and diseases aren't usually a problem.

ABOVE
The foliage of
Echium fastuosum
is beautifully soft
to the touch.

Echium pininiana
Tree Echium

Echium pininiana reigns supreme as King of All the Exotics. If your garden is a mild one, this woody herb is essential. Warm inner city gardens are ideal, but milder coastal gardens are best of all, as this plant thrives in the salty sea air. It looks spectacular in large groups, but if this is not possible due to lack of space, try to find room for a small gathering of at least five.

Plants have a life cycle that spreads over two years, starting with the planting of small seedlings in early spring. These will grow fairly rapidly during their first growing season, forming leafy masses 1.2–1.5m (4–5ft) tall by the end of the summer. The stems will be quite thick and woody, and the leaves large and lush, with a tropical aura. Getting plants through their first winter is the real challenge, as they are difficult to wrap up and protect from frost.

Assuming they have come through winter unscathed, this is when the fun begins. Growth starts early, usually at the beginning of spring. With surprising rapidity, the stem starts to get longer and longer, and the new foliage smaller and smaller, as the stem romps away into the air. By late spring, the stems can be towering 3.7m (12ft) into the air, and the flower buds are becoming more obvious. They cover the entire top half of the stem, which by now has reached its maximum height and tapered off at the top. The flowers are a truly wonderful sight, opening out into hundreds of purplish-blue blossoms. They last for many weeks but then the plant dies. One compensation, though, is that many seeds will probably be scattered around the garden and will pop up in the most unexpected places for many years to come.

These plants are rarely successful in pots. They need to be planted out in full sun or light shade in any good-quality soil. Good drainage is vital. Never transplant them – they hate root disturbance. Watering is required only when newly planted. If planted late in the season, the two-year cycle can extend into a third growing season. Pests and diseases aren't usually a problem. Propagation is easy, providing the seed is really fresh.

ABOVE
The woody stems are densely covered with bristles that rub off easily, causing an itchy rash if they get under the skin. Take care when handling the stems, and always wear gloves.

BELOW
The purplish-blue blossoms are not only a joy to look at, but also sheer heaven for the local bees.

Ephedra
Mormon's Tea

There are several species of this weird-looking plant, all so similar that even the experts have difficulty telling them apart. They are all evergreen, many are fully hardy, and they are wonderfully different from most other plants found in the garden. *Ephedra* consist of thick, feathery bright green masses that creep along the ground or tumble over walls and banks, providing total cover. The stems are slender and jointed with small scale-like leaves, giving the appearance of a conifer crossed with the horsetail weed. Small, pale lemon catkins are produced on mature plants during a hot summer, sometimes followed by red, edible fruits. *Ephedra* are of great botanical interest, rather than plants of great beauty, but once a mature clump that's growing well has been viewed, they are usually given greater respect. Large swathes can cover a considerable area.

These are very easy plants to cultivate, as long as they are planted directly into the ground – container-grown plants are hopeless and take on a sparse, leggy look. To keep them looking good, plant in full sun in light, exceptionally well-drained soil. Suitable sites include sunny slopes, where all excess rain can drain away immediately. They are also unusual additions to rockeries, and are great in gravel gardens mixed in with other drought-loving plants. They love draping over stone walls where they can hang down in 'curtains' and make marvellous groundcover beneath spiky plants that enjoy the same growing conditions. They are ideal for coastal gardens too, where they like to creep across pebbles and be blown about by salty sea breezes. Plant in large groups, as growth is unbelievably slow. After ten years, one plant will still only cover an area of around 90cm (3ft) square.

Virtually no maintenance or pruning will be required. Even weeding will be eliminated, because of the thick groundcover that this plant provides.

Water newly planted specimens until they settle in, then irrigation can be dispensed with. Full sun is preferred, but a bit of light shade does no harm. Propagation is easiest from fresh seed, although stock can also be increased by taking cuttings or layering. Pests and diseases do not usually cause any problems.

ABOVE
Ephedra looks its best when planted in large drifts.

Eryngium agavifolium

A spiny perennial plant from Argentina. The leaves are wide, look highly polished and are a bright emerald-green. They feel leathery and are edged with hooked barbs, which look more ferocious than they actually are. *Eryngium agavifolium* usually manages to stay evergreen through the winter except in really cold areas. However, if the frost is severe enough to cut the foliage back to the ground, it always regenerates the following spring and takes only a few weeks to regain its previous form.

Away from its native country, the ultimate height and spread is rarely more than 60cm (2ft). Plants grow in clumps from a stemless base. The flower spikes, which are sent up during early summer, look like large greenish-yellow thimbles on short stalks. Although not exactly things of ravishing beauty, and it is tempting to cut them off, bees, wasps and flies flock around them in large numbers, so it would be a pity to spoil their enjoyment.

These plants are very easy to cultivate and look better in groups of at least three to make them more noticeable. In large gardens, bold clumps of at least ten make a striking display.

They are ideal for the front of borders, in rockeries or planted in gravel gardens. They complement other spiky plants such as *Yucca*, *Dasylirion* and *Agave* beautifully, but they are not suitable for growing in pots, as the roots are very vigorous and tend to dry out quickly unless watered frequently.

Light, sandy free-draining soil in full sun would be the perfect planting position. Water in new plants until they become established. After a few weeks, they can fend for themselves and irrigation is not usually necessary. Remove any older leaves as they turn yellow or brown. If the winter has been especially harsh, the foliage can become tatty and unattractive. The whole plant should then be cut right back to the ground with a sharp knife. It will soon regrow. A light feed of blood, fish and bone can be sprinkled around the base annually during spring if the soil is particularly poor or chalky.

Propagation is best from fresh seed, although larger plants can be divided up. Slugs can be a nuisance, and green aphids are fond of the new shoots.

Eryngium horridum
Horrid Eryngium

Eryngium horridum is a bristly evergreen perennial from Uruguay that isn't at all horrid (*horridum* is Latin for shaggy or bristly). It has lots of long leaves that drape across the ground. It is stemless, with all the foliage emerging from a central rosette. The leaves are edged with spiny bristles that look much sharper than they really are. Each year, more rosettes are sent up from the roots, forming larger clumps as the plants age, although mature plants away from their native habitat are unlikely to be more than 90cm (3ft) across and 60cm (2ft) high.

During the summer, tall flower spikes are sent up from the middle of the plant. They tower above the foliage and open up into yellowish thistles. They are interesting rather than beautiful but, as all the local insects love them, it would be a pity to chop them off.

They can grow in sun or light shade. Most types of soil are suitable, as long as they drain well, but light sandy soil that is fed annually would be ideal. A couple of handfuls of blood, fish and bone applied each spring is enough to keep everything looking healthy. New plants should be watered in well for the first few weeks,

but after they have become established they can usually take care of themselves, unless the summer is exceptionally hot and dry.

Eryngium horridum is a versatile plant and looks as much at home at the front of a traditional herbaceous border as it does mixed in with spiky desert planting schemes. It can be planted in gravel gardens, copes well in seaside gardens and looks perfectly okay among Mediterranean-style plantings. As it enjoys sharp drainage, it could also be planted as an unusual feature in a rockery or be positioned to hang over a stone wall. In large gardens, plants look effective in larger groups rather than as individual specimens.

Any older brown leaves should be removed with secateurs, cutting them as far back to the base as possible. Old flower stems should also be cut off as soon as they have finished. Pests and diseases are not often a problem on the foliage, but aphids are sometimes a nuisance on the flowers. Propagation should be by division, separating the individual rosettes. Although new plants are raised easily from seed, the results can be variable.

ABOVE
Although they look sharp, the spiny bristles on the leaves are not capable of inflicting any damage to the skin.

Eryngium pandanifolium

SYN. *Eryngium decaisneana*

This massive evergreen plant from Uruguay takes the form of big rosettes of long glaucous-green leaves, each edged with soft spines. It looks a real brute of a plant but it isn't sharp at all. The leaves can stretch out to 1.2m (4ft) in length, and the whole plant can fill a large space in the garden. The flower spike is amazing and can reach up to 3.7m (12ft) before opening out into masses of little purplish-pink bobbles. It is quite a sight in the summer and always gets lots of attention.

After flowering, the plant seems to have used up most of its energy and can look a bit tired. Once the dead flower spike has been removed, and providing the remaining foliage appears okay, then leave it to regenerate. Otherwise, this plant is best treated as a biennial, disposing of it and replanting with fresh stock the following spring. During its first year, it can be enjoyed as an unusual foliage plant while it gains more and more bulk, preparing itself for the flowering display the following year.

A leafy plant of this size needs lots of food and water to keep the foliage looking its best and to support its mad flowering phase. Prepare the ground before planting by introducing lots of well-rotted manure and digging it in thoroughly. After planting, keep the soil moist by irrigating regularly, especially during the main growing season of its first year. Make sure that any excess water drains away quickly, as the roots will not tolerate any waterlogging.

Eryngium pandanifolium needs lots of sun and should be planted in a prominent position to be enjoyed as a focal feature. It can be planted as a single specimen, with nothing around it except an ornamental mulch, or it can be put at the back of any large border where it will tower over everything else in front. It looks just as effective with traditional herbaceous plants as it does with other spiky architectural plants. If the ground tends to hold too much water, choose a sloping site for better drainage.

Although this greedy plant must have plenty of food and water initially, it needs very little maintenance once established. Pests and diseases are rarely a major problem, except for the odd slug or snail on the foliage and an occasional visit from aphids on the flowers. Propagation is from fresh seed.

ABOVE
This massive plant is ideal for planting in large borders.

Eucomis bicolor
Pineapple Lily

A large chunky bulb that produces a splendid plant with attractive leaves, stems and flowers. The large, floppy leaves, which spread out across the ground, are bright emerald-green and very fleshy. The tall flower stems, sent up during the summer, are the same emerald-green as the leaves, but with purple spots all the way up them. The flower heads are fat cylinders consisting of many blooms. Each flower is pale green, with a narrow purple strip all around its perimeter. They give off an unusual scent. The flower head finishes off with a tufty rosette of little, pale green leaves perched on the top like a rather fancy hat.

Eucomis bicolor likes rich moist soil and stays the nicest colour in light shade. Plant it in a sheltered spot. The flowers and foliage tend to be a bit top-heavy – gusts of wind would knock them flat. They look better in groups rather than single specimens, and can be planted in any shady spot in the garden where they can be clearly visible during the flowering season.

These plants are also quite happy growing in containers. Use a good quality soil-based compost, such as John Innes no. 3, and keep the pots well watered throughout the growing season. At the end of the year, the leaves will start to turn yellow and die back. Stop watering at this point and allow the bulbs to dry off during their dormant period. Cut back any old foliage and flower stems with a sharp knife.

In cold gardens, or if the soil retains too much moisture during the winter, the bulbs are best dug up each year and stored in dryish peat in a cool greenhouse until they show signs of new growth the following spring. Plant them back into the same positions as the previous year, after adding some well-rotted manure to the soil.

These bulbs are native to the Natal province of South Africa. Propagating can be done by separating any offsets produced by the parent bulbs. However, if extra stock is required, it is much more satisfactory just buying in extra flowering sized bulbs from a reputable nursery. The offsets can then be left on the original plants to increase in size and produce even more flower stems. Slugs and snails adore the appetizing foliage and munch on it constantly during warm, wet summers.

ABOVE
The overall appearance of the flower head gives us this plant's common name of Pineapple Lily.

Euonymus japonicus
Evergreen Spindle

A familiar sight along many coastlines, as the salt resistance of this tough, evergreen shrub is almost unmatched. The dark green leaves are thick and leathery, with a highly polished sheen to the top surface. The insignificant little yellowish blooms are followed by lots of bright orange berries, which are held onto the plant by small rigid stalks, or 'spindles', as they are referred to in their common name.

Growth starts very early in the season, sometimes as early as mid-winter. The new shoots are bright emerald-green, adding very attractive splashes of colour to the garden. Although brilliant for a seaside garden, *Euonymus japonicus* can also be used inland where a strongly shaped architectural foliage plant is required. It responds very well to clipping, and plants can be formed into hedges or planted singly and shaped into domes or curved shrubs. The lower growth can also be chopped off to form a miniature tree. They make fantastic windbreaks for any garden, whether by the sea or on exposed hilltops, and can be used to shelter more delicate plants positioned in front of them.

Their dark green colouring makes a perfect backdrop for highlighting other plants.

This Japanese plant is slow-growing and takes at least ten years to reach 2.5m (8ft). It can grow in sun or shade, and prefers rich, moist soil. Keep well watered, especially during hot dry summers, as it is prone to powdery mildew. Feed heavily with blood, fish and bone in early spring and again in mid-summer to keep the foliage a deep rich green.

Although not particularly suitable for growing in containers, the dwarf form 'Compactus' can sit in a large pot for years if it is regularly clipped with shears. It is even more slow growing than the straight form, and produces about twice as many leaves to make a really dense specimen plant. A pair of these planted either side of the front door would make a refreshing change from the usual box or bay.

Variegated versions – pale cream and green or loud yellow and green – are often available. Both need a sunnier spot than the green form to succeed, and they are less hardy, although their wind resistance is as efficient. All varieties can be propagated easily from cuttings.

Euphorbia mellifera
Honey Spurge

One of the most beautiful members of the *Euphorbia* family, and essential for almost any garden. The evergreen foliage is of such a bright emerald-green that it's almost luminous. Fast-growing, it can reach a height and spread of 2.2m (7ft) within five years. It grows into a neat, dense dome and nestles in between surrounding plants, conveniently filling in any gaps. The common name of honey spurge refers to the flowers, which are not only honey-coloured but have a delicious honey smell too. They appear in liberal quantities in late spring.

Considering *Euphorbia mellifera* is native to Madeira and the Canary Islands, it is surprisingly hardy. It performs hopelessly if confined to a container, so plant it out into rich, fertile soil in a sunny or lightly shaded spot. If planted in deep shade, it becomes very leggy, although this can be resolved by annual pruning, cutting back to the base each spring. Wear gloves when doing this, as the milky white sap that exudes from the cut leaves and stems of all *Euphorbia* can be an irritant to the eyes and skin.

Plant in a sheltered position away from strong winds. If the garden is exceptionally cold in the winter, plant it in the warmest spot possible, preferably in the shelter of a sunny wall. In perfect conditions, it could reach 3m (10ft) across, but it can be clipped with shears if it gets too big. Clipped plants look awful to start with, as the bare exposed stems are unattractive. But, within a short time, new growth appears, making the plant even bushier than it was before.

Water well to start with but, once established, this plant can usually take care of itself. Enrich poor soil annually with a few handfuls of blood, fish and bone. Plants can be raised easily from cuttings, but superior plants are produced from fresh seed. Make regular inspections for capsid bugs and aphids. During very hot dry summers, as well as under glass, there are also whitefly and red spider mites to contend with. On the plus side, if your garden is plagued with rabbits, this is one of their last choices, as the bitter sap makes for an unpalatable lunch.

ABOVE
Euphorbia mellifera has masses of shapely leaves of a vivid emerald-green hue.

ABOVE
The flattened clusters of flowers give off their wonderful honey aroma when fully open on a warm, sunny day.

Euphorbia myrsinites
Creeping Spurge

An unusual evergreen for groundcover that complements taller spiky and succulent plants such as *Agave*, *Dasylirion* and *Yucca* brilliantly. It looks like a typical desert plant itself, being equipped with blue fleshy-looking leaves but, on closer inspection, the foliage is actually quite flat. *Euphorbia myrsinites* sends out long runners from a central rosette, and each runner is edged with blue leaves, which are small and attractively shaped into a point.

It adores full sun and drapes itself all around the base of every plant it encounters, providing a thick undercover. The denseness is something of a surprise because nursery plants growing in pots can look straggly. This is because they loathe being in a container and, once in the ground, they show their appreciation by bulking up and doing what groundcover plants are supposed to do. One plant can cover an area of about 0.5sq m (2sq ft) in a couple of years. They can also be planted on the top of stone walls or along sloping sunny banks and left to hang over them as trailing plants instead.

The flowers (which are actually called bracts) are bright greenish-yellow and appear during early spring. Inside each one is the true flower, which is just a tiny yellow dot. This plant is totally hardy and remains evergreen, even in the harshest winters.

Older plants can sometimes become a bit leggy, but this can be solved by pruning them back fairly hard. This encourages new growth to sprout from the central rosette. Wear gloves when cutting into *Euphorbia*, as the milky sap that pours from the cut stems and leaves can be irritating to the skin and eyes.

Full sun is essential to keep the plants really bushy. Poor soil is quite acceptable, and good drainage is vital. Too much water collecting around the roots is a guaranteed way of killing the whole plant very quickly. This plant is very easy to cultivate. Once established, watering is unnecessary, except in long periods of exceptionally dry weather. After flowering, cut back the old flower stems. Apart from this, virtually no maintenance is needed. Even annual feeding can be dispensed with.

Apart from the occasional aphid appearing on the flowers, nothing else is likely to be a problem. Propagation is easy from fresh seed.

ABOVE
The strong blue colouring of the leaves makes *Euphorbia myrsinites* an excellent choice as an unusual groundcover plant

Euphorbia wulfenii
Spurge

A dramatic, evergreen perennial that is totally hardy and easy to grow. The foliage is a dark, steely blue and produced in abundance to make a very bushy plant that can reach 1.2m (4ft) tall and the same in width within five years. The showy flower heads are made up of startling sulphur-yellow bracts, surrounding a tiny yellow dot, which is the real flower.

This versatile plant can be incorporated into most planting schemes, looking just as good with spiky plants as it does in a shrubby or flowery border. It is particularly fetching in gravel gardens, where the colour of the leaves can be shown off to good effect. In spacious gardens, it looks wonderful planted in large groups. It can also be used in coastal planting plans, as it copes marvellously with sea winds.

This plant is unfussy in its requirements, but, given the choice, it does have several preferences. A sunny spot will give the best results, but it seems quite content in light shade too. Good drainage is essential. Any soil will do, although it does have a penchant for chalky conditions. Otherwise anything will suffice, whether the soil is sandy, loam-based or clay. Poor soil is quite acceptable, but rich fertile conditions get the plant off to a quicker start. The only place it hates to be is in a small container, where root restriction will turn it into a hideous leggy-looking object fairly rapidly.

Water new plants in well. Once established, however, they become very drought-tolerant. Remove old flower heads when they turn brown. If older plants become straggly, prune back the stems hard to the base where lots of new shoots will usually regrow. Take care of the milky sap that oozes from the stem when it is cut, which can be an irritant to the skin and eyes.

Very few problems afflict this plant, although the odd aphid might appear during the flowering season. Propagation is easy from seed, but use seed from a reputable company instead of collecting it yourself. These plants hybridize easily and can produce variable adult plants. Alternatively, buy a mature plant – then you know exactly what you are getting.

ABOVE
The distinctive blue-grey foliage makes an attractive feature in the garden for the entire year.

ABOVE
The sulphur-yellow bracts last for many weeks throughout spring.

Fatsia japonica
Fig-leaved Palm or **False Castor Oil Plant**

This Japanese plant is a fantastic addition to a jungly garden. The deep green leaves are huge, lobed and leathery, with a glossy sheen to the upper surface. *Fatsia japonica* is sometimes seen on sale as a houseplant, so it is often assumed that it cannot be hardy enough for the garden. However, not only is it hardy, it is so tough that it can be planted outside in virtually any climate. Mature plants can easily reach 2.5m (8ft) tall and 2.2m (7ft) wide, so plenty of space must be left around them when planting. Growth is slow, though, and it can take many years to reach these dimensions. There is nothing delicate about this plant. It is large and heavy-looking with plenty of dense growth – perfect for filling a large, shady corner.

In late summer, cream-coloured flowers appear from the centre. They look like drumsticks and are followed by bunches of black, inedible fruits.

Fatsia japonica must have full shade. The leaves can go a horrid yellow colour in the sunshine. Growth is slow enough to make it suitable for a container for the first few years of its life, if required. Rich, fertile soil is preferred, and plenty of moisture is needed throughout its life to produce the leafiest results. If the plants become too tall for their space in the garden, chop off the plant through the stem at any height during the spring or summer – new leaves soon appear from the cut end. An alternative pruning idea is to remove all the lower branches and retain one single stem with foliage on the top. This way, it looks even more exotic, closely resembling a papaya.

Feed heavily with either well-rotted manure or lots of blood, fish and bone annually each spring. Remove any older leaves as they turn yellow or brown. Although a perfectly hardy plant, late frosts can sometimes scorch the new tips. If this happens, cut off the damaged bits – they soon regrow.

Black aphids are often a nuisance on the new shoots. Capsid bugs can be a pest too, so make regular checks for these rotters. Propagation is easiest from cuttings.

ABOVE
Fatsia japonica is fully hardy and totally evergreen, which makes it an essential addition for shady gardens.

ABOVE
The cream flowers are not very exciting and can be removed, to channel all the plant's energy back into leaf production.

Fremontodendron 'California Glory'
Flannel Bush

Not exactly a climber, but not a free-standing plant either, so it's probably best described as a wall shrub. It is not self-clinging, but enjoys resting against a sun-baked wall where it can spread out flat. If growing conditions are right, it could reach 5m (16ft) in height within five years. The eventual width is around half its height. It is almost evergreen, but can be a bit sparse in the winter. The leaves are mid-green and covered in a dusty powder. This dust is harmless to most people but, occasionally, it can cause an allergic reaction if inhaled. Sensitive fools like myself cannot get close to it without experiencing a mild asthma attack.

The main reason for growing this gorgeous plant is its beautiful flowers. They are wonderful, just like giant buttercups. Loud yellow in colour, they are produced in copious amounts and last for many weeks during early summer.

This plant is a bit of a fusspot and can take a while to get going. Choose the planting site carefully because, once planted, it cannot be moved – root disturbance of any kind can kill it. The base of a sunny wall would be an excellent position. A wall offers the required support, and is also likely to be one of the hottest places in the garden, with the sun reflecting off the bricks. This extra heat helps to produce even more flowers. The drier conditions that are likely to occur there will also be appreciated. Once established, this plant can become exceptionally drought-tolerant.

Full sun is essential. The soil should be poor and very well drained; chalky or sandy soils would be best. Water frequently until established. Feeding is not usually required, and the only regular maintenance is to tie in the stems onto a supporting wall or trellis as growth increases. Pruning is not usually necessary, but if any is needed to restrict its spread, prune immediately after flowering.

This plant generally doesn't suffer from pests or diseases, although sometimes it is rather short-lived. If, after ten or fifteen years, it suddenly curls up and dies, it won't necessarily be your fault. Propagation is from cuttings.

■ Geranium madarense

Grown equally for its beautiful flowers and exotic leaves, this evergreen Madeiran plant is an essential acquisition for a mild garden or conservatory. The enormous leaves are delicate and ferny. Grown from seed, this plant spends the first few years of its life putting all its energy into producing fine arrays of foliage. After around four years, odd things will be noticed about the centre of the plant.

Rising above the foliage, a massive flower stem will appear, opening up into hundreds of bright magenta blooms. The flowering display lasts for several months. Alas, when this stage has finished, the whole plant collapses and dies, but the chances of fresh seed being dispersed around the garden are high. When seedlings appear, they can be dug up and potted on.

Geranium madarense loves the sunshine. It can be planted outside in any well-drained gritty soil or, in colder gardens, cultivated in a container and brought under glass for the winter months. Pot up in John Innes no. 3 and stir in some extra grit to ensure that drainage is really sharp. Keep the soil moist, but never soggy. Regular irrigation is vital during

flowering. The size of a mature plant will not be more than 90cm (3ft) tall and 60cm (2ft) wide.

These plants are perfect for a Mediterranean-style garden and also blend in beautifully with palms and spiky plants.

The central plant stalk is pink and fleshy, and has to support the weight of all the foliage and the heavy flower stem. To stop everything from becoming top-heavy and falling over, when the older leaves turn yellow or brown, don't cut them right back to the base, but leave a long-enough piece of the leaf stem to act as a stilt to prop it up.

Under glass in a greenhouse, porch or conservatory, whitefly could be a nuisance; green aphids sometimes appear on the flowers, too, both in the garden and indoors. The leaves sometimes turn fiery red. Although attractive, this colouring is usually a sign that something is amiss: either vine weevils are nibbling at the roots or the plant has got too cold or stressed in some way.

Griselinia littoralis

An attractive evergreen plant from New Zealand with lots of fleshy, apple-green foliage. The leaves have a leathery feel to them and an attractive gloss to their upper surface. *Griselinia littoralis* can be grown in a number of ways. It is not only useful and versatile, but it is also as tough as an ox, and can be grown in the kind of coastal conditions that would make most plants nervous just thinking about them. Its salt-resistance is brilliant, and it doesn't flinch when confronted with salty gales coming straight off the sea. The name *littoralis* comes from the Latin word meaning 'of the seashore'.

It can be shaped into squared hedging or rounded specimen shrubs. It can also have all of its lower growth removed and be trained as a little tree. Growth is steady enough to produce a height of about 2.5m (8ft) in five years, with an ultimate height of approximately 13ft (4m) away from its native country.

Griselinia littoralis can grow in any aspect except really deep shade, and in almost any soil, although fertile, moisture-retentive soil will give the best and fastest results. Clipping should be done little and often. The flowers are small, yellow and insignificant, so any pruning or shaping can be done when it's convenient, without the worry of cutting off any flower buds. The more this plant sees a pair of shears, the better. The denseness and smart look of the foliage is totally dependent on the frequency of cutting.

Feed annually with a mix of blood, fish and bone in the spring. Water new plants well throughout their first season. After this, watering needs to be thought about only if the soil is exceptionally poor or during a very hot and dry summer. Pests and diseases aren't usually a problem. Propagation is easiest from semi-ripe cuttings.

There are some variegated versions on the market too, mostly with green and very pale cream colouring. These are less hardy than the straight green version, and need full sun to remain a rich colour. They are just as salt-resistant, however, and can be planted as successfully in seaside gardens.

ABOVE
Griselinia littoralis can be clipped into domes or formal hedges.

ABOVE
The bright apple-green foliage shrugs off salt-laden gales, making it essential for coastal gardens.

Gunnera manicata
Giant Rhubarb

This is the kind of plant you'd expect to find in a science fiction novel. It is definitely not a plant for the timid gardener. With practically no care at all, it can be big; with proper care and attention, it can be an absolute giant.

The leaves are enormous, reaching around 1.5m (5ft) across, with a surface that is rough and crinkled. The stems can become so large that it is possible to stand underneath fully mature plants and look up into the leaves that form a canopy far above. The leaves and stems grow from a central crown that gets bigger and bulkier each year. This is the delicate part of the plant, which can need some protection during the winter, especially in its early years.

As the leaves die back every year after the first frosts, it is both practical and traditional to fold the brown frosted foliage over the crown to give it some on-site protection. This can be left on all winter until growth starts again in spring. The previous year's foliage can then either be disposed of or trodden in around the plant to provide extra nutrients as it rots down. Flower spikes – huge, dark pink and quite unmistakable – are often sent up from the middle of the plant.

Gunnera manicata is suitable for any boggy area where the roots have unlimited access to plenty of water. It is excellent for planting around lakes and ponds or along riverbanks and streams, although even a small bog garden could perhaps accommodate one plant. Even though it requires masses of water, this plant will not tolerate its roots being permanently submerged in water, so it is quite unsuitable as an aquatic plant. It should always be planted in a sheltered position away from strong winds.

The soil should not only be moist, but also rich and fertile. Feed annually in spring with masses of well-rotted manure or any food with a high nitrogen content. It is happy in sun or shade, but a shady spot will draw the plant up, making the stems even longer and the leaves even larger. A regular supply of water will be required for its entire life to ensure the very best results from this Brazilian plant. By removing any flower spikes, the plant's energy won't be wasted and it can all be concentrated on leaf production.

Pests and diseases are uncommon with this plant. Propagation is easiest from fresh seed.

ABOVE
Hundreds of waxy barbs cover the stems and extend along the veins on the undersides of each leaf.

Hebe parviflora angustifolia

A beautiful mass of emerald-green foliage that is fully hardy and evergreen. Soft and feathery, the foliage forms a rounded shape that looks like a large and comfortable cushion. Apart from its good looks, this plant is immensely tough and very versatile. It can be grown in a wide range of conditions but is particularly useful in dry shade where little else will grow. It is perfectly happy growing under trees, where there is often very little water or nutrients left in the soil.

Because the foliage is so dense, *Hebe parviflora angustifolia* makes a wonderful hedge that gets thicker the more it is clipped. Clipping should be done little and often with shears, taking care not to cut back into the old wood, which could be fatal for the plant. Clip at any time during the growing season. There is no need to time any cutting around the flowering season, as the greyish-white flowers are not attractive enough to worry about.

This New Zealand plant is a pretty choice as a specimen shrub in any prominent part of the garden. In full sun, it will keep its rounded shape with foliage down to the ground. In deep shade, the plant will be drawn up, leaving it bare underneath and allowing it to take on the shape of a small tree with a lovely rounded top. It looks like a miniature willow, with the added bonus of being evergreen.

This plant will grow in any soil, whether it's clay, chalk or loam, and can tolerate lots of moisture or cope with virtually none. Keep sheltered out of very strong, cold winds. If your soil is rich and moist, this *Hebe* looks particularly good planted in deep shade near a *Fatsia japonica*. The delicate bright foliage of the *Hebe parviflora angustifolia* next to the large, leathery, dark green leaves of the *Fatsia* makes a splendid contrast in a dark corner of the garden.

The only place this fast-growing plant will refuse to thrive is in a small pot – it does not like having its roots checked at all. Planting directly into the ground is essential, where dimensions can easily reach 2.2m (7ft) tall and wide in five years. A light annual feed in spring can be given if the soil is especially poor. Use just a small measure of blood, fish and bone.

Pests and diseases are rarely a problem, although green aphids can be a nuisance in hot summers. Propagation is easy from cuttings.

Hebe rakaiensis
Veronica

Another fine plant from New Zealand, with a mass of tiny, fresh green leaves forming curved mounds. The regular use of shears can produce really dense domes, which can give the same effect as box (*Buxus*) plants. They are a shapely addition to the garden. They can also be grown in very large terracotta pots.

Larger groups of them can act as groundcover, especially if they are planted close enough to be clipped as one continuous undulating outline, spreading out into each other like a series of small hills. Grown this way, they look extremely effective planted beneath taller architectural plants such as *Yucca recurvifolia*, *Cordyline australis* or *Trachycarpus fortunei*. These plants contrast beautifully with each other, not only in shape and texture, but also in their different shades of green. The height of mature *Hebe rakaiensis* will be only 60cm (2ft) maximum; the width after ten years will be around 90cm (3ft).

White flower spikes are sent up during the summer. Although not unattractive, they are not beautiful enough to postpone any clipping that needs to be done to keep the plants in good shape.

Plant in full sun or light shade. Any well-drained soil is suitable. They seem just as happy in soil containing clay or loam as they do in soil containing chalk or sand. Watering is important for new plants until they become established. Then they can fend for themselves, unless confined to a container where they will need regular irrigation throughout their lives. *Hebe rakaiensis* is also useful for planting in exposed positions. The growth is so dense that salt-laden gales from the sea or windy hilltop locations present no problems at all. Choose the planting spots carefully, as they hate root disturbance, and the transplanting of older plants isn't usually successful. Once planted, leave them where they are.

Very little maintenance is necessary with this unfussy plant, although annual feeding in the spring with a light helping of blood, fish and bone would be appreciated. Pests and diseases aren't usually anything to worry about, although leaf spot can occasionally be a nuisance on container-grown plants if they have become stressed due to insufficient or irregular watering. Propagation is easiest from cuttings.

ABOVE
The naturally curved shape of *Hebe rakaiensis* can be accentuated by clipping.

LEFT
Plants resemble
a posh and exotic
type of sweetcorn.

Hedychium coccineum 'Tara'
Tara's Ginger Lily

A tropical-looking perennial that gets bigger and better with age. The large pointed leaves surround a thick fleshy stem that can reach a height of 1.5m (5ft) during each growing season. The flower head is made up from dozens of individual orange blooms massed together in a cylindrical shape at the end of each stem.

The plants grow in clumps, which spread slowly, bulking up just a little bit more each year. They are best planted in groups of at least three, with each trio covering less than 1sq m (1sq yd) after five years. Flowering starts after three years, and the number of flower stems increases each year. Once planted, they are best left undisturbed.

Their life cycle begins in spring. They perform much better if planted directly into the ground in rich, fertile soil, but a large container is an acceptable option. As soon as growth starts, constant watering will be required for the whole season to get good results. These plants are very greedy and will consume as much food and water that is sent their way. However, the drainage must be first class so that water doesn't gather around the roots.

At the end of summer, the stems will have reached their full height and odd lumpy-looking things will start to protrude. These will open up into flowers, which will be in their full glory in autumn. After this, the foliage will gradually turn yellow and die back, although in mild gardens, it could stay green right through the winter. Cut off the old foliage when it becomes unsightly.

Feed with generous amounts of well-rotted manure each spring. In colder areas, mulch the ground with straw in winter for extra protection. These plants can grow in sun or light shade. If grown in containers, either store them somewhere dry during the winter or tip them on their sides so that all the water drains out, keeping the rhizome dry until new growth recommences the following year. Propagation can be done by division. Pests and diseases are rarely a problem in the garden. Red spider mites can be a nuisance under glass.

BELOW
The flowers are
an unusual deep
orange, lightly
fragrant and last
for many weeks.
Bees adore them.

Hedychium forrestii
Ginger Lily

This is the hardiest of the ginger lilies and can be grown in nearly all gardens, unless they are very cold and wet. It is also one of the tallest. The large, dark green leaves encircle a central fleshy stem, which can reach a height of 2.2m (7ft) in optimum growing conditions. The flowers are pure white and massed together to form a cylindrical shape at the end of each stem. These plants are too tall to confine to a pot and should therefore be planted outside in groups directly into the soil for best effect.

Choose the planting position carefully, as they prefer to be left undisturbed once planted. The rootstock increases in size each year, sending up more flower stems every year as the plants mature. They are slow to spread out and can take many years to fill a decent-sized space.

They are late to commence growing in the spring, but once they start, growth is rapid and they quickly reach their full height. The typical lumpy growths that emerge from the stems and open up into flowers become noticeable at the end of summer. The flowering season is throughout autumn. After this, in cold gardens, the foliage starts to turn yellow and die down for the winter. In milder areas, the leaves tend to remain green until well into winter.

To get the very best from these greedy exotic plants, rich growing conditions must be given, accompanied by large helpings of food and drink. The soil should be enriched at the start of the year with something strong, such as a generous helping of well-rotted manure. They are happy in sun or light shade, and need a sheltered spot away from strong winds. Lots of water is required throughout the growing season, but good drainage is vital so that water doesn't collect around the roots.

Hedychium forrestii can be propagated by division in spring but, as older plants resent being dug up out of the ground, it is better to buy in any extra stock needed. Cut down older yellowing foliage as it becomes unsightly. In very cold gardens, mulch the ground with straw in winter to provide extra protection. Pests and diseases do not generally cause any problems.

ABOVE
The leaves are large, dark green and attractively tapered.

ABOVE
The pure white flowers are a popular meeting place for local bees.

Hedychium gardnerianum
Ginger Lily

A showy plant from northern India, blessed with lavish good looks and an exotic presence. Huge, rounded leaves grow out from a central fleshy stem. These attributes on their own are a fine addition to a tropical border, but it is for the flowers that this plant is usually grown. Each stem produces a large cylindrical head consisting of many individual flowers that mass together. The colouring is exquisite, comprising mainly a strong lemon-yellow interspersed with long orange filaments. On warm, sunny days, they can give off a sweetly scented fragrance.

Hedychium gardnerianum can be grown permanently outdoors only in mild gardens. Plants need a sheltered, warm spot in either full sun or light shade. Rich, fertile soil is essential for good results, and each year the surrounding area should be fed with lashings of well-rotted manure. Plenty of water is another necessity, and regular irrigation should be done throughout the growing season. Within a couple of months they can reach their maximum height of around 1.5m (5ft). They can add a jungly feel to the garden, and look good planted alongside bamboos, palms or bananas (*Musa*).

In colder gardens, they could be grown in a large container in John Innes no. 3 compost, supplemented by a foliar feed every time they are watered. During the growing season, plants may need watering every day if the weather is hot and dry. When the leaves have died back for the winter, the container could be moved somewhere sheltered from the rain and frost.

If you are lucky enough to own a conservatory or greenhouse with a border for planting directly into the ground, this would be the perfect planting position. The roots would have enough room to spread and the rhizomes would be able to increase in bulk every year without being disturbed. Planted this way, they would still need lots of food and water while actively growing.

These plants are generally free from pests and diseases if grown in the garden but, under glass, red spider mites can sometimes be a nuisance. They can be propagated by dividing up existing plants but, as they are slow to develop into large clumps, buying in extra stock as required would probably be the best option.

LEFT
Helleborus foetidus
looks its best
during the winter.

Helleborus foetidus
Stinking Hellebore

An excellent evergreen plant that can cope wonderfully well with shade and chalk, a combination of two awkward features in any garden. The leaves are finely cut, dark green and glossy. The flowers are lime-green, and the flowering period lasts for several months – for most of the winter and into the following spring. Young plants grow rapidly to 60cm (2ft) and then stop, but each year the flower heads get larger. Once plants have settled in, seeds are regularly produced and then scattered all over the garden. Unwanted seedlings are easily removed and not invasive enough ever to become a nuisance.

Although suitable for difficult planting sites, *Helleborus foetidus* would still prefer to be in richer soil. Despite its common name, there is nothing unpleasant about the smell of either the leaves or the flowers. Plants look much more effective in large drifts; one or two on their own look a bit lost unless the garden is really tiny. They are perfect for shady borders or for planting in groups underneath trees. They are also tolerant of seaside locations and do not seem to mind being on the receiving end of the occasional blast of salty air. This plant has the reputation of being able to cure madness, but quite how it supposedly manages to do so is a mystery.

This is an easy plant to cultivate. It can cope with all levels of shade, down to really deep shade. Poor soil can be enriched with a little blood, fish and bone every spring. Dry soil can be tolerated well, but some extra irrigation in really hot dry weather would be beneficial. The only maintenance is the removal of old flower heads when they age and start to turn brown.

Plants can be grown in containers for a couple of years but, after that, they prefer the freedom of being planted out in the ground.

The main pests likely to be encountered are green aphids. They should be dealt with at the very first sign to stop them from building up into large numbers and spoiling the appearance of any late blooms. Propagation is easy from fresh seed.

BELOW
Mature flower
stems can be
smothered
with well over
a hundred
individual blooms.

Hydrangea aspera

Although it's difficult to find the right spot in the garden for *Hydrangea aspera*, given the right conditions, this Chinese plant can become a fine asset. It forms a large shrub that can reach 1.8m (6ft) tall and 1.2m (4ft) wide within ten years. Its huge glaucous-green leaves are fuzzy to the touch due to the thick bristly hairs covering each one. The flowers appear in the summer and are very showy. They form enormous heads made up of many smaller individual flowers clustered together. The inner flowers are a dark shade of pinkish-purple, and are surrounded by much bigger pinkish-white flowers.

The soil can be alkaline, acid or neutral, as long as it is rich, moisture-retentive and well drained. *Hydrangea aspera* will not tolerate drying out at all, but the roots hate being in permanently boggy conditions. The more shade the roots have, the better for keeping them cool and moist. The foliage also appreciates some shade – but only light shade – to keep the leaves a rich colour. Deep shade for the top part of the plant can cause it to become drawn up and leggy. A sheltered spot protected from any strong winds will also be needed.

Because of the large leaves, this plant can fit into any jungly garden, complementing palms, bamboos and other large-leaved exotics such as *Paulownia tomentosa* and *Fatsia japonica*. But this plant's size and bushiness, together with its flowers, also make it a suitable addition to a more traditional woodland planting.

As long as the balance of rich soil and adequate moisture can be achieved, very little other maintenance is required. Pruning will be necessary only in very small gardens where it outgrows its given space, or simply to tidy up its shape. Do any pruning after the leaves have been shed in autumn, or the following spring just before the new season's growth commences.

This plant is relatively trouble-free from pests and diseases, providing all the cultivation instructions are followed. Annual feeding with some well-rotted manure will give good results. Propagation is quite tricky and is usually from cuttings.

ABOVE
The gorgeous fuzzy foliage looks good in any type of planting scheme.

ABOVE
The contrasting inner and outer flowers make an unusual blend of texture and colour.

Iris confusa
Confused Iris

This plant cannot quite make up its mind about what it wants to be, and is therefore fully deserving of its common name. It doesn't look or behave as most irises would, but has traits characteristic of both bamboos and palm trees. The stems are definitely reminiscent of bamboo canes, being quite hard and woody. These grow to around 60cm (2ft) in height. They are topped by what looks like a type of palm leaf with fronds that are about 20cm (8in) across and made up of individual 'fingers' that are broad and flat. *Iris confusa* is fully evergreen and hardy if correctly sited. The flowers, which are white, tinged slightly with mauve and with the occasional yellow dot, are of secondary interest but quite pleasing to the eye. They are long-lasting and appear during late spring.

These plants are suitable for most types of garden and look much more effective planted in larger groups, rather than as single specimens.

Iris confusa prefers full sun. Light shade is fine for the foliage but tends to result in fewer flowers. A planting position in fertile soil and sheltered from the wind would be ideal. Plants do well at the base of a sunny wall, with extra heat reflected from the bricks behind. Soil at the base of walls also tends to be drier, which would suit these plants admirably.

They do quite well in containers, as long as the pots are a decent size. Try planting a group of three plants in a pot at least 45cm (18in) across to produce a nice leafy clump. Container-grown specimens need regular irrigation throughout the growing season, unlike those planted directly into the ground.

Feeding is not not that important, but a light feed of blood, fish and bone can be given annually in spring, if desired. Remove any older yellowing leaves as they appear, cutting them off as near to the base as possible. Propagation can be by division immediately after flowering.

Iris confusa is a magnet for every slug in the vicinity, and the use of a commercial slug repellent is essential. They not only eat the leaves, but the rotters chomp every bit of the plant right down to the ground.

Isoplexis spectrum

A pretty evergreen shrub from Madeira for mild gardens or for growing in a large pot under glass. The fresh green leaves are large and held almost horizontally up the length of the stem. Flowers, which are produced on mature plants usually after about three years, are showy and held high above the foliage. They are like miniature foxglove flowers, consisting of individual bell-shaped blooms held together on one large head. They last for at least a couple of months.

This is a small woody shrub with a height and width of only about 90cm (3ft). It looks perfectly presentable planted as a single specimen in the garden, although if you have a large garden, groups of them would look more effective.

Plant in a lightly shaded or sunny position, sheltered from strong winds. Most types of soil will do, whether acid or alkaline, as long as it retains some moisture without being boggy. This is quite a hungry plant, and richer soil will give much better results. Small helpings of well-rotted manure applied annually in the spring should keep everything looking healthy and vigorous. In really cold winters, the leaves may become scorched,

but the plant usually regenerates from its main woody structure during the following spring.

Under glass, the best place to plant would be directly into the soil in a conservatory or greenhouse border. If you don't have the luxury of such growing conditions, a large container will suffice. Pot up young plants into good-quality compost, such as John Innes no. 3, with some extra grit stirred in for improved drainage. Make this its final-sized pot, as it resents being transplanted as it matures. Keep well watered throughout the growing season and just about moist during the dormant winter period.

Remove any older yellowing or brown leaves as they appear. Cut off the flower stems immediately after flowering. Pests and diseases aren't usually a problem outdoors but, under glass, aphids and whitefly can be regular visitors. Propagation is from fresh seed.

Kniphofia caulescens
Red Hot Poker

There are many different types of *Kniphofia* available and all of them seem to share the common name of Red Hot Poker, which describes the flowers beautifully, but could lead to confusion unless the Latin name is strictly adhered to. Most *Kniphofia* are grown for their splendid flowers alone but, sometimes, the foliage is special enough to be the main attraction, as it is for *Kniphofia caulescens*.

Lovely rosettes of blue-grey foliage give it the kind of tropical appearance that many *Yucca* have, but without the sharp bits. It is a slow plant to get going but, gradually, the rosettes send up more baby plants from the base, which spread to form larger clumps. They are tough, hardy and evergreen. Woody stems, 60cm (2ft) long, are sent up from the centre of each mature rosette in the autumn. These open out into tubular flowers massed together to form a cylindrical shape that is fiery orange-red at the tip and yellow underneath. They last for many weeks.

This plant is found growing naturally in many parts of South Africa, usually in areas of high altitude where the ground is hilly and the soil light and free-draining. So, it almost requires being treated as an alpine plant, where the ground is never allowed to become boggy and the planting position is in full sun. Plenty of moisture is required, but its naturally sloping location would obviously cause any excess rain to drain away immediately. These preferences need some thought when choosing a good site in a garden.

It is happy at the front of a border and blends in well with most planting schemes. Rich soil is important, and well-rotted manure applied every spring would produce good results. Once established, mature plants can become almost drought-tolerant.

This plant is really unbelievably reluctant to grow with any speed at all. A trio I planted five years ago has virtually the same spread now as it did then. Next time, I shall plant at least ten to make them more noticeable.

Cut off any old leaves and flower stems as soon as they look unsightly. Plants can be propagated either by seed or by division, if you are lucky to have large-enough plants to split up. Slugs and snails can be a real nuisance.

Kniphofia northiae
Red Hot Poker

The evergreen leaves of *Kniphofia northiae* are wide, curving straps up to 1.5m (5ft) long and 10cm (4in) wide, edged with small, sharp serrations. Short, stubby stems form the base of each rosette, making the whole plant look like a giant pot leek. They rarely grow as clumps, preferring to put all their energy into one enormous, single specimen. The height of a mature plant is usually about 90cm (3ft).

Short, rather squat flower spikes appear in autumn, and open out into torch-shaped blooms made up of coral-red flowers on the top and creamy yellow ones underneath.

These plants fit beautifully into any architectural garden, and look wonderful in gravel gardens. They can also sit quite happily for several years in a large terracotta pot.

Kniphofia northiae is a greedy plant that needs lots of food and water. In their native South Africa, plants are seen growing in large colonies along streams and riverbanks, where they have access to a constant supply of water. They are nearly always found on a sloping site, so that any excess rain can run away without collecting around the roots. The conditions they enjoy in the wild should be mimicked exactly in cultivation to achieve the same vast proportions. Once planted out, they loathe root disturbance, so choose their planting position carefully.

Choose a planting spot in full sun and sheltered from strong winds. The soil should be rich, fertile and free-draining. Large dollops of well-rotted manure applied annually during late spring will be greatly appreciated. Lots of water will be required throughout the growing season for newly planted specimens; established plants can usually fend for themselves unless the summer is exceptionally hot and dry. Remove any older brown or yellow leaves as soon as they appear.

Propagation is from fresh seed, which always seems to be in short supply. Slugs delight in scraping off the surface of the leaves, leaving large grazed areas – on quiet summer evenings, this scraping is actually audible.

ABOVE
This massive plant is definitely grown primarily for its foliage.

BELOW
The stubby little flowers are an added extra.

Kniphofia rooperi
Red Hot Poker

The very best flowering Red Hot Poker that deserves to be planted in great swathes everywhere. The more this plant is massed together, the more effective it is, forming large clumps of evergreen foliage. The densely packed leaves completely hide their planting area underneath, so that this plant could almost be classed as groundcover. Long and arching, the leaves measure around 1.5m (5ft) from base to tip. They are slender, glaucous-green and rather droopy. The total height of the clumps of foliage is no more than 60–90cm (2–3ft).

The flowers are spectacular, and I couldn't imagine having a garden without them. They are at their best in late autumn and early winter. Tall, straight flower stems tower above the foliage and can easily reach 1.5–1.8m (5–6ft) in height. The more mature the clumps, the more flower spikes that are produced each year. A trio of mature plants clumped together could easily send up twenty spikes by their third season. Each flower head is made up of many smaller florets, which are a beautiful fiery orange above and a strong yellow on the lower section. They last for many weeks before slowly fading. When they reach the brown stage, chop them off as low down into the plant as you can reach.

The foliage is fully evergreen, but sometimes, after a cold, wet winter, older clumps can look a bit tired and in need of some attention. They can be chopped back hard right to the base, if required, and will regenerate fully by the end of the following season.

Choose a sunny spot for *Kniphofia rooperi*, and make sure the soil is enriched annually to keep it fertile – large helpings of well-rotted manure is as good as anything. Masses of water will be needed throughout the growing season, especially for young plants; once established, they can usually fend for themselves. These plants need to be in a prominent place in the garden where they can be fully on show during the flowering season. They look just as good planted in traditional herbaceous borders as they do with groups of spiky plants, but for maximum effect, just plant large numbers of them all in one place.

Slugs and snails adore them. Propagation is from fresh seed or by dividing up larger plants.

Libertia formosa

A pretty evergreen perennial from Chile with tufts of grassy leaves emerging from a central clump. The leaves are long and slender, growing to about 60cm (2ft) in height, and are sent up in numerous quantities, which makes the plant more substantial with each growing season. The whole plant has the appearance of a miniature *Phormium*.

Tall flower spikes emerge from the centre during late spring and are usually fully open by early summer. Each spike consists of wiry stems adorned with many clusters of orchid-like flowers. They are tri-petalled and are bright white with yellow stamens. They last for many weeks and sometimes several months. A mature *Libertia formosa* can be about 90cm (3ft) across, and a plant this size will produce around thirty or forty flower stems per year.

This plant suits almost any planting scheme. It is a particularly good choice for a large terracotta pot, and can give good results year after year, although planting directly into the ground will give superior results.

This plant will grow practically anywhere, but light, crumbly soil is preferred. For a container,

use John Innes no. 3 compost. Find a planting position in either sun or light shade. Clumps stay tidier if planted in a sheltered spot away from strong winds. The soil should be rich enough to hold onto some moisture without becoming waterlogged. To achieve adequate drainage, add plenty of grit to the planting hole or container. New plants should be well watered until established. Mature clumps can usually manage to rely just on the rain but with a little extra help if the summer is especially hot and dry. Plants confined permanently to a container will always need regular irrigation.

This is an easy plant to keep looking good. Remove any older leaves that have become brown or yellow, cutting as low down into the plant as possible with secateurs, and remove flower stems as soon as they have faded. An annual feed in the spring with a couple of handfuls of blood, fish and bone should be enough to keep everything looking healthy.

Propagation is easy from fresh seed. Pests and diseases are rarely a problem, except for the occasional aphid on the flower buds.

ABOVE
Libertia formosa is a gentle, well-behaved plant, suitable for even the tiniest of gardens. The name *formosa* is well-deserved – it is Latin for handsome.

Lobelia tupa
Devil's Tobacco

A huge, perennial herb with an intriguing common name. Mature plants can easily put on 2.2m (7ft) of height during each growing season. They form large, towering spikes consisting of thick stems which are covered in soft foliage on the bottom half and a magnificent spire of red flowers on the top half. The leaves are pointed, downy, mid-green and 25cm (10in) long.

Despite its stature, *Lobelia tupa* stands up well to sea breezes, making it a good choice for a coastal garden. It also fits in with most other styles of gardening, but it is hopeless if confined to a container – it must be planted directly into the ground. It looks much better in larger groups than as a single specimen.

Young plants are best planted in the spring after that year's frosts have finished. In their first year, they will grow to about 1.2m (4ft) and then flower. It is during their second year, when they have become established, that their full height develops. Growth usually starts in early spring and will reach its 2.2m (7ft) mark within four months if the growing conditions are right. Although these plants bulk up and spread slightly after a few years, planting at least five to start with is advised.

The common name of devil's tobacco refers to the fact that if huge numbers of this plant are chopped back in the confined conditions of a nursery glasshouse, the air around them can become toxic. In normal growing conditions outside, this is not a problem.

The soil should be very rich and free-draining; adding lots of well-rotted manure each spring would be highly beneficial. Either full sun or light shade produces good results. Plants should be very well watered during their first season, especially when actively growing. Established plants require regular irrigation only if the soil is especially poor and sharply drained, such as on thin chalk. Remove dead flower spikes as they fade. The foliage will continue to grow until the autumn, when it starts to become brown and tatty and should be cut right down to the base.

Propagation is from fresh seed. Pests and diseases are quite rare, apart from an occasional visit from green aphids, which love to congregate on the new growing tips.

ABOVE
The flowers, which appear during the summer, are made up of hundreds of deep red tubular blooms. They are the perfect shape to be pollinated by hummingbirds, which live along the hilly coastal regions of Chile where this plant grows wild.

Lomatia myricoides

A very unusual evergreen shrub from south-east Australia and a plant for someone who likes a challenge. The leaves are a fresh green and have an attractively crinkled appearance. Mature plants will not reach much more than 1.8m (6ft) in height and 1.5m (5ft) in width. They make fine specimen plants for a focal position in the garden. Older plants flower regularly each year during the summer. The flowers are small but exotic, creamy white in colour and fragrant, but it is for the foliage that *Lomatia myricoides* should be grown.

Once these plants have found a spot in the garden where they are happy, then growing them is a joy – it's finding the right place that's the problem. Decent-sized plants are rarely seen for sale at specialist nurseries. These plants hate to be in containers, even when young, which makes their commercial cultivation rather tricky.

Whatever size plant you buy, whether it's a reasonable specimen or just a baby, plant it outside at the first opportunity. Choose a spot in shade where there is good light but no direct sun during the hottest part of the day. Plant in a sheltered spot, away from any cold or strong winds, in soil that retains some moisture without ever becoming boggy. The soil should be neutral to acid, with no trace of lime or chalk. It should also be free-draining and light in texture, preferably containing some sand. Heavy soils such as clay won't be appreciated.

Assuming all of these requirements can be met, then you are halfway to ending up with a beautiful shrub that none of your neighbours is likely to have. But, there are other points to consider: *Lomatia myricoides* is a member of the *Proteaceae* family and, like others in the family, loathes phosphates, which are found in many types of plant food. Take great care when feeding other plants nearby because any phosphates will kill it. It will blacken and look miserable within a very short period of time. However, it still appreciates an annual feed with something that contains nitrogen but not all the other usual ingredients. Some larger garden centres stock a mix made specially for *Protea*, and this is what to look out for.

Pests and diseases are unlikely to be much of a problem. Propagation is from semi-ripe cuttings.

▪ Mahonia lomariifolia

This large, evergreen and supremely architectural shrub could reach 3m (10ft) in ten years. It has thick, corky stems, each one ending in a flourish of wide-spreading foliage, made up of many pairs of spiny leaves that look something like holly. Large clusters of bright yellow flowers appear at various times of the year, but usually during late autumn.

Although a fine shrub if left to grow naturally, this Chinese plant can be improved hugely by wielding a pair of secateurs and doing battle. Wherever the stem is cut on a young plant, more foliage will appear. With this in mind, try to create a plant that consists of five or six stems, all of different heights and all topped with a head of foliage that has enough room to spread out fully, without being entangled with its neighbouring stem. From a distance and with a bit of imagination, the whole plant can resemble a mini grove of palm trees.

Find a shady spot in the garden, sheltered from any strong winds. Plants like being tucked underneath the canopy of larger trees, as long as the ground stays moist. The soil should be rich, fertile and moisture-retentive, without

ever becoming boggy. Poorer soil should be enriched annually in early spring with something like a good helping of well-rotted manure or generous amounts of blood, fish and bone.

Young plants should never be allowed to dry out. Water them frequently for the first few seasons, after which time, the roots should be sufficiently established to search for their own water. These plants will live in a large container for several years in a shady spot, but will need regular watering during every growing season.

Although hardy, any new growth produced early in the season can be damaged by late frosts. If the new tips become scorched, snip them off; others will soon be sent out to replace them.

This is an easy plant to cultivate, if suitable growing conditions can be provided. Pests and diseases are not often a problem. Propagation is easiest from fresh seed, although plants grown this way can take years to reach a decent size.

ABOVE
Mahonia lomariifolia is by far the most imposing *Mahonia*. available. It is much more delicate in appearance and much less loutish than many of the more commonly grown ones.

BELOW
The bright yellow flowers are lightly fragrant and are followed by bunches of blue-black fruits.

Melianthus major
Honey Flower or **Honey Bush**

The pale blue-grey leaves of this perennial are beautifully sculpted and exude a strong smell of peanut butter when touched. A height of at least 1.5m (5ft) can be reached in one year, with most growth occurring in autumn.

Mature plants send up tall flower spikes that soar above the foliage and open up into slender cone shapes that are coloured blood-red. The flowering period is usually around early summer. The outer parts of the flower contain a honey-like substance, hence the plant's common name. The size and colour of the leaves contrast well with virtually all other architectural plants, and plants can be used in all types and styles of gardens. Don't try growing this plant in a pot – the result will be very disappointing unless the container is of gigantic proportions.

This South African plant is not very hardy and is often cut back to the ground by frosts, but as the growth on older plants can sometimes become leggy, hard pruning is no bad thing, whether done deliberately with secateurs or accidentally by frosts. The new growth that follows a severe hacking is much improved, giving extra bushiness to the entire shape.

Full sun or light shade is preferred, but this plant can be grown in deep shade if it is hard pruned every year to stop it becoming too leggy. As it is quite a delicate plant, it should be planted in a sheltered spot away from strong winds. Constant moisture is required throughout the growing season, but the ground should never be allowed to become waterlogged. Good drainage is essential, and rich, fertile soil produces the best results. Well-drained loam would be the perfect choice.

Remove older leaves as soon as they become brown, using secateurs instead of just tugging at them – the fragile stems can easily snap with rough treatment. Do any pruning just before new growth starts in spring, so that only a minimum amount of time passes waiting for new leaves to appear.

Propagation is easy from seed as long as it is very fresh. Pests and diseases are not usually a problem for plants growing outdoors in the ground.

ABOVE
This very popular and decorative perennial has huge, deeply cut leaves that smell of peanut butter when touched.

ABOVE
The tall flower spikes, which are best described as interesting and spectacular, rather than beautiful, open up into slender, blood-red cone shapes,

Musa basjoo
Hardy Japanese Banana

The most exotic, architectural plant of all
and an essential addition for any garden.
It's the sort of plant that makes neighbours
question your sanity. No one believes there
is really such a thing as a hardy banana, but
there is and this is it. It is the most absurd
tropical-looking plant that can be grown in
temperate climates.

With the right growing conditions, *Musa
basjoo* can easily reach 2.2m (7ft) in one year
and eventually grow as tall as 6m (20ft). Huge
leaves can be produced at the rate of one per
week at the height of the growing season.
These unfurl to reveal a large green 'paddle',
which is bright vivid green and 1.8m (6ft) long.
The leaves grow from a base that eventually
forms a fibrous, watery trunk. Suckers are
produced from around this base, which grow
to form a small grove of extra plants. These
can be cut off, but look much better if left to
grow as a multi-stemmed clump.

Mature stems can produce flowers, which
are large and lumpy, and extend from a curved
stalk. Behind the flower bud, tiny bunches of
bananas appear. These are hard, green and
inedible, but to have them growing in a non-
tropical climate always brings on a feeling of
total disbelief. They are truly amazing, and
visitors to my garden always suspect some
sort of skulduggery on my part.

The stem dies after fruiting, but sends
up new plants from the roots to replace it.
Frost always destroys the foliage. In milder
gardens, the trunk stays hardy through the
winter and new growth starts from the top
the following year. In colder
areas, the trunk can be left
as it is for the frost to kill,
and new growth will appear
from the base the following
spring. Alternatively, the
plant can be wrapped for
the winter by covering the
main stem with a tower
of flue liners and stuffing
the inside with straw (see
instructions opposite).

Wrapping the plants up
in this way means that
there is still something

1. Cut off all the frosted and droopy leaves with a sharp knife, so that you are left with just the main stem.

2. Place a flue liner (you can buy these from a builders' merchants) over the stem.

3. Make a tower of flue liners over the stem, and stuff the inside with straw as the liners pile up.

4. Place a ridge tile on the top of the flue liners as a waterproof lid. Clear up any loose bits of straw with a garden rake.

interesting to look at during the winter months. The time of year that you carry out this procedure depends entirely on how cold the weather is. There is little point in chopping off leaves if they are still fresh and verdant. The main reason for winter wrapping is that, by keeping the trunk alive, the next season's growth will sprout from the top of the trunk instead of having to start again from ground level. This not only produces taller plants, but also allows it to become mature enough to fruit and flower.

Musa basjoo must have vast amounts of water to sustain such large, fast growth. It also requires rich soil, and it is almost impossible to overfeed. Give it generous amounts of well-rotted manure in the spring, and add foliar feed each time it is watered. Every four to six weeks throughout the growing season, give it extra supplies of blood, fish and bone or rotted kitchen waste from the compost heap. All of this food needs to be well watered in.

For the best colour green, choose a spot in light shade; too much sun gives a bleached effect, while too much shade draws the plant up, making it less bushy. Plant *Musa basjoo* away from any winds, as even the slightest gust can tear the delicate foliage.

Pests and diseases become a problem only if the plant is stressed in some way, such as being confined to a container or not having enough to eat and drink.

Propagation is tricky for the amateur. Offsets can be separated from the parent plant but they are successful only if there is a piece of root attached, which is difficult to accomplish. Most commercially grown plants have been produced with the aid of a micropropagation laboratory.

Musa ensete
Abyssinian Plantain or **Abyssinian Banana**

SYN. *Ensete ventricosum*

Something exciting, exotic and fast-growing for the conservatory. This huge leafy banana can easily reach 3.7m (12ft) within five years. The stem is a stout watery trunk, and the massive leaves unfurl to a length of almost 2.2m (7ft). These plants sound far too large for most conservatories, but don't let this put you off – they can be easily controlled by slicing through the stem at any height whenever they outgrow their given space. Wherever they are cut, a new sprout of growth appears, to carry on as before until it hits the ceiling once again.

These plants need a brightly lit spot but prefer to be kept out of the scorching midday summer sun. The container must be gigantic to support such leafiness successfully. Use John Innes no. 3 soil-based compost and stir in some grit for extra drainage. While actively growing, they need copious amounts of food and water. Feed every four to six weeks with blood, fish and bone or, if you find this too smelly for indoors, use any high nitrogen food. Apply a foliar feed with each watering. Never let the plant sit in pools of water for any length of time – the roots will hate this.

During the dormant season, stop feeding and reduce the irrigation to keep the soil only just moist. Overwatering during the winter can lead to rotting. Plants can survive almost down to freezing point, but prefer a couple of degrees of warmth.

There is also a stunning red version of this plant, variously listed as *Musa ensete* 'Rubra', *Ensete ventricosum* 'Rubrum' or *Ensete* 'Maurelii'. The leaves are a dark purplish-maroon. It is smaller than the straight green form, reaching no more than about 1.5–1.8m (5–6ft) and is even less hardy, preferring a temperature of at least 6°C (43°F) in winter.

Musa ensete is susceptible to various pests, especially green aphids, whitefly and red spider mites. Check for all of these creatures regularly, especially in the warmest summer months. Unless the plant is too big to move, transferring it out into the garden for the summer will be highly beneficial and help to keep these bugs at bay.

Although the green version can be propagated easily from seed, the red form must be reproduced vegetatively, which is best left to the experts.

LEFT
The flowers
smother the
whole plant
in the summer.

Olearia macrodonta
New Zealand Holly or **Daisy Bush**

A tough evergreen shrub from New Zealand that can cope with the most severe salty gales and exposed coastal conditions, making it a useful, as well as attractive, addition to the garden. It is fairly slow-growing and, away from its native country, unlikely to exceed 2.5m (8ft) in height and 1.2m (4ft) in width after ten years.

The leaves are silvery green, rough-textured and edged with sharp teeth around the entire perimeter. The flowers are large, white and fragrant, consisting of lots of little daisies clustered together. They are produced in such large quantities during the summer that they sometimes completely conceal all of the foliage. Most text books mention the plant's musky odour, but I can't say it's something I've ever noticed.

This shrub can be grown as a single specimen plant and, if desired, can be clipped with shears into a tidier shape. Plants make wonderful screening, not just for coastal gardens, but for those inland too. *Olearia macrodonta* also makes an unusual choice for a formal hedge and can be clipped into the normal squared shape, as with other hedging plants. Any clipping and shaping should be done in the spring or early summer.

Full sun is essential. The soil doesn't have to be particularly rich, although fertile soil can give quicker and better results. This shrub can grow on chalk, sand, peat, clay or loam, and is easy to cultivate.

Drainage is another vital element to consider. Waterlogging won't be tolerated, even for a short period of time. Very poor soil could be enriched annually with a couple of handfuls of blood, fish and bone in the spring. This plant performs very badly if confined to a pot and should be planted outside directly into the soil as soon as it is large enough to handle.

These plants can be prone to sudden dieback, but this is most likely to occur on plants that have been overwatered, which causes the roots to rot.

No particular insect is attracted to *Olearia macrodonta*, and plants grown in the correct conditions should stay free from pests and diseases. Propagation is from cuttings taken at the end of the summer.

Phormium cookianum
Mountain Flax or **Wharariki**

SYN. *Phormium colensoi*

Phormium cookianum is found in all parts of New Zealand, where it used to be grown just for its fibre. Arching, sword-shaped leaves grow from fan-shaped bases in copious amounts to create clumps 1.2m (4ft) tall and 1.2m (4ft) wide within three years. The number of leaves on a plant this size could be 150, making a strongly architectural shape for the garden. Flower spikes are sent up from the centre during the summer. They are slightly taller than the foliage, and could be classed as interesting rather than as things of stunning loveliness. They open out into large yellowish-green angular blooms and, when these fade, seed pods begin to form. As the pods are much more attractive than the flowers, they should be left on the plant to be enjoyed visually. They are long-lasting and much admired.

Phormium cookianum is a plant of varying hardiness – some forms are worthy of the green hardiness colour code, but the provenance should be checked before planting out in very cold climates. The variegated form, *Phormium cookianum tricolor*, has striking leaves of cream and green with subtle red edges. It is not only attractive, but also just as hardy as the green version. The market is flooded with many named cultivars, most of them with hideously loud colouring, although most tend to lose their colour after a couple of years. They are also fairly short-lived, and should be regarded as temporary additions to the garden.

Plant out in full sun or light shade in fertile, free-draining soil. They are excellent in exposed coastal gardens and reasonably good in pots. Water well until established. After this, watering will be required only in periods of drought. This, of course, applies only to plants in the ground – container-grown plants will need watering regularly throughout their lives.

Feed annually in late spring with blood, fish and bone. When planting, make sure the central base is not planted too low, otherwise water could gather in the crown and cause rotting. Remove any older leaves with a sharp knife as soon as they turn brown. Propagation is easiest from division. Seed-grown plants can be variable whereas division ensures the small plantlets will be the same as the parent plant. The pests most likely to be encountered are mealy bugs.

ABOVE
The foliage is strikingly architectural.

Phormium tenax
New Zealand Flax

This is an easy plant to cultivate, and its strong shape has made it the basis of many architectural gardens over the past decade. Massive sword-shaped leaves up to 2.2m (7ft) tall grow from fan-shaped bases to create enormous clumps of upright foliage. The flower spikes are extraordinary. Towering above the foliage, they open up into angular reddish-brown flowers similar in shape to the Bird of Paradise Plant (*Strelitzia reginae*). The flowers still manage to look attractive even when they are dead and their colour has faded and turned black.

Plant in full sun or light shade. *Phormium tenax* is excellent in exposed coastal gardens and also a reasonably good candidate for growing in large containers. The soil should be very free-draining and preferably fertile. Any type of soil will be fine, whether it's clay, chalk or loam. Enrich poor soil annually in the spring with a few handfuls of blood, fish and bone.

Water well for the first season. After this, watering should be necessary only during periods of drought. If plants are confined to containers, however, they will require watering for their entire lives. When planting, make sure the central base is not positioned too deeply, otherwise water can gather in the crown, causing rotting. Plant them at exactly the same level as they were in the pot they came in from the shop or nursery. Brown-bitting – the removal of all older brown or yellowing leaves – should be done as required to keep the foliage looking neat and tidy.

The variegated version – *Phormium tenax variegatum* – is worthy of a mention (see photographs, page 276). It is smaller, growing to around 1.8m (6ft), and slightly less hardy than the straight green version. The leaves are green striped with pale cream. The purple version – *Phormium tenax purpureum* – is also a popular alternative (see photograph, page 276). It is much smaller, growing to 1.5m (5ft) and even less hardy, although some seriously low temperatures can still be tolerated, so that it still qualifies for the orange hardiness colour code. Both of these plants have the same reddish-brown flowers, which are produced annually.

ABOVE
Phormium tenax is a huge stately plant, essential to viritually all architectural planting schemes.

There are hundreds of other named cultivars available, all with embarrassingly awful names such as 'Apricot Queen', 'Bronze Baby' or 'Dusky Maiden' (sigh!) and all with distressingly loud colours on their foliage. Few are hardy and most will have either died or reverted to a mucky brown colour within two years. They have all been overbred to such an extent that the plants are very unreliable. If you must plant them, they are best regarded as temporary bedding plants and discarded at the end of each season. Their hideous colours are often quite difficult to place in a garden and can disturb the otherwise peaceful tranquillity of a tasteful architectural planting scheme.

Phormium tenax is a very variable plant, both in looks and hardiness. Propagation is therefore best done by division, using a plant that has been carefully chosen for its looks and has proved itself to be of superior quality.

Pests and diseases aren't usually much of a problem, although mealy bugs can be a nuisance, tucking themselves down into the shelter of the leaf bases.

Pieris 'Forest Flame'
Andromeda

A fine mix of two evergreen shrubs, producing what seems to be rather a traditional-looking plant. However, it slips into the exotic class because of its beautiful spring growth and its lovely flowers. And its evergreen shape gives it an architectural presence in the garden.

The leaves are leathery with a glossy sheen. They are produced in sufficient quantities to form plants with nicely layered shapes, which become more apparent with maturity. The gentle roundness of larger plants can always be exaggerated with a pair of shears. The new spring growth is spectacular – a bright flaming red that looks almost artificial. This colouring is on all the new shoots, both on the tops of each plant and also on all of the lateral growth. Large bunches of bell-shaped waxy flowers that are pale cream then follow. The delicate colouring of the flowers contrasts well with the remaining red leaves and the older dark green ones.

These plants perform best in a shady spot, where their colour appears stronger. They need to be in a sheltered position out of the way of any cold, drying winds, which can scorch the leaves. The soil should be moist at all times, but never boggy. Peaty, lime-free soil is preferred, but they will grow in most types except heavy chalk. These plants will sit in containers for years as growth is slow. Leave pots in a shady site and use ericaceous (lime-free) compost for potting.

These plants are perfect for any type of garden and make a fine focal feature if planted singly as a specimen shrub. Plant it where it is easily viewed throughout the spring season when it is at its most interesting.

If growth starts early, late frosts may burn all the new tips, turning them from an attractive red to a very unattractive black. If this happens, cut them off with secateurs. Usually, a second flush will be produced within a few weeks, depending on the weather.

Because it is a hybrid, propagation cannot be done from seed. The easiest method is from cuttings in late summer or from layering. Pests and diseases aren't usually much of a problem.

Pittosporum tobira
Japanese Pittosporum

Pittosporum tobira is one of the most versatile evergreen plants available. It can be trained as a small tree, clipped into a hedge or left as a shapely shrub. The ultimate height is not usually much more than 2.5m (8ft). The leaves are large and leathery and look as though they have been sprayed with leafshine. The pale creamy white flowers are borne in clusters in early summer. After a hot summer, the flowers are followed by bunches of green seed pods the size and shape of cob nuts. When ripe, these split open to reveal bright orange seeds, which remain on the plant for many weeks.

This fantastically salt-resistant plant is an excellent addition to a coastal garden, especially when grown as a long, fragrant hedge. It can be a difficult plant to site correctly, though. Lots of sunshine produces masses of flowers but, if planted in a shady spot, the foliage becomes larger and looks healthier, glossier and a stronger colour. A position somewhere between the two is what to aim for.

Any soil suits this plant, although poor chalky soil will benefit from annual feeding in spring with blood, fish and bone. Once established, it becomes wonderfully drought-resistant. Newly planted shrubs, plus those left in containers, will need plenty of regular irrigation. Just before the new growth starts in the spring, older leaves can become yellow and drop off in alarming amounts. This is all perfectly normal and, providing this phase lasts for only a few weeks, there is nothing to worry about.

The pruning of shaped plants or hedging should be done in early spring or immediately after flowering, which would still leave enough time in the season for the stems to produce a bit of cover to conceal the freshly cut ends.

There is a dwarf version of this plant frequently offered for sale – *Pittosporum tobira* 'Nanum' – which is a compact form suitable for growing in containers. A variegated form, with beautiful silvery cream markings on the leaves and the same deliciously perfumed flowers is also available. Unfortunately, it is hardy in only very mild gardens.

Propagation is easy from semi-ripe cuttings. Black aphids can be a nuisance on new shoots and flower buds and should be removed at the first sign to halt the spread of any virus.

ABOVE
The creamy white flowers change to butter-yellow as they age. They have a fabulous scent, similar to that of gardenias.

Poncirus trifoliata
Japanese Bitter Orange

Unlikely though it seems, *Poncirus trifoliata* is a genuinely hardy type of *Citrus*. It is the only member of its genus and, apart from its novelty value, is a real asset to any exotic garden. It is very slow-growing, reaching only 4.5m (15ft) after several decades. It matures into a gnarled, craggy shape with branches that twist and curl, so it stays interesting even in winter after the leaves have dropped. Although usually deciduous, sometimes the leaves are retained all year round if the weather is especially mild.

It can either be left as an untidy shrub or trained as a tiny single-stemmed tree by removing the lower branches as the plant grows. The leaves are small and leathery and, as with most other *Citrus*, dark green and glossy when young and healthy. These turn butter-yellow in the autumn just before they drop. The stems are covered with brutally sharp spines up to 8cm (3in) long – a wonderful deterrent to would-be intruders if planted near a window or as a hedge near a boundary.

The pretty white flowers are a beautiful sight in spring. They are followed by fruits the size of tangerines, which are fragrant, wrinkled and gradually change from green to yellow as they swell and ripen. These are covered in a lovely soft down and, although they are not edible straight from the plant because of their rather bitter taste, they can be made into jam or jelly. Few fruits are produced unless the plant is very old, so they are probably best left unpicked.

This plant deserves a prime spot in the garden so that it can be viewed all year round. It looks very effective as a single specimen shrub. It always seems to be in short supply at specialist nurseries due to its slow speed of growth so, if you find one, treasure it. It is tough enough to grow in any climate and can be grown successfully in coastal gardens.

Poncirus trifoliata must have full sun and a good loamy soil that is very well drained. It is too slow-growing to need much maintenance, except for an occasional trim to remove overlapping branches, or a light clipping once a year if grown as a hedge. Feed annually in spring with a little blood, fish and bone.

Propagation is easy from fresh seed, or semi-ripe cuttings can be used. Pests and diseases are rarely a problem.

Prunus lusitanica
Portuguese Laurel

One of the hardiest evergreen plants on the market, capable of withstanding mind-blowing temperatures of -32°C (-25°F) without flinching.

Prunus lusitanica is a mass of shiny, leathery leaves of a rich deep green. It is slow-growing and, if left to its own devices, can reach 3m (10ft) after fifteen years. It makes a wonderful hedge and can be formally clipped into a strong angular shape without any difficulty. It can also be clipped at almost any time of year. Keeping a neat and tidy appearance should come before worrying about whether any flower buds are being chopped off. The flowers are okay and the berries that follow are also quite nice. But being 'okay' and 'quite nice' are not good enough reasons to leave this plant unclipped. It is the foliage that deserves the most consideration.

These plants can be grown successfully in containers for several years and, when clipped into cones or lollipop shapes, make a great alternative to the box and bay plants usually found on either side of front doors.

However, they are at their most beautiful when shaped into wide-headed small trees, exposing their fine, sturdy trunks below. It is quite tricky for amateurs to grow these shapes from small plants, and they are usually offered for sale ready clipped. They are not cheap, but their price reflects their old age. The more mature they are, the better the effect. Thirty-year-old plants can have trunks 15cm (6in) in diameter and heads 1.5m (5ft) across. They look stunning when clipped into mushroom shapes, that is, curved across the top of the head and dead straight along the bottom.

These plants look their best in shade where the foliage stays a richer colour. They appreciate fertile conditions and require enough water to keep the soil moist at all times. Any type of soil will do, even chalk or clay, as long as it is enriched annually in spring with something like blood, fish and bone. Annual feeding is even more important if the plants are confined to containers.

Propagation is easy from cuttings but, as the plants take such a long time to achieve a decent size, it is hardly worth the effort unless they are being produced commercially. Keep a watch out for caterpillars.

ABOVE
Prunus lusitanica is the perfect plant for some seriously creative pruning. With a pair of shears and a fertile imagination, beautiful results can be achieved.

Rhamnus alaternus variegata
Variegated Buckthorn

A useful and pretty evergreen shrub from Portugal. The foliage is small and delicate with pale cream variegation on all the leaves. The rather inconspicuous flowers appear in summer. They are tiny clusters of greenish-yellow but are followed by lots of bright orange berries, which are much more noticeable.

Rhamnus alaternus variegata is fast-growing and does a fine job of filling any gaps in the garden. It blends in well with most types of planting scheme, and within ten years could be 2.5m (8ft) tall and 1.2m (4ft) wide. Its ultimate height could be as much as 3.7–4.5m (12–15ft), but this can be controlled easily with shears to make it more suitable for a small garden. It can be planted as a single specimen shrub or in a row for screening or hedging purposes. It also makes a fantastic windbreak for breezy coastal gardens and can cope well with salty sea winds, although planting in permanently windy places, such as on the seafront or on a clifftop, is not advised. This plant is similar in looks to the variegated *Pittosporum tenuifolium* but is much hardier and can therefore be grown more successfully in colder inland gardens.

The variegation makes a noticeable contrast to other exotic plants, not just because of the colour, but also the leaf size. One of these planted near a large-leaved *Fatsia japonica*, a bright green *Hebe parviflora angustifolia* and a spiky glaucous-green *Yucca* x *floribunda* would fill a shady corner of the garden well, giving a good combination of leaf shape, texture and colour.

The planting position can be in sun or shade, but avoid really deep, dank shade. The soil should be light and well drained. Waterlogging won't be tolerated, and heavy clay should also be avoided. Light loam, peat or chalk would all be good options. Poor soil is not a problem, although annual feeding would be beneficial and speed up the growth: a light dose of blood, fish and bone in spring is all that is required.

Propagation is usually done from cuttings. *Rhamnus alaternus variegata* is an easy plant to cultivate, and pests and diseases aren't usually much of a problem.

ABOVE
The cream variegation stays bright even in the shade, unlike many variegated plants, which revert to plain green in shady conditions.

ABOVE
The bright orange berries are produced every autumn in copious amounts on mature plants.

Richea dracophylla

This strange little plant from Tasmania is hard to describe and even more difficult to grow, but it's just the plant if you enjoy a challenge. It has the appearance of a miniature *Cordyline* with green recurved leaves emerging from a central stem, but the leaves are the stiff and waxy texture of a monkey puzzle tree. An evergreen and one of the slowest-growing plants imaginable, it can sit quite happily in a pot for years before it is large enough to plant out. Gardeners who are lucky enough to be able to grow one of these plants to maturity will be rewarded with a fine show of white flowers.

Getting the right conditions for *Richea dracophylla* is not easy. The effect of any errors in cultivation are not immediately apparent, so its demise could be the result of something that didn't meet with its approval six months earlier. It takes months to die, gradually losing its glossy sheen, then very slowly losing its deep colour and taking on a yellowish hue. By the time you notice that something is wrong, closer inspection usually reveals that the plant is just a desiccated version of its former self, with no roots left at all. You feel rather silly when you

realize that the treasured plant you've been nurturing has probably been dead for ages.

Assuming it will rarely get large enough to plant out, pot it up in a terracotta container with ericaceous (lime-free) compost with some chipped bark stirred in for extra drainage. Good light levels are required, but keep it slightly shaded from the midday sun. Watering is the tricky part. Tap water isn't generally liked; if possible, use stored rainwater from a water butt. The soil should never be allowed to dry out and, ideally, should remain just about moist at all times. *Richea dracophylla* needs constant vigilance, so forget about ever taking a summer holiday again unless you take it with you.

Expert gardeners like to have rare plants in their collection. Just because something is rare doesn't necessarily make it beautiful. However, it is worth persevering with *Richea dracophylla* because it really is a pretty little plant.

Other maintenance isn't usually required. An annual feed with the tiniest of doses of blood, fish and bone can be given in the spring. Pests and diseases are not often a problem. Propagation is very slow from seed.

Rosmarinus repens
Creeping Rosemary

Hurrah! At last, a groundcover rosemary that not only grows lush and dense, but is hardy too. Thick, bushy growth hugs the ground and provides the perfect underblanket for sunny Mediterranean-style gardens. The fragrance from the crushed leaves is unbeatable, and the pretty mauve flowers can appear sporadically throughout the year on the previous year's growth, although the main flowering season is early summer.

Rosmarinus repens looks good if allowed to crawl over gravel or left to dangle over the edges of pots, troughs and walls. Plants also look rather splendid hanging out of window boxes. The aromatic leaves can still be used for culinary purposes in exactly the same way as any other rosemary. Unfortunately, this plant is not very long-lived. Older plants become less vigorous as they age and also seem to become less hardy. If used as groundcover, one small plant per 60sq cm (2sq ft) should be enough to provide a dense mat within five years. Plant larger plants at a rate of one per 90sq cm (1sq yd). They not only look attractive, but also provide a dense mulch to keep out the weeds.

There is much confusion over the naming of this plant, so check that you really are buying the correct one.

Full sun is preferred. It is wonderful for coastal gardens, as it copes brilliantly with salty sea winds. Poor, sandy soil is best, but it is generally happy growing anywhere with sharp drainage. Young plants must be watered regularly. Once established, they develop outstanding drought-resistance, but this applies only to plants in the ground.

Feeding is usually unnecessary. Pruning the leaf tips maintains a bushy appearance. Occasionally an entire stem will turn brown for no apparent reason. If this happens, cut it off as far back into the plant as you can reach.

Propagation is easy from cuttings. If sited correctly, pests and diseases are not usually much of a problem, apart from a few leafhoppers in summer. Plants in damp shade, where there is poor airflow, can develop various moulds and mildews.

ABOVE
Large drifts of *Rosmarinus repens* look far better than single specimens.

BELOW
The pretty flowers appear throughout the year.

Solanum laciniatum

Kangaroo Apple or **Poropo**

The leaves of this vigorous evergreen are enormous and beautifully shaped. A young seedling plant can put on almost 1.8m (6ft) of growth per season, and the more plants are hacked back, the bushier and faster they grow. New shoots are sent out from wherever the stems and branches are cut.

From mid-summer onwards, copious amounts of large purple flowers appear all over the plant. The flowering season, which lasts for several months, is followed by the production of green berries, which ripen to a rich yellowy orange. When ripe, I'm told, they make quite a decent jam, but don't eat them when they're still green – they are poisonous at this stage.

Plant in either full sun or light shade. They tolerate breezy coastal gardens surprisingly well for such a large-leaved plant. Any type of soil will do, providing it drains well. They are easy plants to cultivate if planted directly into the ground. Because they cannot survive low temperatures, it is tempting to try to grow them indoors under glass. Try to resist doing this, though, as they grow far too quickly to be kept in containers unless the pots are vast. Under glass, there are the added problems of attracting almost every bug known to man. Outside they remain free from most pests and diseases.

If your garden is cold but you find *Solanum laciniatum* irresistible, plant one out in spring after the frosts have finished. It will grow rapidly during spring and summer, flower, produce berries and reach 1.8m (6ft) before the first frosts of the next winter cut it back. In other words, treat it as an annual and discard it at the end of the season. It seeds quite freely, so you might find seedlings popping up all over the garden the following spring. And, occasionally, after an especially warm winter, it might even survive a second year.

In mild gardens, *Solanum laciniatum* could easily reach 4.5m (15ft). If it outgrows its given space in the garden, prune it hard in the spring. A light annual feed of blood, fish and bone can also be given at this time of year, if required. Propagation is easy from fresh seed harvested from the berries.

Sparmannia africana
House Lime or **African Hemp**

The perfect choice of plant for filling the corner of a large conservatory. *Sparmannia africana* has large jungly leaves that are lime-green and fuzzy; it's difficult to resist stroking them every time you walk past this plant. It is very fast-growing and can soon become the focal feature of an indoor exotic planting scheme. The flowers are wonderful, too, and are produced in copious amounts over a period of several months during late spring and summer.

The best planting position would be directly into the ground, in an indoor border of a greenhouse or conservatory. Unfortunately, most of us aren't lucky enough to possess such facilities, so a container will have to suffice. Make sure the pot is the largest you can possibly obtain – the bigger the pot, the more magnificent the plant will be. Pot up in a soil-based compost, such as John Innes no. 3. Don't bother adding any extra material for drainage.

Water very regularly during the growing season, keeping the soil moist at all times. Leaves this size need lots of irrigation to keep them looking good. However, don't let the roots sit in pools of water, as this will lead to rotting. Feeding is also important. Sprinkle several handfuls of blood, fish and bone into the container during early spring and then give another large dose in early summer. Water it in well. If you find the smell of this food too unpleasant for indoor use, use any high nitrogen food instead.

Sparmannia africana can produce 1.8–2.5m (6–8ft) of growth per season. If it becomes too large or too leggy, it responds to pruning very well. In fact, it can be cut right down to the base and will soon send up new, vigorous and bushy growth. Shears and secateurs are not much use when dealing with mature specimens – you'll need a saw.

Under glass, whitefly will be the main nuisance, and regular inspections should be carried out to catch them at the first sign. The little devils like to hide on the undersides of leaves and pretend they are not really there. Propagation is easy from cuttings.

Spartium junceum
Spanish Broom

A tough evergreen plant that thrives in hostile conditions. The foliage is sparse and whippy, although the overall shape of mature plants is one of billowing curves if planted on the coast, where salty gales keep the growth short and stubby. Inland, the growth becomes rather lush and leggy, and the same curving shape has to be helped along by the occasional use of a pair of shears. It is a wide-spreading shrub, often with a width almost twice that of its height. After ten years, it could reach 2.5m (8ft) across and be 1.5m (5ft) tall.

In summer, large quantities of bright yellow flowers smother the whole plant. Their sweet fragrance can be experienced from some distance away. A constant display can be expected to last for several months. These are followed by numerous slender seed pods.

Apart from being an essential choice for coastal gardens, it is perfect for Mediterranean-style gardens, blending in beautifully with Italian cypress (*Cupressus sempervirens*), dwarf palms (*Chamaerops humilis*) and umbrella pines (*Pinus pinea*). It can also be planted as a single specimen plant in more traditional gardens.

Plant in full sun in exceptionally well-drained soil. *Spartium junceum* cannot tolerate any water gathering around the roots. Choose the final planting position carefully, as it won't survive being transplanted later on. Once established, it can survive in really poor conditions, such as in shallow chalk or on poor, flinty slopes and banks. The more this plant has to struggle, the better its shape. Water in new plants for their first season, then leave them alone; they quickly become very drought-resistant. Even the annual chore of feeding can be dispensed with. These plants are seen all over the Mediterranean, especially Spain, where they grow on virtually nothing. Even the poorest scrubland or steepest cliff can support them.

Pruning should be done either in early spring before the flower buds start to form or in late summer, immediately after flowering. Very little other maintenance is required.

Pests and diseases don't seem to bother this plant either, making it really easy to cultivate. However, take care if your garden is plagued by rabbits: this is one of their favourite snacks. Propagation is from fresh seed.

ABOVE
Mature plants of *Spartium junceum* are beautifully shaped.

Strelitzia reginae
Bird of Paradise Flower

Despite its flamboyant good looks, this plant is surprisingly easy to cultivate. It can sit in a large pot for years and enjoys conservatory conditions. Large flat leaves hold themselves upright on long, fleshy stalks – both the leaves and stalks are bluish-green. Young plants will have only three or four leaves, but each year more and more are sent up, eventually achieving a bushy mass. Growth is very slow: to fill a 60cm (2ft) diameter pot to capacity would take at least fifteen years. The height of the foliage usually reaches no more than 90–120cm (3–4ft).

The main reason for choosing *Strelitzia reginae* is its beautiful flowers. Held up high on sturdy stems, they open out into orange and purple, and last for many weeks.

Flowers are not produced on plants until they are at least five years old. After this time, just one or two will appear in early spring. More and more will be produced each year, if conditions are right. Pot plants up in a soil-based compost, such as John Innes no. 3, and stir in a little extra grit to provide sharp drainage. Keep the soil only just moist during the growing season, and allow it to dry out slightly in winter. Plants will tolerate a fair amount of neglect, but better results will be achieved if given proper attention. A position in light shade is better than one in full sun.

The feeding can be tricky to get a good balance of lush foliage and lots of flowers. Start off by feeding annually with a handful of blood, fish and bone in spring. If this produces healthy-looking leaves and the plant performs well during the flowering season, continue with this feeding regime. Sometimes, though, the foliage can be plentiful and lush, but no flowers. If this happens, try tomato food instead. This will add more potash to the soil, which encourages flower production. However, if there are lots of flowers but the leaves take on an unhealthy yellowish tinge and decrease in size, then add high-nitrogen feed to restore their appearance.

Repot only when the plant is almost bursting out of the container. Pot it up into something only slightly larger, as being rootbound helps to give a better floral display.

Apart from a few aphids, nothing much seems to bother this plant. Propagation is easy from seed, but it's a slow process, so buying a mature plant is advisable instead.

ABOVE
Strelitzia flowers take on the shape of an exotic bird's head, clearly depicting the beak and the feathery crest found on the heads of certain birds in lush jungle areas.

■■ Telanthophora grandifolia

SYN. *Senecio grandifolius*

An exciting and unusual Mexican plant for the conservatory. The foliage and the flowers get equal billing – both are magnificent. The leaves are large and furry with a jungly appearance. The flowering season lasts for most of the winter, when lots of individual flowers combine together to make huge heads of brilliant yellow. They give off a very pleasant scent and are attractive to any bees still around at that time of year.

To get the very best from this plant, it must be grown in a container that measures at least 60cm (2ft) in diameter. *Telanthophora grandifolia* can easily reach 2.5m (8ft) in height and 1.2m (4ft) across, although its size can always be controlled with secateurs. In fact, pruning keeps the plant looking bushy and encourages new growth. Pot it up in soil-based compost, such as John Innes no. 3. There is no need to add anything extra for drainage, as moisture-retentive soil is required for optimum growth. Position the pot somewhere sunny, but away from the full scorching effect of the midday sun.

With such huge leaves and flowers to support, lots of regular irrigation is required throughout the growing and flowering season, but never let the soil become saturated. After flowering has finished, let it dry out slightly until it begins to put on the next season's new growth. Feed with generous amounts of blood, fish and bone in early summer. This food is perfect, even though it's a bit smelly for indoor use, but it can be forked in lightly to help mask its unpleasant pong.

For such a large leafy plant, *Telanthophora grandifolia* is rarely bothered by pests and diseases. If it gets too wet or cold, grey fluffy mould (botrytis) can be a nuisance on the lower leaves. Remove any affected leaves at the first sign to prevent its spread. Increasing the airflow and the temperature in winter will also help.

Any pruning can take place right at the start of the growing period, but any dead flower heads should be cut off as soon as they become unattractive. Propagation is easiest from cuttings.

ABOVE
The yellow flower heads can be more than 30cm (1ft) across. They last for several months and make a fine display in even the largest conservatory.

BELOW
The large floppy leaves are topped with huge flower heads in winter.

Tetrapanax papyrifera
Rice Paper Plant

SYN. *Aralia papyrifera*
   Fatsia papyrifera

A fantastic addition to jungly planting schemes and essential for gardeners who love big leaves. *Tetrapanax papyrifera* is a large evergreen shrub, although, by removing the lower leaves on older plants, it could almost be classed as a small tree. It has an unruly manner, wilfully refusing to grow straight. The deeply lobed leaves, as well as the stems, are covered in white powdery stuff that is quite harmless but occasionally causes violent sneezing if too much is inhaled.

Small plants stay neat and tidy for the first few years, then, as they gain height, the stems become gnarled and twisted. *Tetrapanax papyrifera* often grow as multi-stemmed plants, and the extra stems can be removed if a more tree-shaped effect is required. A mature plant of ten years old could reach 3.7m (12ft); sometimes older plants are seen nearly 6m (20ft) tall, but this would happen only in mild gardens. In cold gardens, the leaves won't survive the winter but the plant remains root hardy, so will usually regenerate from the base the following spring.

There are several forms of this plant available; some are much hardier than others and could fit into the orange hardiness category. However, unless the exact form being purchased is known, it is best to assume that they are not reliably frost-resistant. Flowers are produced in the autumn. Long and cream in colour, they are passably attractive, but can be removed to channel the plant's energy back into the leaves.

Plant in a very sheltered spot away from any wind that could tear the leaves. This plant prefers rich, heavy, moist soil, but never let it sit in water, as the roots will rot. It is particularly fond of clay soil, which often holds moisture well. Water in new plants, but watering becomes less necessary as the plant ages. Plant in light shade; too much sun can bleach the leaves and too much shade draws the plant up to make it even leggier than normal.

Feed annually in the spring with something rich, such as well-rotted manure. Leggy plants can be pruned back hard in late spring. Capsid bugs can be a nuisance and ruin the appearance of the leaves. Green aphids are also quite fond of the new shoots. Propagation is easiest from cuttings, as fresh seed can be difficult to find.

ABOVE
The leaves of *Tetrapanax papyrifera*, which can easily be more than 30cm (1ft) across, grow on the end of very long stems. These are filled with pith, which is used for making Chinese rice paper.

■ ■ Tibouchina urvilleana

Another wonderful plant for the conservatory, although it might just be worth trying outside in really mild gardens. The foliage is a mass of glaucous-green leaves, each one covered with a soft velvety coating.

Bright pink, fuzzy flower buds start to form in late summer. They open out into a dazzling shade of royal purple and are produced in large quantities for most of the winter. Each delicate-looking flower is 5cm (2in) across.

This plant needs a good-sized pot to live in if it is going to last for more than a few seasons. Use John Innes no. 3 compost, with a bit of extra grit stirred in for good drainage. Position the container in a brightly lit spot but away from the scorching effect of the midday sun. When it is actively growing, water frequently enough to keep the compost just moist at all times. Don't allow it to dry out, otherwise it will shed copious amounts of leaves almost overnight. After the flowering has finished, water it slightly less until more new growth can be seen.

Tibouchina urvilleana is a fast-growing Brazilian plant that, without regular annual pruning, can become too tall and leggy to look good in a container. The best time to cut it back is in late spring just as it starts the new season's growth. Cut back really hard to within 30cm (1ft) from the base to just above a leaf node (where the leaf bud pokes out from the stem). This will keep the plant nice and bushy. Alternatively, grow it unchecked for two or three years and then discard it when it looks a bit tatty and replace it with a new plant. Feed every spring with a handful of blood, fish and bone.

If it's grown under glass, make regular checks for all manner of nasty bugs. Everything likes this plant, and any outbreaks must be dealt with immediately they are spotted. The most likely unwanted visitors are whitefly, red spider mites and green aphids. Various large caterpillars might also be seen occasionally. This plant would benefit by spending at least part of the summer outdoors in the garden if the container is of a manageable size. Propagation is from semi-ripe cuttings.

Viburnum cinnamomifolium

There is nothing at all delicate about this plant. It is similar in looks to the more familiar garden varieties such as *Viburnum davidii*, but on a much larger scale. The leaves are large, dark and evergreen, and grow on rather pretty red stems. The overall dimensions for a mature shrub could be 3.7–4.5m (12–15ft) tall and 2.5m (8ft) wide after ten years. The flowers – clusters of little white blooms – are not very exciting, but the berries that follow the flowers are attractive bunches of shiny blue-black. This is definitely a plant to grow for its foliage and size, rather than for its floral display.

It is quite slow to get going, taking at least four years to reach only 60cm (2ft) but, once it settles in, the speed of growth accelerates considerably. It loves being in the shade and fills a dark corner of the garden very well. It is perfect for the back of shady borders and in woodland aspects. It looks just as comfortable among jungly exotic foliage plants as it does in more traditional planting schemes.

This plant requires rich, fertile soil to produce the maximum size of leaves, which can be 15cm (6in) long and 8cm (3in) wide. Feed the surrounding area of soil every spring with lots of well-rotted manure. Moisture is essential , especially for newly planted shrubs. Ideally, the soil should never dry out, but give just enough water to sustain the roots without the ground ever becoming waterlogged. Plant in a sheltered position away from strong winds.

There is little maintenance to be thought about. Pruning shouldn't be necessary, providing some thought has gone into the planting position. Make sure there is enough room around the plant so it can mature into its full size without crowding out anything else. Restricting its size would be a pity, and transplanting isn't really an option, as it would be unlikely to survive such a move.

Pests and diseases are rarely a problem, although a few green aphids might appear on the new growing tips during hot weather. Propagation is usually from semi-ripe cuttings, but this is a slow process and it will take years before a decent-sized plant is produced. Large specimens are seldom seen in nurseries, but it would be worth buying the biggest one possible for instant effect in the garden.

ABOVE
A huge monster of a *Viburnum* from China with a virtually unpronounceable name.

Weinmannia trichosperma

In its native Chile, *Weinmannia trichosperma* grows as a large tree. However, in an average temperate garden, its stature will be somewhat diminished. It will still grow as a handsome evergreen, but expect no more than about 3.7m (12ft) after fifteen years. The leaves are beautifully crafted into little fern shapes that appear soft and delicate but are actually quite coarse to the touch. This plant is very rare in cultivation, and it's definitely one that your neighbours won't have.

The new season's growth is particularly lovely. The little fern shapes are a bright emerald-green with a glossy finish to them. The pleasantly fragrant flowers appear on mature specimens. These are quite odd and very striking: pale creamy cylinder shapes tipped with bright pinkish-red filaments. They are followed by little red seed capsules.

This is quite a fussy plant and it can be tricky finding the right planting position. Plant out as soon as possible after purchasing it from the nursery. They are slow to bulk up, so buying one of a decent size to start with makes sense. The site should be partly shaded from bright

sunlight during the hottest part of the day, while still maintaining good light levels. The soil should be fairly fertile – rich loam would be perfect. Although not a lime-hating plant, poor chalky soils would lack enough nutrients and moisture to keep it happy and healthy. Plant in a sheltered spot away from cold winds.

Water in well to start with, keeping the soil moist at all times, without it ever becoming boggy. If possible, try to plant where the soil retains some moisture but is also well drained so that any excess water quickly runs away.

Weinmannia trichosperma makes a beautiful specimen plant, deserving a focal position in the garden. Leave enough space around it so that it can be fully admired, without being crowded by other plants. As with many other Chilean plants, it doesn't always appreciate being fed. Add just the tiniest helping of blood, fish and bone to the surrounding soil in late spring, if required, to keep the foliage a good colour.

Propagation is from cuttings. Pests and diseases aren't generally much of a problem, but check new growth occasionally for signs of our old familiar pals, namely green aphids.

ABOVE
The new foliage is bright emerald-green in the spring.

Zantedeschia aethiopica 'Crowborough'

Arum Lily or **Lily of the Nile**

A big, leafy herbaceous plant with large jungly leaves up to 60cm (2ft) long and 30cm (1ft) across. They are bright fresh green in colour and rather fragile. The flowers are delightful: enormous pure white trumpets with a real look of the tropics about them. This is a clump-forming plant that increases in width each year, although its height rarely exceeds 90cm (3ft).

These plants look particularly effective in large groups along the banks of ponds or streams, where they can have constant access to water, for which they have an almost insatiable thirst. In very mild gardens, they can be planted directly into a pond or lake margin, providing that the water never freezes and that it is at least 30cm (1ft) deep so that the rhizome (root system) stays a good distance away from any frost.

There are many Arum Lilies available but the 'Crowborough' variety seems to be hardier than all of the others, and it is also much more forgiving of less than ideal growing conditions.

Very rich, heavily manured soil gives the best results. The planting position can be sun or shade, but light shade is best, as this will give the leaves a rich, bright green colour. In full sun, they can become slightly yellow. Shelter from strong winds is advisable, as the large leaves can tear easily. Copious amounts of water throughout the growing season will be needed for the foliage to reach its maximum size.

Zantedeschia aethiopica 'Crowborough' is a fairly good choice for growing in containers and can give successful results, but the watering during the summer has to be done so frequently that it can become a real chore.

These plants die down each winter, with the foliage gradually becoming more and more yellow and unattractive. Remove these older leaves as they become discoloured, until everything is cut down to ground level.

Propagation is easiest from suckers, which can be separated from the main rhizome during early spring. Despite their appetizing-looking leaves, they seem to be remarkably untroubled by pests and diseases.

Spiky & succulent plants

This chapter features an exciting selection of some of the most dramatic and beautiful plants in the world. All of them are architectural and shapely, while some have the added bonus of colourful and exotic blooms.

My fascination with spiky plants turned into an obsession twelve years ago after two trips to Arizona in the early 1990s. To me, the Sonoran Desert is still the most beautiful place in the whole world, even though I have travelled to many other exciting places since.

The memories of trekking in the peace and quiet of the desert on a little horse called Coal, surrounded by the majestic presence of giant *Yucca* and *Agave*, are very special. *Yucca*, in particular, are plentiful in this region, where they're all left to reach their full size and age. They are an awesome sight, and are used to the full by the local wildlife. Desert rodents burrow into the trunks, and birds use them for nesting, creating little neighbourhood colonies. I became well and truly addicted to *Yucca* and have remained so ever since.

As for succulent plants, everyone seems to like them. Their range of shapes and sizes is huge, and they seem to crop up in almost every country I visit. Many of them are small and collectable, and they seem to span almost the entire spectrum of colour, from blue *Echeveria* to purple-black *Aeonium*, with every shade of green in between. Many are hardy, but those that aren't are quite often small enough to be accommodated on the windowsill for the winter.

Spiky and succulent plants are probably the most architectural of all.

All the spiky and succulent plants in this chapter are evergreen, and they all have a strong shape. They can make a really bold statement in the garden. Many are decorated with sharp spines and thorns, some having the ferocity of daggers. All of this adds to their appeal. These plants are not for the meek and timid! A leaflet published by the Arizona Native Plants Society eloquently sums up the varying degrees of sharpness on a scale of zero to four: 0 = soft tips, 1 = not offensive, 2 = painful, 3 = injurious and 4 = positively dangerous.

Most of the plants discussed here are easy to look after and will cope with virtually any soil. The Sonoran Desert, for example, is very alkaline and all the plants that grow there are blissfully content. They need no special requirements, and most can be grown to a good size without too many problems. Some can experience very low temperatures, despite their provenance. These plants are very adaptable, and many can cope with the winter cold of cooler climates. What spiky and succulent plants really hate, however, is being too wet in the winter. They have no natural immunity to the damp, foggy weather found in many places; they are used to crisp, dry air. This can be partially overcome by choosing the hottest and driest part of the garden as a planting site. Adding masses of extra grit to the soil to ensure perfect drainage will also help.

In really cold areas, smaller plants can be protected by keeping them in pots and bringing them under cover for winter. Larger plants can be treated with a copper-based fungicide in autumn, which is applied as a drench every six weeks throughout the winter. This acts as a partial substitute for their non-existent

immune system, and should help to act as a preventative for rots and other leaf spots that can occur if there's an excessive amount of rain.

The leaves on many of these plants turn brown as they age but do not fall off. They can accumulate as drooping thatch as their numbers increase over the years. In the desert, this is fine because the thatch provides hiding places for animals and helps shade the plant from the intense summer heat. However, in smart cultivated gardens, brown leaves look messy and a plant's appearance is greatly improved by their removal. Removing the brown bits of a plant is called 'brown-bitting' (see left).

Propagating this group of plants is very easy and rewarding. Many can be propagated from fresh seed, such as *Dasylirion* and *Furcraea*, although tracking down good suppliers is sometimes difficult. *Yucca* and *Agave* send up little plantlets from the root system. These are referred to as 'toes' and can be cut away from the main plant with a sharp knife. Do this in late spring or early summer. Cut as near to the base of the parent plant as possible. It does not matter if the toes come off without any roots on them. Leave the cuttings on a sunny windowsill until the cut end has dried off – this takes only a couple of days. Pot them into some gritty compost, water in and then leave them alone until signs of new growth appear – a sure indication that some roots have developed. The only way to fail is to ignore warnings of leaving them alone and, instead, be tempted into giving them more water – this will probably lead to rotting. Once the plant is growing well, pot it up into its permanent position in the garden or into a larger pot.

Most spiky and succulent plants can be grown in containers with much success. Use a soil-based compost, such as John Innes no. 3, and stir in up to 50 per cent of extra grit. Just because these type of plants can cope with poor, dry soil, it doesn't mean that's what they prefer. Give them regular doses

1. The lower leaves of this *Yucca* have been left on for a few years, which gives the plant an unkempt appearance.
2. Start cutting the lowest leaves off one at a time as close to the trunk as possible with very sharp secateurs. Work up through the plant until only lush green leaves are left.
3. For extra neatness, make sure that the remaining stumps of the leaf bases are all the same length. This creates a rather attractive 'pineapple' effect.
4. The task completed.

The flowers of
Colletia cruciata
have a rich
almond fragrance.

ABOVE
Carpobrotus edulis
is a fleshy
groundcover plant,
essential for
seaside gardens.

RIGHT
Puya chilensis is
a seriously spiky
relative of the
pineapple plant.

of blood, fish and bone at least once every year in late spring, plus plenty of moisture during spring and summer, and their growth rate and appearance will improve hugely.

Succulents such as *Aeonium* are also easy to propagate from cuttings. Sometimes these plants become top-heavy – the size and weight of their heads are too much for the stems to support. When this stage is reached, cut off the top of the plant, with around 10cm (4in) of stalk attached. Let the cut end dry off on a sunny windowsill for a couple of days, just as before with *Agave* and *Yucca* 'toes'. Then push the stem into very gritty compost and leave it to root. The remains of the old plant will look a bit sad – just a bare stem in a pot – but don't throw it away because, after a few weeks, new tiny plants will emerge in clusters from the top and sides of the stalk. Within a few months, a splendid new multi-headed *Aeonium* will have formed.

This group of plants all has similar requirements, and it is, therefore, possible to grow many different types of them in the same planting area. They all complement each other brilliantly. *Yucca* and *Colletia* provide height; *Agave*, *Beschorneria* and *Dasylirion* provide bulk. Then there is *Carpobrotus* and *Lampranthus* to finish off the whole look as groundcover. Ornamental mulch spread around each plant not only keeps the weeds down, but emphasizes each sculptural shape too. It can also help to stop rain splashing mud onto the leaves and spoiling their pristine condition. Use either pea shingle or slate chips, or anything else that takes your fancy.

If using a lot of these lovely spiky beasts seems rather overpowering, plant a few of them through the garden beds as occasional statements. They can really add drama to unexciting herbaceous borders.

ABOVE
The tropical-looking flowers of *Beschorneria yuccoides* last for several months.

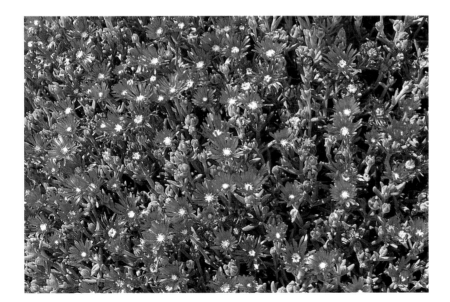

LEFT
Lampranthus spectabilis gives a dazzling floral display during the summer.

■■ Aeonium

There are many different *Aeonium*. All are beautiful, all need similar care and none is hardy.

They are delicate succulent plants with rosettes of foliage comprising numerous 'petals' clustered tightly together. The leaves are often very shiny, which adds to their appeal. Young plants start off with a single rosette. Mature plants often have many heads at the ends of each branched stem. None is likely to get any taller than 90cm (3ft) in an average temperate climate. Flowers appear on older plants as large bunches of daisy-like blooms, which are nearly always yellow. They are so numerous that they can upset the balance of the plant and cause it to topple over. Either support them with canes or, better still, chop them off. The foliage is much prettier than the flowers.

Aeonium are perfect for conservatories. They enjoy the heat of the summer and require frost protection under glass during the winter. They can tolerate low temperatures but must not be allowed to freeze. All require good light but not necessarily full sun. Larger specimens can be taken outside for the summer and grouped together on the terrace, and then brought in

for just the winter months. Younger and smaller plants can sit on windowsills to overwinter. All require very well-drained compost. They look good planted individually in terracotta pots or they can be planted as several together in larger containers. Water generously during summer, but keep them much drier in winter when they are dormant. A light dose of a balanced fertilizer can be given annually in late spring. Pests and diseases aren't much of a problem, apart from the occasional aphid. Overwatering is by far the most common cause of death. All can be propagated from cuttings.

Aeonium balsamiferum is a lovely, compact plant with pale green leaves. In strong sunlight, it gives off the wonderful scent of balsam, which can be detected from some distance away. *Aeonium* 'Schwarzkopf' has foliage of such a deep purple that it is almost black. *Aeonium cuneatum* has pale matt green, cup-shaped rosettes up to 45cm (18in) long. *Aeonium tabulaeforma* is one of the smallest and prettiest, with very flat rosettes made up of masses of green petals, so tightly intertwined they look almost artificial.

Agave americana
Century Plant

This is one of the largest spiky plants that can safely be grown outdoors in most temperate climates. Although it has a red hardiness colour code, its hardiness increases with size. A more mature specimen of 90cm (3ft) is much tougher and could almost be promoted into the next colour category.

Large, heavy leaves curve gently outwards forming an enormous tulip shape. They are blue-grey and have the appearance of being lightly dusted with white powder. They are edged with painfully sharp spines. Each leaf ends in a long pointed needle, perfect for repelling unwelcome visitors. The central core of the plant, from which each new leaf unfurls, is a solid mass that remains unforgivingly rigid and capable of inflicting savage wounds. Growth is very slow. Each leaf takes such a long time to emerge that the shape of the teeth from the leaf next in the queue remains as a permanent imprint.

Plants of thirty years old could reach a height and width of 1.5m (5ft) if growing in a suitable site. The flower spikes are extremely impressive but they're rarely seen on plants younger than twenty-five years old. Most take about forty years to bloom. The common name of century plant was given because it was once thought that it took one hundred years to flower. After flowering, the whole plant dies, but it is usually replenished with offshoots sent up from the old rootstock.

A variegated form is often available with leaves striped yellow and green. This is *Agave americana* 'Variegata', which gets as large as its blue counterpart but is less hardy. A wonderful rare form that is always in short supply and blessed with the name of *Agave americana* 'Mediopicta Alba' is probably the most beautiful of all the *Agave*. It is much smaller and much less hardy than the type. The leaves are dark green and striped with a lovely pale silvery cream. It cannot be propagated from seed and sends up only the occasional offset, so material for propagation is scarce.

Full sun is essential, and so is a very gritty, well-drained compost. If *Agave americana* is planted outdoors in colder areas, position it

on a sunny slope, if possible. This will ensure that excess rain runs straight off instead of settling around the central core and the rootball. The variegated form, being less hardy, requires milder conditions than the blue-leaved type. It is more suited to coastal gardens or warmer inner cities. All *Agave* can cope with strong sea breezes and add a Mediterranean feel to any seafront. The white-striped *Agave* is best kept in a pot and brought under glass for the winter. It isn't even remotely hardy, and is too rare and expensive to risk leaving outside.

All *Agave* are excellent choices for pots. They are slow-growing, so do not require frequent repotting, and if they dry out occasionally, no lasting damage is done. Blue *Agave* look particularly effective contrasted with the colour of a terracotta pot. Use John Innes no. 3 compost with lots of extra grit stirred in for really perfect drainage. Water as much as you would for any other plant during late spring and all through the summer, but keep fairly dry during the autumn and winter. Low temperatures can be endured if the plant is kept dry. If a plant becomes soggy, freezing weather will kill small specimens and cause rotting in larger ones.

Feed annually with either some well-rotted manure or a mix of blood, fish and bone, sprinkled around the base of the plant. Poor soil can be tolerated, but a richer one will give very rewarding results. Take care not to get any food onto the leaves – they are sensitive and could become scorched.

Propagation is best from offsets sent up from the root system of the parent plant. Mealy bugs can sometimes be a problem, especially if the plants are kept in pots under glass. Plants growing in the conservatory would benefit from being taken outside during the hottest months of the year. Various rots and fungal infections can also occur if the soil is poorly drained and water is allowed to collect around the roots.

LEFT
Agave attenuata
is a perfect choice
for a shady
conservatory.

Agave attenuata
Tulip-leaved Agave

Shapely rosettes of bluish-green succulent leaves on stout arching stems make this *Agave* one of the most beautiful in its family. The leaves are similar in shape to those of a tulip, tapering to a point. The tips are soft to the touch, unlike most *Agave*. The foliage of *Agave attenuata* appears to be lightly dusted with powder. A handsome plant indeed. The flowers are absurd, arching spikes up to 3.7m (12ft) long. After flowering, the whole plant dies, but there are usually plenty of baby plants around to take their place. In temperate climates, *Agave attenuata* is unlikely to flower, even if kept in a warm, bright conservatory.

Although native to Mexico, *Agave attenuata* does not have the heat of the desert to contend with – it is found in higher altitude areas that are less hot and more humid. Therefore, it is perfect for the shadier, cooler part of the conservatory. Grow it in a huge terracotta pot and keep the compost just moist. Too much water will cause rotting, and too little will make it dry out and shrivel. Light levels are important as well. Too much direct sun won't kill it, but the colour will change to a yellowy green. Shade helps it stay a lovely blue-green hue. Position this plant in the conservatory out of the way of passing dogs and people – the delicate foliage can tear very easily.

Feed during late spring with just a light helping of blood, fish and bone. Make sure that the food is put directly onto the soil, avoiding all contact with the leaves. It is also important to water carefully so that none is splashed onto the foliage. Drops of water can spoil the appearance by leaving marks. Older leaves that have aged and gone brown can be removed by cutting them off as near to the stem as possible. Don't try to pull them.

Transporting one of these *Agave* can be tricky. They are very fragile and need to be kept very still for the journey home. Wedge the pots with whatever is to hand, so that all movement is kept to the absolute minimum.

The main pests of these plants are red spider mites, which are regular visitors to conservatories. To help reduce infestations, move the plant outside into the garden during the hottest months of the year. Propagation is by the removal of offsets.

■ Agave celsii

Agave celsii is a beautifully shaped spiky plant with foliage that can range in colour from bluish-green to dark bottle-green. The leaves are artistically arranged to form a perfect rosette. The outer edge of each leaf's perimeter is covered with lots of little reddish-brown barbs, all spaced at exactly the same interval, just like tiny teeth. These are fairly sharp, but not dangerous. However, the final 'needle' at the end of each leaf could give quite a fearsome jab to unsuspecting flesh.

The flower spike is enormous, held way above the plants, and flowers form on the top third of this. They could be described as interesting, rather than lovely.

In very mild gardens, these plants look good in groups, and contrast well with other spiky plants and succulents, especially groundcover ones such as *Lampranthus*. They require lots of light, but not necessarily full sun all day long. If given maximum sunshine, they remain happy but tend to be less clump-forming.

In gardens where cold and wet winters are guaranteed, grow *Agave celsii* in good-sized terracotta pots. They can then stand outside for the summer and be brought in under glass when the temperatures dip. The size of a mature plant won't be much more than 60cm (2ft) across, so transporting them indoors is not too much of a problem. Use a loam-based compost, such as John Innes no. 3, and stir in masses of extra grit. Water regularly throughout the growing season.

Keeping these plants dry during the winter is the most important part of their care. Water collecting on the leaves can cause all sorts of rotting and leaf spots if the weather is very cold. Older plants can gather dust or become mucky from chalky deposits from years of watering. If this happens, use a soft, dry cloth to clean off each leaf gently until it shines again. Feed annually in late spring with any balanced feed – blood, fish and bone is as good as anything. Old leaves that have become brown can be removed with a sharp knife. Cut them off as close to the stem as possible. Pests and diseases are generally not a problem, but mealy bugs could infect plants that are kept indoors permanently. Propagation is easy either from fresh seed or by removing offsets.

ABOVE
Each fleshy leaf emerges from the centre of the plant, then widens into a slightly dipped scoop before tapering to a final point at the end.

Agave parryi

Agave parryi has wide, chunky leaves arranged in a dainty rosette. It is one of the prettiest *Agave* in the world, and it also has the distinction of being one of the hardiest. The foliage is blue-grey and each leaf is edged with hooked barbs. The leaves taper to a curved needle.

The flowers are huge spikes, which open up into yellow 'candelabra'. They last for many months and then the whole rosette dies. Away from its native habitats of New Mexico and Arizona, flowering is rare. Propagation can be done in the usual way by removing offsets from around the base of the parent plant. However, sometimes this *Agave* produces little bulbils on the flower stalks, which can be removed and used for growing on. Seed can also be used, but there are quite a few different types of *Agave parryi*, so propagating in this way can be a bit of a gamble as you can't be sure what the plants will look like when mature. The best one by miles is *Agave parryi* 'Truncata', which always seems to be in short supply. It has a beautifully curved, compact shape, like a rather posh cabbage. Fully grown plants are almost round.

This is a small *Agave* with each rosette not much more than 45cm (18in) across. It can sit in a large pot for years, and is easier than most to carry indoors for the winter. Although hardy, it must stay dry to cope with low temperatures. In many countries, rain is part of the winter climate, so it needs the protection of a conservatory or porch, otherwise the whole plant could disintegrate into a soggy mess.

If planted outdoors in the garden, choose the sunniest spot possible, so that any rain can drain away immediately. Exceptionally well-drained soil is vital. Chalky soil is particularly good, as it drains quickly, and *Agave* are quite happy growing in alkaline conditions. They look good planted in groups, rather than as individual plants. Make sure slugs are kept away – they enjoy scraping off the surface of the leaves, which leaves a permanent scar.

Very little maintenance is required. Keep plants watered during spring and summer, and give a light feed of blood, fish and bone in late spring. Remove any old leaves with a sharp knife. Repotting can be done in early summer, removing any offsets at the same time.

ABOVE
Agave parryi is an excellent choice of plant for growing in a container.

■ Agave salmiana 'Ferox'

A magnificent brute of a plant and king of all the *Agave*. Each leaf is a weighty affair: long, wide and fleshy. The leaves are dark olive-green and edged with painfully sharp hooks, but the really dangerous part is the leaf tip. This finishes with an exquisitely sharp point, about 10cm (4in) long. Being pierced with one of these tends to dominate future conversations for quite some time....

A mature plant can be enormous and extremely heavy to move around if it is planted in a terracotta pot. But, as this *Agave* can be planted in the ground only in fairly mild areas, there may be no other alternative. Warm coastal areas are ideal because it can then be planted directly into the ground, where it can be allowed to reach full size without being a burden. Twenty-year-old plants can be 1.2m (4ft) tall and 1.2m (4ft) wide. As each thick leaf holds its own water supply, this adds up to some considerable weight.

Choose a planting position in full sun, ideally on slightly sloping ground to maximize drainage. It can be planted as close to the sea as you wish because it is virtually hurricane-proof. Being

blasted by strong salty gales on a cliff top would not cause any difficulties whatsoever – the whole plant is completely solid, leaving nothing for the wind to move around. Larger specimens are much hardier than smaller ones and can take several degrees of frost, providing the weather remains fairly dry. A really wet winter, together with prolonged periods of frost, can turn it all to a mushy heap.

Any sharply drained soil is suitable, and watering should be done regularly in spring and summer. It is only during winter that watering becomes harmful. Feed with well-rotted manure or several handfuls of blood, fish and bone in late spring or early summer. This is rather a greedy plant, having large leaf areas to keep healthy.

In colder inland areas, keep confined to a huge terracotta pot, so that it can be moved under cover at the start of the winter. A pot standing on a wheeled base would be the most suitable, to make transporting it less of a burden. Pests and diseases aren't usually a problem, but various rots and fungal infections are possible in overly wet conditions.

ABOVE
Away from its native country of Mexico, *Agave salmiana* 'Ferox' is unlikely to flower, but it can be enjoyed as one of the most exciting foliage plants in the world.

Aloe aristata
Hardy Aloe

This is the hardiest *Aloe* in the world, able to cope with really low temperatures and a wide variety of climates. It is a slow-growing plant made up of individual rosettes of up to 25cm (10in) across. These gradually spread to form thick clumps. The foliage is dark green and fleshy, and each leaf is streaked with white, dotted lines (tubercles) and ends with a soft curling tip. The leaves contain a lovely slimy gel, which can be used to soothe minor burns, just like its famous cousin *Aloe vera*. The rosettes are stemless and therefore hug the ground closely. Its total height is about 20cm (8in).

Tall flower stems, which last for many weeks, rise out of the centre of each rosette in summer and open out into orange-red elongated bells. Full sun is essential for plants to flower.

These plants can be used as unusual groundcover or as rockery plants. They also look very effective in large drifts in gravel gardens or planted individually throughout any exotic planting scheme. Young plants can be potted into containers small enough to sit on a window sill. Mature plants look especially attractive in large terracotta dishes. Plant in generous numbers as they are slow to spread. A 60cm (2ft) diameter dish planted up with four mature plants will take about six years to become full to overflowing. Little offsets are sent up at regular intervals to fill in all the surrounding spaces. These can be left to form larger clumps or be separated from the parent plant and used for propagation. Offsets can be pulled off – there is no need to cut them.

Aloe aristata can be planted in full sun or light shade, but the more sunshine it receives, the more flowers it will produce. Well-drained, gritty soil is important for good drainage. Very little maintenance is necessary. A light feed of any balanced fertilizer can be given annually in late spring. Water frequently during spring and summer, but keep much drier in winter.

Pests and diseases are rarely a problem, apart from the odd slug scraping the fleshy leaves. Mealy bugs could be occasional visitors on plants kept indoors all year.

ABOVE
This native to the Cape Province of South Africa is an easy choice for novice gardeners.

BELOW
Copious amounts of orange-red flowers appear in the summer.

■ ■ Aloe ferox

A big and bold succulent from the Cape Province of South Africa and a perfect choice for conservatories. The large fleshy leaves are bluish-green and covered with lots of rubbery barbs and thorns, which look far more menacing than they really are. Each leaf is filled with a thick syrupy liquid, the trademark of most of the *Aloe* family.

The flowers are amazing spikes of fiery orange-red. They are produced annually and can last for several months.

Aloe ferox can cope with all of the hostile conditions often found in conservatories. The summer heat and scorching sunshine will be enjoyed; the stuffy atmosphere and hot, dry air is also no problem. It can cope with no heating in winter, as long as it doesn't actually freeze. On top of all this, it can live in a pot for years.

Choose a good-sized terracotta pot. *Aloe ferox* is very slow-growing, but repotting is quite difficult due to its bulk. Therefore, choosing a large pot will make this chore a less frequent one. Choose a good quality soil-based compost, such as John Innes no. 3, and stir in lots of extra grit to provide a free-draining

mix. This eliminates the need for putting the usual pile of broken crocks at the bottom of the pot to aid drainage.

Irrigation should be done frequently during the growing season and while the plant is flowering. When flowering has finished, cut off the old stems and ease up on watering, keeping it only just moist until signs of growth are seen the following year. Feed annually in early summer with any balanced fertilizer. Liquid feed is the easiest to use; powder or granules are tricky to apply when plants are mature, as the top of the pot can be obscured by the mass of leaves, and residue on the foliage can leave scorch marks.

If plants spend all of their life under glass, they may become susceptible to mealy bugs. Plants stay much healthier if they can be moved outside for the summer to give them some fresh air. The odd shower of rain also helps to keep them clean. This tough plant can be killed only by excessive overwatering, or if it's not watered at all. Propagation can be done by removing unwanted offsets from the base of the parent plant.

Aloe striatula

An upright, branching succulent with long, pointed, fleshy leaves that are filled with a thick, syrupy jelly. Plants can easily reach 1.2m (4ft) tall and 90cm (3ft) wide after just five years. The bright yellow flowers are produced in summer and last for many weeks. These South African plants are hardy anywhere except in bad frost pockets, but they are especially suitable for coastal gardens and seem to thrive in the salty sea air. However, they need some shelter from the strongest sea winds, otherwise they can topple over.

Choose a planting site in full sun with very well-drained soil. Plants can become top-heavy as they age, so the support of a wall can be useful. If planted in the middle of the garden, either support their weight with some kind of prop or cut them back to half their size every few years. This encourages more offsets to be produced from the base, and bushier plants need less help in standing up straight. Only very young plants are suitable for growing in pots, as older ones become too branched and bulky.

Water young specimens well when first planted. Once they become established, they are very drought-tolerant and can last for long periods without rain. Feed annually in late spring with blood, fish and bone, taking care not to get any in direct contact with the foliage, as this can cause scorching. Remove older brown leaves with secateurs, cutting in as close to the stem as possible for a tidy appearance. Remove any old flower stems, cutting as far down into the plant as you can.

Plants can be raised from seed but it is quicker and easier to produce new stock by removing offsets. Cuttings can also be used. Allow the cut end to dry off for a few days before potting into gritty compost. Slugs can be a real nuisance, leaving unsightly scrapings across the surface of the leaves.

These plants blend well with any other type of spiky or succulent plant, and they look good when grouped together and mulched with pea shingle or slate chippings.

◼ Beschorneria yuccoides

This plant is similar in appearance to some types of *Yucca* and vaguely related to *Agave*, but without the sharp and spiky bits. It can form huge clumps of evergreen, glaucous foliage made up of individual rosettes all massed together. Each strap-like leaf can be over 90cm (3ft) long and 5cm (2in) wide.

The flower spikes are stupendous. Massive coral-red stems 1.8m (6ft) long arch out of the centre of each mature rosette, followed by numerous rose-red bracts. These develop into dozens of nodding green flowers. The whole flowering process lasts for several months and each stage is an awesome sight. After flowering, large fruits appear. They look just like fat green figs, 5cm (2in) long, but they're not edible. Each individual rosette dies once it has flowered but the whole plant carries on as normal, producing more and more clumps of foliage.

Not much seems to be known about *Beschorneria yuccoides*. It probably comes from Mexico and, considering its provenance, can cope with remarkably low temperatures. It is an easy plant to grow and can become the centrepiece of any exotic planting scheme.

To get the very best from this unusual plant, give it as much sun as possible. Plant it in rich, moist soil that is well drained. Anything less than good-quality loam or clay will need a helping hand. Enrich poor soil with copious amounts of well-rotted manure before planting. Feed annually in early summer with yet more helpings of manure or generous amounts of blood, fish and bone. Water frequently during spring and summer, allowing the soil to dry out a little during the winter months.

The only likely pests outdoors are slugs. If *Beschorneria yuccoides* has been grown under glass in a container for a couple of years before planting out, check for red spider mites. Propagation is easy from seed or by division.

These plants look fine as individual specimens, but if your garden is huge, larger groups look very effective and they are guaranteed to receive lots of attention from your gardening chums.

ABOVE
This massive plant can produce arching flower spikes over 1.8m (6ft) long.

BELOW
The coral-red flower spikes are a brilliant contrast to the glaucous foliage.

Carpobrotus edulis
Hottentot Fig

SYN. *Mesembryanthemum edule*

This succulent groundcover plant for salty seaside gardens is fast-growing and can cover large expanses of ground very speedily. In mild coastal areas, it can often be seen cascading down cliffs or romping along beach perimeters. Despite its rate of growth, it is easy enough to control in smaller gardens just by tugging out unwanted bits as they escape from their allocated space.

The evergreen foliage is made up of thick chunks, strung together like little sausages. In milder areas, mature plants have large daisy flowers, which can be white, magenta, vivid pink, pale pink, red or yellow. They have an exotic, almost Caribbean, look to them. In hot summers, these are followed by luscious edible fruits that are sweet and sticky.

This is one of the most salt-resistant plants available, easily on a par with seaweed! The fiercest salt-laden gales can be tolerated and it is virtually indestructible – even fire can't destroy it. *Carpobrotus edulis* can grow on almost anything, even poor sandy soil that cannot sustain anything else. It forms a dense mat and covers the ground totally, eliminating the task of weeding. In extremely cold winters, the frost can sear all the top growth, but it always regrows with a vengeance the following season.

Carpobrotus edulis grows far too quickly to be successful in small pots, and even young plants produced in nurseries need more space. Using large, deep seed trays instead of pots achieves the best results. Plants can become stringy if confined to small containers, and for dense healthy growth they need the surface of a tray to cling to.

Although able to survive in poor dry conditions, newly planted specimens need regular irrigation until they become established. A light feed at the beginning of each spring season is also beneficial to keep the foliage a nice deep green colour.

Very little bothers this plant but the occasional slug can scar the leaves. Propagation can be from either fresh, fully ripened seed or cuttings.

Colletia armata

SYN. *Colletia hystrix*

An unusual prickly shrub from Chile. The foliage is so tiny that proper leaves can hardly be detected. What can be seen is a mass of evergreen wiry stems, covered with thorns. These aren't sharp enough to do too much damage to skin, but brushing past them will result in the same sort of scratches inflicted by an angry cat. The whole plant looks like a giant pile of barbed wire.

The size of a mature plant away from its native country is unlikely to be more than 2.5m (8ft) after fifteen years. It grows naturally as a large shrub but, with a bit of pruning, could be transformed into a tiny tree by removing all of the lower growth.

The flowers are delightful and a complete contrast to the rather brutal appearance of the foliage. They are delicate, pale creamy white in colour and exude a beautiful almond fragrance. Butterflies throng around the clusters of blooms, thoroughly enjoying their presence. A variety called *Colletia armata* 'Rosea' is often available. This has flowers of the very palest pink.

Colletia armata is slow-growing and very easy to cultivate. There would be room in any garden for one of these peculiar plants. They would blend in well with other spiky plants or make a good contrast to the sort of leafy, flowery plants found in herbaceous borders. Mature specimens could be trained as miniature trees to provide some height to the kind of planting schemes found in gravel gardens.

They need full sun to flourish and gritty well-drained soil. Rich and fertile soil that retains some moisture gives the best results, while poor soil can be enriched with a generous heap of well-rotted manure before planting. Feed annually in late spring with a couple of handfuls of blood, fish and bone.

Pests and diseases are rarely a problem. Even slugs keep their distance from this spiny plant. Propagation is a painful affair, best done from semi-ripe cuttings towards the end of summer. Growing this plant in a container is a very unrewarding experience. They manage to survive but never really thrive, staying the same size year after year. As soon as pot-grown plants are put directly into the ground, new growth can be seen almost immediately.

ABOVE
Bees and butterflies adore the strong almond fragrance of *Colletia armata*.

Colletia cruciata

SYN. *Colletia paradoxa*

The 'leaves' of this wonderfully vicious spiky plant are technically modified branches, arranged in pairs and set at right angles to the pair directly beneath them. They are flat, fleshy and triangular, with each one ending in a sharp tip.

The flowers are dainty little bells of the palest cream that waft the delicious scent of almonds around the garden from late summer to early spring. Before winter sets in, every butterfly for miles around is drawn to the blossom, and every autumn *Colletia cruciata* is alive with red admirals, tortoiseshells and cabbage whites. Bees also enjoy this plant immensely.

This plant is usually seen as a large shrub, although it can be trained into a little tree by removing the lower branches. The height and spread after ten years will be no more than 2.5m (8ft). Taking off the lower growth also exposes the rather attractive trunk, which can be a nicely gnarled shape. The bark is quite corky.

Although slow-growing, this plant is hopeless in a container. It sits and sulks for years, refusing to grow at all. When planted directly into the ground, growth speeds up considerably. It needs full sun and well-drained gritty soil. Adequate drainage is essential, but poor soil will not give good results. Fertile conditions are best and anything substandard can be improved by adding decent quantities of well-rotted manure before planting. Feed annually in late spring with blood, fish and bone to keep the plant a healthy colour.

This plant is brilliant in a seaside garden as strong salt-laden winds don't seem to bother it at all. Choose the planting position carefully. It needs to be where it can mature without having to be transplanted later on – it hates being moved and usually dies. Leave plenty of space around it so that it doesn't encroach onto paths. Walking past this shrub is always a risky business because of its spiky bits.

Colletia cruciata doesn't seem to be prone to any particular pests or diseases, and it's an easy plant to maintain. Propagation is from semi-ripe cuttings; wear protective gloves when doing this.

Dasylirion acrotrichum
Green Desert Spoon

A fantastic plant and one I really cannot live without. Mere words cannot do justice to this amazing desert plant. From the centre of each rosette emerge hundreds of very thin, serrated leaves, all of which are tipped with a feathery tuft. As more and more leaves develop, the older ones are pushed down until a beautiful arrangement begins to form, gradually building up into an almost perfect sphere.

The overall size of a thirty-year-old plant can be 1.5m (5ft) in diameter. After many years, a little stubby trunk starts to form. Mature plants send up dramatic-looking flower spikes, which would be classed as interesting, rather than pretty. These can reach 3.7m (12ft) in height. Once flowering has finished, chop off the old flower stalk as low into the plant as possible.

When planting, leave plenty of space around them so that their shape can be fully admired. They are the ultimate landscape plant, and their shape can be noticeable from quite a distance away. Single specimens look wonderful, but groups planted together look even better in larger gardens. Plant in full sun in gritty compost that drains well. They make excellent coastal plants, as they are virtually hurricane-proof. They are very slow-growing and would make good choices for containers. They work especially well on windy roof terraces. Although used to desert conditions, they give much better results if they are watered regularly until established. If grown in a pot, water as frequently as you would anything else during spring and summer.

Dasylirion acrotrichum is almost maintenance-free. Older leaves can be removed as they turn brown with age. Feed with generous amounts of blood, fish and bone in late spring. Apart from an occasional bout of mealy bug, these plants are generally free from pests and diseases. Propagation is easy from fresh seed, but plants grown in this way take at least ten years to grow to 60cm (2ft). Serious overwatering can lead to rotting.

ABOVE
Dasylirion acrotrichum is always the first thing I plant when I move to a new garden.

BELOW
The flower spikes can either be left on the plant or, because they may spoil its symmetry, removed.

■ Echeveria glauca

A pretty little succulent plant made up of fat, fleshy leaves. The foliage is a beautiful shade of blue, and the leaves are delicately interwoven to form a perfect circular rosette.

They are easy to include in a garden. They can be grown in drifts through gravel gardens or as groundcover under other spiky plants such as *Colletia* and *Yucca*. After a few years they start to clump up nicely. They can be added to rockeries or grown in terracotta pots, either singly or in groups. If planted towards the front of borders, using large numbers is much more effective than just one or two.

Flowers are produced annually. Each rosette send up a flower spike that opens up into many tiny bell-shaped blooms, which are dark pink with yellow tips. They are about 30cm (1ft) tall and last for many weeks.

Plant out in full sun. Drainage needs to be extra sharp, as excess water gathering around the roots won't be tolerated at all. Either incorporate masses of grit into the compost or plant on a slope, which will allow the rain to run off immediately. Whether planting directly into the ground or in pots, cover the area surrounding each plant with an ornamental mulch. A dressing of slate or pebbles not only enhances the plants' shape and colour, but stops the rain from splashing any mud onto the leaves and spoiling their appearance.

Water sparingly during summer to keep the compost just moist. Irrigation is not necessary in winter unless small pots have been brought indoors to overwinter under glass. Pests and diseases aren't much of a problem, although slugs can be a nuisance as they scrape off the surface of the leaves. Vine weevils can be real pests on plants grown in containers.

Apart from removing old leaves or flower stems that have become brown and crispy, this plant can take care of itself. Even feeding is unnecessary. The easiest method of propagation is by dividing clumps of rosettes. It is also easy with seed but, due to frequent hybridization, plants of varying size, shape and quality can result.

Fascicularia bicolor
Firewheel

Fascicularia bicolor is closely related to the pineapple and is the hardiest member of the Bromeliad family. This unusual plant from Chile is made up of tightly packed bundles of narrow, prickly leaves. The leaves mass together forming individual rosettes that pile up on each other, gradually creating huge clumps of impenetrable foliage. They either spread sideways or hang down over walls. They can be gently coaxed into any direction required, but take many years to form decent-sized thickets. They are one of the slowest-growing plants in this chapter.

During late summer, the middles of mature rosettes produce astonishing vivid scarlet inner leaves, circling a centre of bright turquoise flowers. A *Fascicularia bicolor* in flower and a mandrill's bottom look unnervingly similar!

If grown correctly, this lovely exotic plant can cope with surprisingly low temperatures. Sharp drainage is the one essential requirement. If grown in the ground, a sloping site is preferred, so that all excess water drains away almost at once. It is a perfect choice for planting in stone troughs or small terracotta pots. It can be grown on rockeries or left to hang over stone walls. It can be tucked into the crevices of any tree trunks and it can even be tied onto the trunks of hairy trees such as the *Trachycarpus fortunei* palm tree, where it will cling to the fibrous matting and gradually haul itself up and around the trunk.

Plant in either full sun or light shade in gritty compost. All types of soil can be tolerated, even thin chalky ones. Exposed, windy positions such as hilltops or next to the coast can be coped with well. Very little irrigation is required; even regular feeding is unnecessary. The only maintenance needed is to chop off any old rosettes as they become scruffy. Propagation is best by division. Pests and diseases are not much of a problem, except during the flowering season. The blue flowers seem to act as a magnet for all the local woodlice, which really seem to enjoy chomping at them.

ABOVE
Fascicularia bicolor has amazing scarlet inner leaves surrounding a flat blue flower head.

ABOVE
Fascicularia pitcairnifolia is even more beautiful but a bit less hardy.

Furcraea longaeva

This exotic masterpiece from Mexico is suitable for either large conservatories or mild coastal gardens. The leaves are glaucous with a tough, leathery texture that is slightly rough to the touch. They are long, wide and arching, finishing with a neatly tapered tip.

For the first two or three years, the plant concentrates on producing bulk so, with each growing season, the height and width steadily increase. By year four, it could be 1.2m (4ft) tall with a span of nearly 1.5m (5ft). A short, sturdy trunk will also have started to form. This can be made more visible by removing any older leaves from the base of the plant. Remove any old brown leaves with a sharp knife, cutting as close as possible into the plant's centre. Do this chore little and often, as the cut ends of the leaves have an unpleasant odour.

Usually around years five or six, odd things start to happen. The central core starts to produce leaves that are stubbier and paler, and the plant takes on a distinctly unhealthy pallor. Don't worry, this is just the flower spike starting to do its thing. Fairly soon, a giant swelling will emerge, becoming bigger with

alarming speed. The flower spike can increase by about 10cm (4in) per day until it is at least 4.5–6m (15–20ft) tall. This will then start to open up into huge 'candelabra' of pale lemon. The flowers last for many weeks before starting to turn brown. Don't cut the old flowers off just yet, though – there's more fun to come. After a few months, glimpses of green start to appear. Within a few more weeks, huge quantities of mini *Furcraea* are dangling from every available space. These turn into large fat 'fruits', which eventually fall off. They can either be gathered for future propagation or left to root where they fall. The flower spike will now start to fade and can be cut off at any time. The whole plant then starts to die.

Grow *Furcraea longaeva* in full sun in gritty compost. Plants in pots never reach the proportions of those planted directly into the ground.

Lampranthus spectabilis
Hardy Mesembryanthemum

A hardy, succulent plant from South Africa that can be grown either as exotic groundcover or as a trailing plant, perfect for hanging down over walls or steep banks. It grows as a dense mat, so it can almost act as a mulch to keep down the weeds. The leaves look like greyish-green jelly beans and have a rubbery feel to them, while the flowers are large daisies of the most glorious magenta-pink. They look far too tropical to be hardy.

Lampranthus spectabilis is evergreen and looks wonderful planted underneath larger spiky plants such as *Yucca*, *Agave* and *Furcraea*. It also complements Mediterranean-style gardens and looks good when planted with *Cordyline* or palm trees, such as *Trachycarpus fortunei* and *Chamaerops humilis*. They are especially suitable for coastal gardens, as they cope well with salty winds.

This plant adores hot, sunny, sharply drained aspects, and can be used to cover sloping banks or rockeries, or left to cascade down over walls or the edges of large stone troughs. A plant covering 30sq cm (1sq ft) can easily increase tenfold within two years of planting. The big daisy flowers open up during the summer whenever the weather is sunny.

Water in new plants for the first few weeks only. Once they become established they are extremely drought resistant. They are generally trouble-free, but slugs can sometimes be a nuisance. They are easy to propagate from either fresh seed or cuttings.

Although poor soil is perfectly acceptable, an occasional light feed with a small helping of blood, fish and bone scattered around the edge of the clump gives good results. Feed in late spring, taking care not to get any food on the delicate foliage. As an extra precaution, hose down the plant afterwards to prevent scorching. After a few years, growth can start to become straggly, so trim back the ends to encourage new, bushier tips. The bits that have been cut off can be used for propagation or just discarded.

ABOVE
This pretty groundcover plant is covered with magenta flowers in the summer.

Opuntia phaeacantha
Prickly Pear

There are lots of different *Opuntia* found in the various desert regions of the United States. Most are hopelessly tender but, occasionally, one or two behave differently and can adapt to colder conditions. *Opuntia phaeacantha* is one of them. In the right position, this cactus can cope with ridiculously low temperatures.

This plant is an essential addition to any desert planting scheme and mixes beautifully with *Dasylirion*, *Yucca* and *Agave*. It grows as a series of fleshy pads that pile up on top and to the side of each other. They are all covered with prickly thorns, which can inflict various wounds and scrapes if they get too near unprotected skin. These act more as an irritant, rather than causing any lasting damage. The thorns can also become easily detached from the plant's surface and anchor themselves into the skin like little darts. Attempts to pull these thorns out usually result in breaking them off, leaving the tip embedded under the flesh. Tweezers often help at this stage, or you can put Sellotape over the afflicted part and peel it off gently. This usually takes everything away painlessly.

Plant out in the hottest part of the garden in very sharply drained gritty soil. These plants may be hardy, but excess water won't be tolerated. Plant them on a sloping site if possible, so that the rain drains off immediately. They are not good choices for growing in terracotta pots, as they can become top-heavy and topple over.

During the winter, the drier the season, the more cold they will take. If the winter is very wet, they may rot without some sort of cover. The easiest way to protect a small clump is to fix a couple of panes of glass together at the top and place them over the whole plant.

Throughout Texas and Arizona, flowering is an annual event, but in cooler climates, the little yellow flowers should be treated as an added bonus because they appear only during exceptionally hot summers. Slugs adore these plants, ignoring the spines completely to chomp at the appetizing foliage underneath. Additional irrigation is rarely necessary, and feeding can usually be dispensed with. Propagation can be either from seed, which is a very slow process, or from cuttings, which can be an uncomfortable task.

Puya alpestris

Each plant grows as a large rosette of arching leaves, edged with sharp, curving thorns. These thorns are not fierce enough to inflict stab wounds, but they are a clever arrangement that allows small, furry or feathery creatures to wander freely under and among the foliage. Unfortunately, when they have had enough of rootling around, they are faced with a barrage of hedgehog-like barbs. They can risk escaping and being torn apart, or they can stay where they are until they die. The latter option is much better from the plant's point of view because they have then snared their own food supply. This acts as a slow-release feed to nourish them over a long period of time. Don't worry, though, this won't happen to pets, which are generally too clever or too large to be captured.

The slightly glaucous foliage is not fleshy, but thin and quite dry to the touch. The leaves can be 60cm (2ft) long and their tapered ends hang down and trail across the ground. It is an excellent choice for a terracotta pot. Once the plant has filled its container, growth seems to stop completely but without causing any lasting harm. After a couple of years, when you're feeling brave enough to face the thorny prospect of repotting *Puya alpestris* into something larger, new growth is immediate.

Better results, though, will be gained from planting directly into the ground. Plants look more effective in groups. A position in full sun is required, preferably on gritty, well-drained soil on a sloping site. Even very poor chalky soil is suitable. Feed lightly with any balanced food in late spring or early summer. Water sparingly unless the plant is confined to a pot, in which case water regularly throughout the growing season. New young plants are sent up from the base of each rosette, forming larger clumps of plants that can spread slowly across the garden.

Mature plants send up the most amazing flower spikes, which open up into incredible colours of metallic blue-green. These last for several months before they, and the rosette from which they emerged, turn brown and die. Pests and diseases are rarely a problem. Propagation is easiest from fresh seed. The only maintenance needed is to remove the lower leaves with a sharp knife once they have become brown with age.

Puya chilensis

The long strap-like leaves are pale green and glossy. Each one is edged with vicious barbs that make it easy for small, woolly animals to be snagged on. The poor beasts cannot always tug themselves free and become trapped, with their bodies rotting down to become a slow-release food supply for the plant. This doesn't just happen in their native Chile. A few years ago, a group of these plants was positioned near a seating area at a seaside resort to stop local yobs loitering there. The ruse worked brilliantly, but pigeons seen wandering into the clump were never seen leaving.... Fortunately, pets seem to have more sense: my cats give these plants a wide berth as they stroll past.

New plants are sent up from the base of each rosette to form larger clumps gradually. Mature plants produce flower spikes about 90cm (3ft) long that open out into spectacular metallic greenish-yellow blooms, which can last many weeks. Unfortunately, the whole rosette dies when flowering has finished, but other smaller rosettes have usually formed to replace them.

These plants are brilliant for growing in large terracotta pots, where they can sit happily for years. However, they look healthier and grow larger if planted directly into the ground. They look good with any spiky planting scheme, whether as individual specimens or in larger groups. They need little water once established, and can be planted with much success on banks of poor, dry soil where little else will grow. The only essential requirement is full sun.

Although these plants are fairly hardy, winter wet is a problem in cool areas. Plants that live permanently in containers should be given some shelter during winter to keep them dry. They can be placed under glass or just be brought nearer to the house where the eaves can protect them from the worst of any rain.

Whether the plants are in pots or in the ground, the compost should be as sharply drained as possible. Stir in lots of extra grit before planting to stop excess water gathering around the roots. Any older brown leaves can be removed with a sharp knife – wear gloves. Feeding is not really necessary, but a light dose of blood, fish and bone can be given in late spring. Pests and diseases are rarely a problem. Propagation can be done from fresh seed.

Sempervivum
House Leek

There are many different *Sempervivum* varieties to choose from. All are fully hardy, evergreen and easy to grow. Many are quite tiny and not really 'architectural', but some are much bigger and make chunky additions to spiky planting schemes, especially if planted out generously in large groups. They make fantastic groundcover and complement all larger spiky plants. Drifts of all the same variety look much more effective than a mix of several different types.

Sempervivum can also be used for stone troughs, rockeries, gravel gardens or planted up individually in terracotta pots for the windowsill. They are excellent for exposed positions such as coastal gardens. They come in a range of colours, usually various reds and greens. They all produce little flower stems, which open up into colours of white, pink or pale yellow. The flowers are rather insignificant, though, compared to the succulent foliage.

Some of the more substantial *Sempervivum* have rosettes of 20cm (8in) across. Varieties like 'Lady Kelly,' 'Commander Hay,' 'Calcareum' and 'Old Lace' are of particular interest and worth searching for at specialist nurseries.

The rosettes send out more and more baby plants each season until much larger clumps are formed. Growth can become so dense that the plants act as a mulch to prevent weeds from growing through. After flowering, the rosette from which the flower spike emerged dies, but this is barely noticeable among mature groups.

Full sun is essential. The soil should be poor and very well drained. Plants can cope with such small amounts of water that they can even be grown successfully on rooftops, where they are totally reliant on rainwater. They seem to thrive in all sorts of poor conditions, needing little in the way of compost and nutrients.

Not much maintenance is needed, apart from the removal of dead rosettes. Larger varieties benefit from small doses of any balanced fertilizer in late spring. Pests and diseases are rarely a problem. Propagation is easily done by separating the offsets.

Yucca aloifolia
Spanish Bayonet

This seriously architectural plant is the most beautiful and most dangerous *Yucca* of all. Its common name refers to the relentlessly sharp spines at the end of each leaf.

This trunk-forming plant often sends up several trunks to form multi-stemmed clumps. Although slow-growing, it could eventually reach 2.2m (7ft). The total height, including foliage, could be 3m (10ft) after twenty years. The dark green leaves cope well with cold temperatures, but they refuse to tolerate very cold weather combined with lots of rain, which could lead to rotting. Therefore, they need either a mild garden to grow in or to be planted in the shelter of a house wall. They can also be left in containers that could be moved to a drier place in winter. Their slow speed of growth makes them suitable for planting into terracotta pots, providing they are repotted every few years into something much larger, otherwise they can become top-heavy and fall over in strong winds.

The soil must be exceptionally well drained with lots of extra grit added. Full sun is best, although some shade is fine. Shelter from very strong coastal gales is recommended. Plants are very drought-resistant once established, unless they spend all of their life in a pot, in which case they will need regular watering every growing season. There is a fantastic variegated version, although it always seems to be in short supply. It has leaves striped with dark green and bright yellow.

Older plants produce wonderful spikes of exotic flowers. Each flower stem is lined with dozens of large, waxy bells of creamy white tinged with purple at the base.

These plants are generally trouble-free, providing their drainage and winter watering needs are met. Black aphids can be a nuisance on the flower spikes. Cut off any old brown leaves. Feed annually in late spring or early summer with a couple of handfuls of blood, fish and bone. The green form can be propagated easily from seed; *Yucca aloifolia* 'Variegata' must be grown from offsets.

LEFT
Yucca x *floribunda* is a hybrid between a trunk-forming and a clump-forming species.

Yucca x floribunda

A handsome *Yucca* with blue-grey foliage, each leaf tapering to a sharp point. After each flowering season, more and more trunks and branches are formed until the whole plant gets into an untidy mess. Lovely though the blooms are, to try to get some semblance of order into these clumps, it is better to try to prohibit them from flowering. This is easily done by growing them in the shade. The foliage takes on a bluer hue and a neater, tidier plant is formed. Flowers can still be enjoyed as, even in full shade, an occasional flower spike is sent up during late summer.

It is a tough, fully hardy plant and prefers rich, well-drained soil. Any type of soil will do, even heavy clay, as long as it drains well. Extra grit can be incorporated in and around the proposed planting area to help prevent any waterlogging. Because it can cope with dry soil once established and because a shady spot makes such a good planting position, *Yucca* x *floribunda* makes a perfect planting choice for those really difficult places where little else will grow. Large trees tend to sap all of the moisture from the surrounding garden, and their canopy blocks out the sunlight. Dry, shady areas such as this have always been a bit of a challenge, so to find that a plant as shapely and interesting as this one will not just survive, but actually thrive there, is a wonderful discovery.

If given richer and more moist conditions, a larger and healthier-looking plant will be the result. They can look fantastic planted sparingly throughout the length of herbaceous borders and also look effective planted in desert-type planting schemes, where a pea shingle or other ornamental mulch can really highlight their colouring.

Yucca x *floribunda* does not come true from seed. Propagation needs to be done using the offsets ('toes') that emerge from the base of the mature plants. Pests and diseases are uncommon except for our old friend the black aphid, which likes to gather in large colonies all over the flower spike.

BELOW
The flower spikes open out into ivory white waxy bells and cover the entire stem.

Yucca glauca
Soapweed

SYN. *Yucca angustifolia*

A small, pretty *Yucca* ideal for smaller gardens, where it can be planted as a single specimen. Larger gardens could accommodate groups of them planted closely together, which would look even more effective. The slender, straight, blue-grey leaves are edged with a narrow white stripe, plus the occasional white fibre. Each leaf is tipped with a small spine that looks harmless but is capable of inflicting a sharp stab.

After many years, *Yucca glauca* starts to develop a short, stubby trunk. Mature plants also produce flower spikes over 90cm (3ft) tall in summer. Each spike carries dozens of individual flowers that are waxy in texture, creamy white and tinged with dark pinkish-red.

This is a very hardy plant and, given the right conditions, can be grown in even the coldest garden. Full sun is one essential requirement and good drainage another. The soil can be made more suitable by adding copious amounts of grit before planting. The thin leaves are excellent for filtering strong winds, so this *Yucca* should do well in any exposed garden, either on a breezy hilltop or near the seaside. Although slow-growing and drought resistant, it is not especially good in a pot and never reaches its full potential.

Brown-bitting (the removal of older brown leaves) should be done as required. Annual feeding is beneficial, and a generous amount of blood, fish and bone can be sprinkled around the base of each plant in early summer. In cold, damp conditions, yucca leaf spot, which shows up as chocolate-brown spots on the leaves, may be a problem. Affected leaves should be removed immediately, as this unsightly condition can spread throughout the plant. Dispose of the foliage carefully, preferably by burning. Black aphids are often regular visitors to the flowers.

The roots contain saponins, which lather up into a perfectly good soap, hence its common name. Propagation is easiest from fresh seed, although many variable forms can result.

Yucca gloriosa
Adam's Needle

This is the *Yucca* that is the most familiar to gardeners everywhere. It was much loved by the Victorians and planted often. Gertrude Jekyll used the plants in virtually all her planting schemes, and they remained popular until the introduction of flowery herbaceous borders, which then became all the rage. *Yucca gloriosa* has a strong evergreen shape that can add structure to any garden and is an essential addition to any exotic planting plan. It has big, bold rosettes of wide, stiff leaves, each one ending in a sharp point. It is very tough and will grow almost anywhere, even right on the coast where it can stand up to the fiercest salty gales. It can develop into a large plant, with clumps reaching 2.2m (7ft) both in height and width after twenty years. Mature specimens gradually form stubby trunks and branches, and can take up quite a lot of space in the garden. For smaller gardens, the size can easily be controlled by sawing off bits that have expanded out of their allocated area.

The flowers are spectacular. The thick red-tipped flower stalk emerges from the centre of each mature rosette in late summer. It

grows rapidly and can reach 1.5m (5ft) before opening out into hundreds of large, waxy blooms. These are pale cream, tinged with purple along the outer edges.

The leaves of *Yucca gloriosa variegata* have bright yellow edges, making a welcome splash of colour to a spiky border. It is unlikely to exceed 1.5m (5ft) in height. Both the green and variegated versions look good planted singly or in groups. They make an unusual hedge, behave brilliantly in terracotta pots and, if planted underneath a window, are a wonderful anti-burglar device.

Both the green and the variegated forms can be planted in sun or shade. Unusually for a variegated plant, the colour remains strong even away from direct sunlight. Practically any soil is suitable, but rich, well-drained loam gives the best results. Water regularly when first planted. After the first year, it can usually take care of itself. If grown permanently in a pot, water frequently throughout every growing season, but allow it to become much drier in winter.

Feed generous amounts of blood, fish and bone each year in early summer. Remove old

ABOVE
Yucca gloriosa is a large majestic beast.

flower spikes as soon as they fade, cutting as low down into the plant as possible. This will leave a flat area in the middle of the rosette to start with, but new growth will soon sprout, forming two or three branches from this point. All older brown leaves should be cut off with a sharp knife as they become unsightly (a process referred to as brown-bitting).

During the flowering season, keep a watch out for black aphids. These wretched creatures breed at such a rate that, within an alarmingly short period of time, the flower spikes can be smothered with them. The main part of the plant is more or less trouble-free. Occasionally the odd mouse or vole might burrow into an old trunk and nest there, although this seems to do little harm. In exceptionally wet winters, yucca leaf spot could be a problem. If the tell-tale chocolate-brown spots are observed on any part of the foliage, remove the affected leaves at once to stop the disease spreading.

Propagation for both the green and the variegated forms is usually done by removing the offsets ('toes') that poke up through the soil from the base of each plant.

Yucca recurvifolia
Recurved Yucca

This is the easiest *Yucca* of all for a cold garden. It is readily available and tolerant of a wide range of conditions. It forms a solid trunk and has generous amounts of dark green, arching leaves, each one tipped with a sharp point. The lower leaves hang down gracefully, skirting the plant with a formal arrangement. The whole plant has a strong outline shape and looks beautiful at night with lights underneath, illuminating its silhouette.

Huge flower spikes up to 1.8m (6ft) appear each year on plants more than five years old. They open up to form hundreds of cream, waxy bells, which can give off a lemon fragrance on hot summer evenings. The flowering period is usually from mid-summer until mid-autumn. After flowering, cut the flower stems off as low into the plant's rosettes as possible. From there, two or more shoots will grow, eventually developing into multi-headed branches above a woody stem. The overall size of a twenty-year-old plant can reach 2.2m (7ft) tall and 2.5m (8ft) across.

Yucca recurvifolia can be grown in sun or shade, and in more or less any soil that drains well. It is hardy enough to grow just about anywhere. It is so tough that it has even been seen thriving in Toronto, where the chilly winter temperatures regularly plunge down to -20°C (-4°F) for days at a time.

Young plants about 60–90cm (2–3ft) tall that haven't yet branched look very attractive in terracotta pots, either singly or planted in rows along the terrace. They make a splendid change from the usual choice of formal topiary. They are wonderful plants for giving extra height to garden beds and borders, and look marvellous among other exotic plants, where they usually provide the main height and bulk.

Because of its bulk, *Yucca recurvifolia* appreciates large annual doses of food. Apply either large helpings of well-rotted manure or plenty of blood, fish and bone. Although established plants can become fairly drought-tolerant, irrigation during the spring and summer produces excellent results. Apart from some black aphid on the flowers, this *Yucca* remains generally trouble-free. Propagate from any offsets ('toes') sent up from the base of the plant.

Yucca rostrata
Beaked Yucca

SYN. *Yucca thompsoniana*

This is a very special *Yucca* and one of the slowest-growing. Mature plants are very desirable and rarely seen because of the time taken to reach their grand proportions. The very slender and straight leaves are light bluish-grey in colour, and each one is tipped with a sharp needle. Each rosette contains so many leaves that their appearance is almost spherical. As the leaves become brown with age, they should be cut off with a sharp knife as near to the main stem as possible. As more and more are removed each year, a small stubby trunk will start to form. The trunk will be covered with the remains of all the old leaf bases, which turn to the colour of straw. This contrasts beautifully with the blue of the foliage. After many years, probably at least thirty, the trunks could be about 1.2m (4ft) tall, with the head of foliage on the top adding an extra 90cm (3ft) of height. It has tall columns of white, waxy flowers produced in summer or, occasionally, in early spring. Its common name of Beaked Yucca refers to the shape of the seed pods formed after flowering.

Although *Yucca rostrata* can cope with low temperatures, this applies only if it is kept dry in the winter – always a challenge for many gardeners. It could be grown in a huge pot, enabling it to be moved indoors under glass for the winter. Or it could be planted outside against a wall or under the eaves of a house to give it extra protection from the worst of the winter weather. Full sun is essential, and drainage must be really sharp. Incorporate masses of extra grit into the soil before planting, so that any excess water runs away immediately.

This splendid plant deserves pride of place either in the conservatory or out in the garden. It is very drought-tolerant, but if kept confined to a pot, remember to water regularly during the summer months. Scale insects are the most likely unwanted visitors to these plants, especially those kept indoors for much of their lives.

Propagation is easiest by separating any offsets from the parent plant. Unfortunately, *Yucca rostrata* is quite shy about producing offsets, which perhaps explains its rarity.

ABOVE
Few plants are more beautiful than *Yucca rostrata*.

Yucca schottii
Mountain Yucca

SYN. *Yucca macrocarpa*

This is the only *Yucca* that grows naturally in the shade and, as its common name suggests, is from areas of high altitude, up to 2,100m (7,000ft), in Arizona and New Mexico. It is found in the mountain forests, nestling under the shady canopies provided by oak and pine trees. It is a very showy single-stemmed *Yucca* that rarely branches. The rosette of foliage is made up from blue leaves that are straight and wide. Each leaf is tipped with a deliciously sharp point; the plant I have in my own garden has brought much pain and misery to unsuspecting visitors over the years.

Yucca schottii is unbelievably slow-growing and, despite lavishing mine with care and attention, it is only 90cm (3ft) tall and 1.2m (4ft) across, with just a hint of a tiny, stubby trunk after nearly fourteen years. It is worth all the patience and effort, though, as it really is a lovely focal feature. Being slow can be an advantage – it means it is suitable for even the tiniest garden.

The flowers of *Yucca schottii* are not often produced, and when they do appear, they are a half-hearted affair – the flower stem is just about visible above the foliage. Each bloom is

almost spherical and creamy white in colour. After flowering, edible fruits form, which can be made into an interesting alcoholic beverage.

Plants stay a better colour if planted in shade, although flowers might be produced more regularly if planted in full sun. However, the flowers should be regarded as an almost unnecessary bonus – the foliage is beautiful enough on its own. Very gritty, well-drained soil is essential. This *Yucca* is one of the best for cold, wet climates, as it shrugs off winter rain remarkably well. The soil should be rich and fertile, and annual feeding is advised. Use generous amounts of blood, fish and bone every spring. Propagation is generally from fresh seed. *Yucca schottii* is not usually prone to any particular pests or diseases. Remove any older brown leaves as they occur.

Planting in containers is not recommended, despite this plant's slowness of growth. Potted specimens grow even more slowly and never reach their full potential. Plant directly into the garden in a prominent position. After all the time it takes to produce a decent size, it would be a pity not to have it in full view.

Yucca whipplei
Our Lord's Candle

Slender grey-green leaves, 45cm (18in) long, radiate from a central base – there is no trunk – into a handsome rosette 90cm (3ft) wide. The foliage is rigid and ends in a sharp tip. Described by the horticultural guru Graham Stuart Thomas as 'one of the most wonderful plants in the whole world', *Yucca whipplei* is usually grown for its amazing flower spike. These are spectacular, reaching up to 3.7m (12ft) tall in just two weeks, usually during late spring. They open up into many hundreds of white, fragrant bell-shaped flowers – an extraordinary sight. Unfortunately, this burst of growth saps the plant's energy to such an extent that the entire rosette often dies shortly afterwards.

Yucca whipplei is a bit of a fusspot, and the planting site needs careful consideration. It doesn't grow well in a pot, so bringing it indoors under glass in winter isn't an option, but it needs shelter from winter wet to prevent rotting. Choose a spot in full sun in very gritty well-drained soil, adding lots of extra grit before planting, if necessary. A sunny wall or a position underneath the eaves would help to shield it from the worst of any wet weather. Planting on a slope would also be advantageous, as any excess water could drain away immediately.

Instead of planting single specimens, try planting in larger groups. This creates a more effective display and, as each rosette often dies after flowering, ensures a continuing supply growing on. All *Yucca* flowers are edible and usually eaten raw because they make a crispy addition to salads. I'm also informed that the flower buds of *Yucca whipplei* can be cooked whole and deep-fried, just like potatoes.

As long as it is kept dry in winter to prevent rotting, little else in the way of pests and diseases seems to trouble this plant. As it doesn't form a trunk, there are very few older leaves to go brown with age, and so brown-bitting is usually unnecessary. Feeding annually with blood, fish and bone is beneficial, especially for older plants that need to gather extra energy for the exhausting process of producing such huge flower spikes. Propagation is best done from fresh seed.

Pests, diseases & other disorders

This is the less glamorous side to horticulture and a subject that just cannot be ignored.

At some time during every growing season, unwelcome visitors will be found somewhere in the garden, feasting and chomping on your prize plants. Instead of automatically reaching for nasty chemicals every time you spot something horrid in the garden or conservatory, learning to recognize the bad guys and learning how to prevent them is a much more pleasant and responsible way of coping.

Making regular checks on all plants helps to find anything unpleasant at the very first sign. Dealing with an initial outbreak is so much easier than ignoring it until plague proportions are reached. For example, green or black aphids love to feed on the young growing tips of plants. If some are seen on the new foliage, just chop off the first few inches of the plant with secateurs. It won't do the plant any harm at all – it will soon send out more new shoots. If these creature are left, they breed at such a rate that, within a few weeks, the whole plant will be smothered with them, making the use of chemicals an unavoidable task.

There are two basic types of insecticide available to the gardener: systemic and contact. A systemic insecticide travels up through the plant's system and into the sap, poisoning any insect that bites into it during the next few weeks. A contact insecticide is sprayed directly onto the offending bug and, hopefully, will kill it almost at once.

It is worth remembering that plants that are lush and brimming with health are much less likely to suffer from pests and diseases. Bugs and other maladies can detect a stressed plant with lightning speed and home in on it immediately. Sick plants don't have the strength to ward off invaders, which is why plants confined to containers or grown under glass are far more prone to cultural problems than plants growing naturally in the garden. In hot conservatories where the atmosphere lacks enough humidity, red spider mites are almost guaranteed. Outdoors, plants grown in pots full of peat-based compost are much more likely to be troubled by vine weevils than those growing in soil-based compost.

Finally, try to develop a more ruthless attitude to sick plants. If a plant is riddled with insects, covered with mouldy leaves and has shed most of its foliage, throw it away or, better still, burn it. It is far better to dispose of something than take on the long and difficult battle of restoring it back to good health. A plant in such a terrible state will also infect other plants growing near it.

Chemicals

All chemicals are unpleasant and are used far too often. They also encourage gardeners to rely on them as some sort of magic cure-all, rather than something that should be used only as a last resort. If plants are inspected regularly for the first signs of any problems, chemicals will be needed only if something very serious takes hold.

Even with the best will in the world, though, most of us are too busy to prowl around the garden every day, and colonies

BOTTOM
Green aphids can reach plague proportions if left untreated.

BELOW
Black aphids seem to get a real kick out of spoiling new stems and flowers.

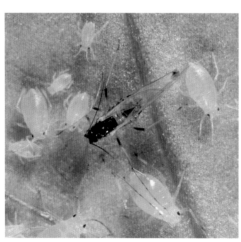

LEFT
Although some
people would
welcome such
visitors, this roe
deer doe and her
kind will nibble
bark and leaves.

ABOVE
Ladybirds
are a friendly
alternative
to chemicals
for getting rid
of aphids.

LEFT
Adelgids are woolly
beasts that love
feeding on the sap
of conifer trees.

of insects can seem to appear from nowhere during periods of warm wet weather. Different arrays of products fill the shelves of garden centres every year. New 'wonder cures' appear every season, while old favourites are suddenly banned and disappear from the shelves. This makes selecting a suitable product a difficult task. Specialist horticultural establishments will probably have an expert on site to offer good advice on what to buy. Every chemical container will also have masses of useful information printed on it. Try to avoid anything that requires the wearing of gloves or masks; choose something that sounds safer. It's not just our own health we need to worry about; it's also the welfare of animals and other creatures visiting the garden. For instance, if a dangerous chemical is used to poison snails, this can be passed on to any unsuspecting creature that eats the snails.

Some products are manufactured as repellents rather than as something that can kill. Putting a slug repellent on or near a juicy-leaved plant will persuade the slimy creature to go and pester something else. The repellent doesn't actually harm the poor beast, which is, after all, only looking out for its next meal.

Biological control

Various types of biological control have been developed over the last few years. What biological control involves is the introduction of living creatures to plants prone to a particular pest. For instance, the biological control for whitefly is a tiny wasp called *Encarsia formosa*, which eats only whitefly and nothing else; *Phytoseiulus persimilis* is a tiny creature that eats only red spider mites. These natural predators are much safer to use than chemicals and do a fine job if used correctly.

Biological controls are normally used in greenhouses and conservatories, where they can be kept in a controlled space. Obviously, if they were put out into the garden, there is little to stop them from disappearing over the fence to help in the neighbour's garden instead of yours. For them to work properly, they should be used at the very start of any infestation. They can eat or destroy only a few insects at a time, and if plagues of nasty bugs are already present, it is expecting too much to hope for a successful result. Natural predators are usually supplied fresh in the post every few weeks throughout the growing season and the hottest summer months.

This method of control needs to be monitored carefully. Chemicals cannot generally be used as well, as these will kill indiscriminately, wiping out all the good guys (the natural predators) as well as the bad guys (whitefly, aphids, red spider mites and so on).

This area of horticulture is still in its infancy, and each year brings a new type of biological control for use against a particular nasty insect. They are usually available from all good garden centres or directly from the suppliers via mail order. Currently there are biological controls for vine weevils, thrips, mealy bugs, aphids, whitefly, red spider mites, caterpillars and some species of scale insect.

LEFT
Remember that using horrible chemicals on slugs and snails will also harm any animal or bird that feeds on them.

Adelgids

Tiny wingless insects, covered with a white woolly coating, that feed off the sap of the host plants. Usually found in fairly large numbers feeding on conifer trees. Difficult to eradicate without frequent attention. Treat at the first sign, spraying weekly until they have disappeared.

Aphids

These aphids can be various colours, including pink and orange, but usually black or green. (Green and black aphids are sometimes referred to as greenfly and blackfly respectively.) They feed off the sap, sucking it from the tips of new growth. They can spread viruses from plant to plant, and can breed quickly, building up into large numbers. They excrete a sticky substance, referred to as honeydew. This attracts fungal spores, which develop into black sooty mould (see page 347), covering the surface of the leaves. Virtually any type of plant can become infected. Root aphids live underground, feeding off root systems. White woolly aphids are also seen occasionally on some species of tree.

Capsid bugs

Small green insects, like elongated greenfly (aphids), usually found on the underside of the leaves. They make hundreds of tiny holes across the new leaves of plants such as *Aralia elata*, *Fatsia japonica* and *Euphorbia mellifera*. They tend to appear on the same plants year after year, so spray with insecticide as a matter of routine every six weeks, even before they have begun to cause any damage.

ABOVE
Aphids come in all sizes and colours.

TOP
Adelgid eggs are easy to spot and can therefore be treated at the first sign.

RIGHT
Capsid bugs can decimate large areas of new foliage.

Deer

The idea of deer roaming across the lawn and through the garden is always appealing to those gardeners such as myself who don't have to witness the damage these lovely creatures can cause. The bark of any tree and the foliage of almost any low-growing plant are vulnerable when there are deer around. Either fence off the entire garden with wire meshing, or protect each plant individually with tree guards or wire netting wrapped around wooden stakes and pushed into the ground.

Froghoppers

Small insects encased in bubbly froth, commonly referred to as 'cuckoo spit', and usually found on herbaceous plants. They feed on the sap of the host plant. Instead of using chemical sprays, just blast them off with a jet of water from the garden hose.

Leaf miners

Minute caterpillars that tunnel inside leaves, making track marks as they go. They disfigure the plant, rather than causing any lasting harm, and it's best to remove and dispose of affected leaves instead of trying to treat the problem with chemicals.

Mealy bugs

Small insects covered in white waxy powder that feed off the sap of plants. They are often found on plants such as *Agave* and *Aloe* in conservatories, or on *Phormium* outdoors. They gather in large colonies and can be difficult to treat, as they tuck themselves deep into the plant's centre or between the folds of the leaf bases. For small numbers, try dabbing them with a cotton wool bud dipped in methylated spirits. For larger numbers, the only cure is by drenching the soil with a powerful systemic insecticide.

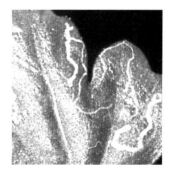

ABOVE
Rabbits are too
cute to harm, so
try to prevent
them entering the
garden instead.

Rabbits

These fluffy creatures can be a real menace if they find their way into the garden – they're able to munch through several dozen plants in just one feeding session. There are various mechanical deterrents on the market that make loud noises to frighten them away. These work well for about two days until these pesky animals realize that no harm can come to them. Rabbits will eat almost anything, and every plant will need to be protected in some way. Unless your garden is vast, the best way of dealing with rabbits is to surround the entire perimeter with small-gauge wire meshing, burying part of it underground to foil their burrowing antics. You may come across various plant lists at nurseries and botanic gardens noting 'rabbit-proof' plants. Unfortunately, rabbits don't seem to be aware of such plants and eat them regardless. One plant that they definitely do steer clear of, though, is *Buxus sempervirens*.

Red spider mites

Mostly found in greenhouses and conservatories, where the air tends to be hot and dry, although they can be seen in the garden during exceptionally hot summers when it hasn't rained for some time. They are tiny reddish-brown dots, barely visible without a magnifying glass. Symptoms are yellowish mottling to foliage, followed by webs over the leaves and stems in advanced infestations. Increasing the humidity helps to deter these beasts.

Sawfly

Insects similar to tiny caterpillars that feed on the leaves of certain types of trees and herbaceous plants. Large numbers can completely defoliate some plants. Once the damage has been done, there is little point in spraying. A check needs to be kept for these creatures, so they can be removed by hand as they appear.

RIGHT
Spider mites are
almost too small
to see with the
naked eye, but
leaves with yellow
mottling give us
a clue that they're
in residence.

FAR RIGHT
The amount of
damage that tiny
sawflies can cause
is extraordinary.

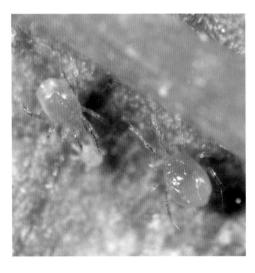
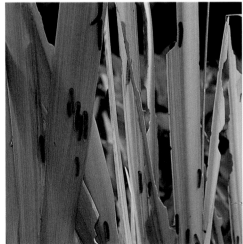

Scale insects

There are various types of scale insects that are often seen, including mussel scale, soft scale, brown scale, peppercorn scale and fluted scale. All of them feed off the sap of their chosen host plants. They are mainly a problem on plants such as palms or olives (*Olea europea*) when grown under glass, although *Camellia* and bay (*Laurus nobilis*) trees are frequently affected outdoors. They are best scraped off as soon as they appear. Chemical means, even powerful ones, are not very effective, and need to be applied regularly. If chemicals do work, the dead bodies will still have to be scraped off by hand, so this method might as well be used in the first place. Either use thumbnails (very unpleasant!) or scrub them off with an old toothbrush.

Slugs & snails

Everyone knows what these blighters look like, and most people recognize the slimy trails they leave all over the leaves they have nibbled. There are many different types, and some are enormous with appetites to match. They can ruin the soft, lush foliage of many herbaceous plants, especially *Canna*, *Kniphofia* and Bananas (*Musa*). They also love the succulent flesh of *Aeonium* and *Aloe*. Either pick them off by hand or use a chemical deterrent, rather than one of the dangerous poisons often seen on sale.

Thrips

Adult thrips are the 'thunder bugs' that many of us are familiar with. Their offspring mainly affect plants in greenhouses or conservatories, as they love the hot, dry atmosphere often found in such environments. They leave tell-tale silvery mottling on the leaves. Most chemical means of attack are inefficient – biological control would be the best method to try indoors. Thrips can also spread viruses between herbaceous garden plants during especially hot, dry summers.

Tortrix

These pretty little stubby brown moths lay their eggs on many different species of plants, mainly under glass, but outside in mild areas too. They hatch into tiny green caterpillars that snuggle down in between two leaves, pulling them together and sealing them tightly with coarse webbing. This webbing ruins the appearance of both leaves, just as much as the caterpillars munching. There is little point in spraying because the creatures are protected by the covering of the sealed foliage. The best way to deal with them is to pick off all affected leaves, seal them in a bag and burn the lot. Tortrix can ruin the appearance of entire trees if their numbers get out of control.

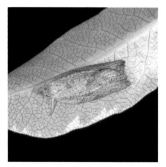

FROM TOP TO BOTTOM
1. Colonies of scale insects can suck the life out of infected plants. 2. *Canna* are a favourite snack of slugs. 3. Silver mottling is always a tell-tale sign of thrips. 4. The sight of tortrix moths always makes me jittery, as their offspring can wreak havoc on trees and shrubs.

Vine weevils

Black, beetle-like insects that appear at night to chomp notches out of the leaves of plants, especially those grown in containers. They lay their eggs underground in the soil, and these hatch out into large, fat, white maggots, which feed on the roots of plants. The maggots can do far more damage than the adults: in large numbers, they can destroy the entire root system of a plant, which leads to the plant's collapse. Avoid using peat-based composts in containers: vine weevil grubs prefer this type of soil because it makes their journey around the pot much easier than if they had to contend with heavier soil-based mixes.

Whitefly

Little white flies shaped like Concorde aeroplanes can be a serious nuisance to glasshouse plants but they can also occur outdoors during hot weather. These horrid things breed very quickly, increasing to such large numbers that when a plant is lightly tapped, great clouds of them immediately take flight. As they mostly congregate on the new leaf tips, the best method of control is by snipping off the affected parts of each plant. If spraying, treatment must take place every three days for there to be any chance of eliminating these pests. Adults feed on the sap, and their honeydew (the substance they excrete) quickly turns into sooty mould (see page 347), giving an unsightly appearance to the host plant. Their eggs can cover the leaves.

Woodlice

These grey, slow-moving miniature 'armadillos' do no harm in small numbers, but if the population causes overcrowding, their feeding habits can cause problems, especially in outdoor containers. They love to crawl into the drainage holes and nibble at the plant roots.

ROGUES' GALLERY: Diseases & disorders

Brown leaves

Many different conditions cause brown leaves. They could be old leaves about to be shed as part of the ageing process. Plants could be too dry, either from excessive heat or from too little water. They could be unsuitable for their planting position – for example, they could be incapable of coping with the salty sea air in coastal gardens. Or they could have been burned or scorched by chemicals such as weedkillers.

Botrytis

Fluffy grey mould usually found on the lower leaves of plants grown in a badly ventilated cold greenhouse or conservatory. This can spread throughout the whole plant if affected leaves are not removed.

Coral spot

Usually found on the diseased old wood of unhealthy trees – *Albizia julibrissin* is a plant that is often affected. It takes the form of numerous pink dots, and diseased branches should be cut out and burned to prevent it spreading to other parts of the tree.

ABOVE
The fluffy mould of botrytis can ruin the foliage.

TOP
This plant has collapsed and turned brown due to basal rot, caused by overwatering.

Honey fungus

This can cause dieback on all woody garden plants and is often accompanied by groups of tawny-coloured toadstools growing around the base of the plant. It is difficult to eliminate, and chemicals rarely work. Any affected tree or shrub should be completely removed, together with the entire root system and all of the surrounding soil. Palms, ferns, bamboos and spiky plants seem unaffected by this fungus.

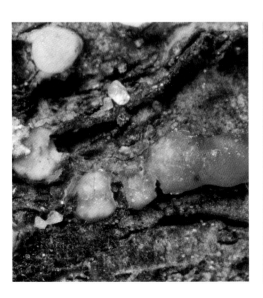

LEFT
Honey fungus is difficult to eradicate, so choose bamboos, spiky plants, palms and ferns for your garden instead of trees and shrubs.

FAR LEFT
Coral spot can sometimes be found on the diseased wood of old trees such as *Albizia julibrissin*.

Powdery mildew

White powdery dustings appear on the leaves of plants during the summer if the weather has been especially hot and dry. *Euonymus japonicus* is particularly susceptible. Watering plants frequently and mulching heavily with something like chipped bark to retain any available moisture around the roots will help to prevent it. Once this unsightly fungus appears, chop out the offending leaves if the damage is slight. For more severe infections, check out garden centres for the latest sulphur-based fungicide on the market.

Rotting

Most plants can be susceptible to rotting, but succulent and spiky plants are particularly prone to having their leaves turn to mush during cold, wet weather or as a result of overwatering throughout the year. Any affected leaves should be removed as soon as possible to prevent rotting from spreading through the entire plant.

Rust

Nasty rust-coloured markings can disfigure certain plants, such as the bamboo *Pleioblastus variegatus*. It is fairly common, especially on plants that are stressed in some way, for example, if they are confined to a container instead of being planted into the ground. Few fungicides are effective in eradicating rust, but frequently changing the products you use may be of some help. Instead of spraying, however, try just cutting down affected plants right back to ground level and letting them start again.

ABOVE
Powdery mildew is frequently seen during hot, dry summers.

RIGHT
Cold, wet weather can turn your delicious spiky plants to mush.

FAR RIGHT
Plants with rust should be cut back hard to the ground to regenerate fresh green foliage.

Sooty mould

This black mould is usually found growing on the excretions of insects such as scale insects, aphids and whitefly. Therefore, it is the insects that should be dealt with first, so that the process can at least be halted. The mould can be removed with a sponge dipped in soapy water and wiped over each leaf. It is a long, boring and messy task, as the sooty black powder is unpleasant to deal with. In severe cases, where the whole plant has been affected, it might be easier to chuck it away and start again with a fresh specimen. Outdoors, bay trees (*Laurus nobilis*) are the most commonly affected plants.

Yellow leaves

There are two main causes for the excessive yellowing of foliage. One is the natural shedding process of certain trees such as *Arbutus* x *andrachnoides*, *Phillyrea latifolia* and *Eriobotrya japonica*. The other is serious overwatering. If it's as a result of the former, don't worry – this will last for only four to six weeks. If it's because of the latter, ease up on watering and improve the drainage as well.

Yucca leaf spot

Although mainly seen on *Yucca* during cold, wet winters, leaf spot can also affect *Agave*, *Eriobotrya japonica* and *Chamaerops humilis*. Dark chocolate-brown spots appear in small numbers to start with; each affected leaf should be removed and burned to prevent it spreading throughout the entire plant. If all parts of *Agave*, *Eriobotrya* and *Yucca* plants are covered with leaf spot, dispose of the plant – there is no point struggling to deal with the problem. If *Chamaerops humilis* palms are affected, cut each section of the plant right back to the ground, even if this means removing every single leaf. The following season usually sees the plant re-shoot with renewed vigour.

ABOVE RIGHT
Yellow leaves are often a sign of overwatering.

ABOVE LEFT
Sooty mould on this *Arbutus* x *andrachnoides* is the result of an aphid infestation.

BELOW
Yucca leaf spot can affect some spiky plants grown in cold, wet climates.

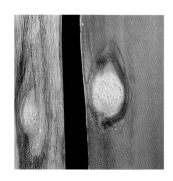

Plant index

General index

Acknowledgments

With special thanks to the best gardener in the world – my Dad, Harry Shaw.

Most of the photographs in this book were taken by the author, Christine Shaw, with the exception of the following:

Tim Sandall: pages 5; 14; 32; 40 top; 41 top left; 41 bottom left; 46; 51 top; 64; 66 bottom; 67 top; 72 bottom; 80; 94; 114; 132; 136 bottom left and bottom right; 141; 163 bottom right; 174 top; 206; 222; 223; 260; 283 bottom; 290; 293; 294; 304 bottom; 344 top left; 347 top left.
Garden Picture Library: pages 231 [John Glover]; 242; 333 top [J.S. Sira]; 337 right [Howard Rice]; 345 bottom right [David England].
Photos Horticultural: pages 174 bottom; 278; 333 bottom.
KM Harris: pages 334; 341 top right; 342 bottom right; 343 second from bottom; 344 top right.
Holt Studio Images: pages 336 top and bottom; 337 top and bottom; 338; 340 all; 341 top left; 342 bottom left;

343 second from top and bottom; 344 bottom; 345 top and bottom left; 346 bottom right; 347 top right and bottom right.
Colin Varndell: page 339.
Stefan Buczacki: pages 341 middle right; 346 top; 346 bottom left.
Rolando Ugolini: page 342 top.
Garden World Images: pages 176; 228.
Marianne Majerus: page 38 bottom.

Architectural Plants, Lidsey Road Nursery, Woodgate, Chichester, West Sussex PO20 3SU (01243 545008).

Architectural Plants, Nuthurst, Horsham, West Sussex RH13 6LH (01403 891772).